Effective Strategies for
Teaching in
K–8 Classrooms

Effective Strategies for
Teaching in K–8 Classrooms

Kenneth D. Moore
Henderson State University

Jacqueline Hansen
Murray State University

$SAGE

Los Angeles | London | New Delhi
Singapore | Washington DC

Los Angeles | London | New Delhi
Singapore | Washington DC

FOR INFORMATION:

SAGE Publications, Inc.
2455 Teller Road
Thousand Oaks, California 91320
E-mail: order@sagepub.com

SAGE Publications Ltd.
1 Oliver's Yard
55 City Road
London EC1Y 1SP
United Kingdom

SAGE Publications India Pvt. Ltd.
B 1/I 1 Mohan Cooperative Industrial Area
Mathura Road, New Delhi 110 044
India

SAGE Publications Asia-Pacific Pte. Ltd.
33 Pekin Street #02-01
Far East Square
Singapore 048763

Acquisitions Editor: Diane McDaniel

Associate Editor: Leah Mori

Editorial Assistant: Theresa Accomazzo

Production Editor: Eric Garner

Copy Editor: Megan Markanich

Typesetter: C&M Digitals (P) Ltd.

Proofreader: Joyce Li

Indexer: Jean Casalegno

Cover Designer: Candice Harman

Marketing Manager: Erica DeLuca

Permissions Editor: Adele Hutchinson

Copyright © 2012 by SAGE Publications, Inc.

Printed in the United States of America

Library of Congress Cataloging-in-Publication Data

Moore, Kenneth D.

Effective strategies for teaching in K-8 classrooms/Kenneth D. Moore, Jacqueline Hansen.

p. cm.
Includes bibliographical references and index.

ISBN 978-1-4129-7455-4 (pbk. : alk. paper)

1. Elementary school teaching—United States. 2. Middle school teaching—United States. 3. Effective teaching—United States. 4. Teacher effectiveness—United States. 5. Lesson planning—Study and teaching (Elementary) 6. Lesson planning—Study and teaching (Middle school) 7. Classroom management. I. Hansen, Jacquelyn Rae. II. Title.

LB1556.5.M66 2012 372.1102—dc22 2010046430

This book is printed on acid-free paper.

11 12 13 14 15 10 9 8 7 6 5 4 3 2 1

Brief Contents

Detailed Contents

Preface

Effective Strategies for Teaching in K-8 Classrooms is designed to prepare future elementary and middle school teachers to meet the challenges of today's complex, ever-changing classrooms. Becoming an effective teacher requires extensive knowledge and skills, as well as hard work, commitment, an inquiring mind, and the ability to learn from experiences. Although this quest for instructional excellence is rigorous, the satisfaction of helping future students realize their potential is well worth the effort. This book will provide aspiring teachers with the pedagogical content knowledge and skills they will need to become exemplary educators.

Throughout this textbook we provide detailed descriptions of effective instructional methods coupled with planning and instructional theory. This approach causes prospective teachers to analyze their ability to translate what they have learned into effective instructional practices in their future classrooms. In short, it is our hope that future elementary and middle school teachers will value this book as a guide to sound educational practices. This text is intended for use in undergraduate general elementary and/or middle school methods courses, but it could be a useful reference for in-service teachers and a variety of courses.

INSTRUCTIONAL THEORY INTO PRACTICE

We have all experienced teachers who earned high grades in college methods courses but weren't able to translate that theory into effective teaching in the real classroom. Therefore, we have integrated a "theory into practice" theme throughout this text. We explore ways to apply research-based practices and learning theories to improve classroom instruction. Whenever possible, we provide specific examples and master teacher's perspectives and experiences.

No one can deny the profound, lifelong impact that effective teachers can have on their students. To make that impact positive, teachers must have both a deep understanding of the powerful principles of effective teaching and a clear sense of how these principles can be applied to the classroom. Effective teachers constantly reflect upon their practices and make instructional decisions based on a clear conception of how students learn best. They know that quality teaching is neither a bag of tricks nor a set of abstract principles; rather, it is an intelligent application of research-based teaching principles to address the reality of the classroom. This text will provide the theoretical knowledge and help you develop the practical skills needed to do the most important job you will ever do—teach.

ORGANIZATION OF THE TEXT

Part I: Setting the Stage for Successful Learning provides an orientation to teaching. In Chapter 1, we explore what you need to know to become an effective K–8 teacher. You will learn about the art and science of teaching, effective teaching skills, constructivism, expectations and standards, accountability, and teacher licensure. Chapter 2 deals with how to meet the needs of an increasingly diverse student population. We discuss team teaching and considerations for teaching children with special needs and children who are gifted and talented. We introduce you to several models of classroom management in Chapter 3. The importance of classroom management cannot be overemphasized. Indeed, a classroom must be well managed if learning is to take place.

Part II: Sequencing and Organizing Instruction focuses upon the importance of careful instructional planning. Chapter 4 deals with the school curriculum and determining instructional intent. We present and discuss a comprehensive model of teaching and teach you how to set instructional goals, write objectives, and use the backward design approach to identify instructional intent. Chapter 5 focuses on developing course, unit, weekly, and daily lesson plans. We illustrate several practical lesson plan formats. Chapter 6 addresses student evaluation and assessment of student learning. You will learn about types and systems of evaluation, information sources, grading systems, and assigning grades.

Part III: Designing Instruction to Maximize Student Learning relates to selecting instructional strategies. Chapters 7, 8, 9, and 10 focus on using the direct, authentic, and integrated teaching methods for instructional delivery. This part also includes a pertinent chapter on skills instruction, which stresses the importance of critical thinking and the development of creative thinking as part of the school curriculum.

FEATURES OF THE TEXT

We have included several special features in *Effective Strategies for Teaching in K–8 Classrooms* to help you apply what you are learning. Each chapter begins with an overview and objectives. Scattered throughout each chapter are innovative focal points. The following sections also appear in each chapter: Reflections on Teacher Practice (two in each chapter), Reflect and Apply (two to three in each chapter), A Reflective Case Study, Through the Eyes of an Expert (except in Chapters 4 and 5), Summary, Discussion Questions and Activities, Tech Connection, Licensing Preparation/Praxis Connection, Portfolio Connection, and Connection With the Field. All these sections provide materials that address your present and future professional needs.

We have created a student website (**www.sagepub.com/mooreteachingk8**) with various enrichment materials plus video clips of excellent teachers and interviews—each tied to a course topic within a chapter and highlighted by a special icon—to help you understand, analyze, and apply chapter concepts. In addition, two appendices provide information on microteaching and reflective teaching and on state licensure/certification and reciprocity.

Before We Begin

To help you make a personal or academic connection with what you are about to read, each chapter starts with a Before We Begin prompt. This will provide you with a cognitive framework for the chapter's information.

Overview

The overview gives an annotated outline of the chapter's major concepts and organization. It represents a quick reference to the chapter content.

Objectives

Because all instructional activities should be tied to an instructional intent, we provide objectives at the outset of each chapter. These will give you an idea of what you are expected to be able to know and do as the result of reading the chapter and completing the chapter activities.

Reflections on Teacher Practice

A real-world feature of each chapter gives you the opportunity to hear directly from teachers in the field about topics to be explored. These reflections show the major principles in the chapter in action. Each reflection is an experience taken from a real-life situation. The reflection describes how principles were applied in classroom settings and the results of each application. They represent brief words of wisdom, strategies, and philosophy from teachers in our elementary and middle schools.

Application Activity

This feature, appearing in most chapters, encourages you to pause and ponder the issues being presented throughout the chapter. These application features reinforce the content, examine contentious topics, and challenge you to explore how your own ideas and beliefs inform your teaching practice.

Reflective Case Study

This feature is designed to encourage you to learn more about the teaching profession by analyzing classroom scenarios and applying what you have learned through your assigned readings. These cases will help you think more deeply about issues and problems encountered in the classroom environment.

Reflect and Apply Exercise

These exercises present the most important ideas of the chapter for review and study. Each exercise uses a series of thought-provoking reflection questions embedded directly in the text material and application questions to help you develop deeper insights into the issues and concepts being discussed.

Summary

At the end of each chapter, we summarize the chapter's main points. The information is presented in bulleted form under each major chapter heading to make it easier to access the information.

Discussion Questions and Activities

The discussion questions and activities that follow each chapter provide critical and creative thinking activities that allow you to ponder and process issues brought up in the chapter. This gives you a chance to take what you have learned in the chapter and apply it to real-world teaching issues or problems in the classroom.

Tech Connection

This feature gives you the opportunity to further explore ways to use technology to enhance student learning and to manage your future classroom.

Connection With the Field

To help you learn how effective teachers apply theory to practice, this section has suggestions for field experiences, classroom observations, interviews with teachers and administrators, and interactions within the schools. We provide questions so you can gain additional insights into the classroom.

ANCILLARIES

Instructor's Teaching Site

A password-protected instructor's manual is available at **www.sagepub.com/mooreteachingk8** to help instructors plan and teach their courses. These resources have been designed to help instructors make the classes as practical and interesting as possible for students.

- A test bank in Word offers a diverse set of test questions and answers for each chapter of the book. Multiple-choice, true/false, short answer, and essay questions for every chapter will aid instructors in assessing students' progress and understanding.

- Carefully selected, web-based video links feature relevant content for use in either independent or classroom-based explorations of key topics.

- Chapter-specific PowerPoint slide presentations offer assistance with lecture and review preparation by highlighting essential content, features, and artwork from the book.

- Sample syllabi—for semester, quarter, and online classes—provide suggested models for creating the syllabus for your course.

- Activities and assignments are lively and stimulating ideas for use both in and out of class reinforce active learning. The activities apply to either individual or group projects.

Student Study Site

An open-access student study site can be found at **www.sagepub.com/mooreteachingk8**. These resources can also be used by the instructor to supplement instruction. For each chapter, the site offers the following:

- Video links feature relevant content for use in either independent or classroom-based explorations of key topics.

- E-flashcards are a study tool that reinforces student understanding of key terms and concepts that have been outlined in the chapters.

- Flexible self-quizzes allow students to independently assess their progress in learning course material.

- Web exercises and activities direct students to useful and current web resources, along with creative activities to extend and reinforce learning.

Acknowledgments

We are, indeed, grateful to hundreds of students and teachers who provided critical feedback and served as invaluable sources in the preparation of this text. Moreover, we would like to thank the many educators who helped identify the major ideas presented in this textbook. Special gratitude also goes to the school districts that opened their doors to us and offered their support.

We would like to thank those who reviewed the text for this edition. Instructors who reviewed this edition include

Elizabeth Sandall, Minnesota State University

Barbara Williams, Longwood University

Frank Brathwaite, D'Youville College

Yolanda Dunston, North Carolina Central University

Betty Crocker, University of North Texas

Danne Davis, Montclair State University

Many professional colleagues contributed to this textbook. We are especially indebted to Dr. Sally Beisser at Drake University, who developed three of the lesson plan formats presented in Chapter 5. We also thank Veronica Russell, Martin Luther King Jr. Elementary School; Karen McCuiston, Kentucky Center for School Safety; Jennifer Dunnaway, Calloway County Middle School; Meagan Musselman, Murray State University; Keri Dowdy, Sedalia Elementary School; Carol A. Withrow, McNabb Elementary School; and Dr. Joy Navan, Murray State University for sharing their viewpoints in the Through the Eyes of an Expert features. We thank the administrators, teachers, and students of the Murray and Calloway County school districts and the Murray State University teacher candidates who volunteered to cooperatively create video clips for online resources. The textbook is much stronger due to the innovative ideas and expert efforts of these talented colleagues.

We would also like to thank the staff at SAGE who helped bring this textbook to life. Diane McDaniel, who got the project started and kept it on track, deserves special thanks. Her leadership will always be remembered and appreciated. Special thanks also go to associate editor Leah Mori, who provided much technical and research assistance. Finally, we would like to thank our spouses, Susan and Allen, for their endless patience, support, and loving encouragement.

Interstate New Teacher Assessment and Support Consortium Correlation Chart

This chart has been designed to indicate how the chapter text relates to sections of the Praxis II: Principles of Learning and Teaching (PLT) Tests and Interstate New Teacher Assessment and Support Consortium (INTASC) standards. The left-hand column of the chart lists the INTASC knowledge standards. The center column contains the topics assessed in the PLT Tests. The right-hand column contains the chapters that correspond to the INTASC standards and the PLT Tests.

INTASC Standard	Description of Teacher Performance	Praxis Topic	Text Chapter/Connection
Principle 1	The teacher understands the central concepts, tools of inquiry, and structures of the discipline(s) he or she teaches and can create learning experiences that make these aspects of subject matter meaningful for students.	I. Students as Learners II. Instruction and Assessment III. Communication Techniques IV. Profession and Community	Chapter 1: Establishing the Foundations for Teaching and Learning Chapter 2: Teaching Diverse Students Chapter 4: Planning and Organizing Instruction Chapter 5: Developing Unit and Daily Lesson Plans

Principle 2	The teacher understands how children learn and develop and can provide learning opportunities that support their intellectual, social, and personal development.	I. Students as Learners	Chapter 1: Establishing the Foundations for Teaching and Learning Chapter 2: Teaching Diverse Students Chapter 4: Planning and Organizing Instruction Chapter 5: Developing Unit and Daily Lesson Plans Chapter 7: Using Direct Teaching Methods Chapter 8: Using Authentic Teaching Methods Chapter 9: Using Integrated Teaching Methods Chapter 10: Teaching Effective Thinking Strategies
Principle 3	The teacher understands how students differ in their approaches to learning and creates instructional opportunities that are adapted to diverse learners.	I. Students as Learners B. Students as Diverse Learners	Chapter 1: Establishing the Foundations for Teaching and Learning Chapter 2: Teaching Diverse Students Chapter 4: Planning and Organizing Instruction Chapter 5: Developing Unit and Daily Lesson Plans
Principle 4	The teacher understands and uses a variety of instructional strategies to encourage students' development of critical thinking, problem solving, and performance skills.	II. Instruction and Assessment A. Instructional Strategies	Chapter 5: Developing Unit and Daily Lesson Plans Chapter 7: Using Direct Teaching Methods Chapter 8: Using Authentic Teaching Methods Chapter 9: Using Integrated Teaching Methods Chapter 10: Teaching Effective Thinking Strategies

Principle 5	The teacher uses an understanding of individual and group motivation and behavior to create a learning environment that encourages positive social interaction, active engagement in learning, and self-motivation.	I. Students as Learners C. Student Motivation and the Learning Process	Chapter 3: Managing the Classroom Environment Chapter 5: Developing Unit and Daily Lesson Plans Chapter 7: Using Direct Teaching Methods Chapter 8: Using Authentic Teaching Methods Chapter 9: Using Integrated Teaching Methods Chapter 10: Teaching Effective Thinking Strategies
Principle 6	The teacher uses knowledge of effective verbal, nonverbal, and media communication techniques to foster active inquiry, collaboration, and supportive interaction in the classroom.	I. Students as Learners B. Students as Diverse Learners III. Communications Techniques	Chapter 2: Teaching Diverse Students Chapter 3: Managing the Classroom Environment Chapter 7: Using Direct Teaching Methods Chapter 8: Using Authentic Teaching Methods Chapter 9: Using Integrated Teaching Methods Chapter 10: Teaching Effective Thinking Strategies
Principle 7	The teacher plans instruction based upon knowledge of subject matter, students, the community, and curriculum goals.	II. Instruction and Assessment B. Planning Instruction	Chapter 1: Establishing the Foundations for Teaching and Learning Chapter 2: Teaching Diverse Students Chapter 4: Planning and Organizing Instruction Chapter 5: Developing Unit and Daily Lesson Plans
Principle 8	The teacher understands and uses formal and informal assessment strategies to evaluate and ensure the continuous intellectual, social, and physical development of the learner.	II. Instruction and Assessment C. Assessment Strategies	Chapter 4: Planning and Organizing Instruction Chapter 5: Developing Unit and Daily Lesson Plans Chapter 6: Evaluating and Measuring Student Learning

Principle 9	The teacher is a reflective practitioner who continually evaluates the effects of his or her choices and actions on others (students, parents, and other professionals in the learning community) and who actively seeks out opportunities to grow professionally.	IV. Profession and Community	Chapter 1: Establishing the Foundations for Teaching and Learning Chapter 4: Planning and Organizing Instruction Chapter 5: Developing Unit and Daily Lesson Plans Chapter 6: Evaluating and Measuring Student Learning
Principle 10	The teacher fosters relationships with school colleagues, parents, and agencies in the larger community to support students' learning and well-being.	I. Students as Learners B. Students as Diverse Learners IV. Profession and Community	Chapter 1: Establishing the Foundations for Teaching and Learning Chapter 2: Teaching Diverse Students Chapter 3: Managing the Classroom Environment Chapter 4: Planning and Organizing Instruction Chapter 6: Evaluating and Measuring Student Learning

National Council for Accreditation of Teacher Education Correlation Chart

This chart has been designed to indicate how the chapter text relates to the National Council for Accreditation of Teacher Education (NCATE) standards. The left-hand column of the chart lists the NCATE standards. The right-hand column of the chart contains the chapters that correspond to the NCATE standards.

NCATE Standard	Chapter
Standard 1: Candidate knowledge, skills, and professional dispositions	Chapter 1: Establishing the Foundations for Teaching and Learning Chapter 2: Teaching Diverse Students Chapter 3: Managing the Classroom Environment Chapter 4: Planning and Organizing Instruction Chapter 5: Developing Unit and Daily Lesson Plans Chapter 7: Using Direct Teaching Methods Chapter 8: Using Authentic Teaching Methods Chapter 9: Using Integrated Teaching Methods Chapter 10: Teaching Effective Thinking Strategies
Standard 2: Assessment system and unit evaluation	Chapter 4: Planning and Organizing Instruction Chapter 5: Developing Unit and Daily Lesson Plans Chapter 6: Evaluating and Measuring Student Learning
Standard 3: Field experiences and clinical practice	Presented and discussed throughout the book

Standard 4: Diversity	Chapter 1: Establishing the Foundations for Teaching and Learning
	Chapter 2: Teaching Diverse Students
	Chapter 3: Managing the Classroom Environment
	Chapter 4: Planning and Organizing Instruction
	Chapter 5: Developing Unit and Daily Lesson Plans
Standard 5: Faculty qualifications, performance, and development	Presented and discussed throughout the book
Standard 6: Unit governance and resources	Chapter 1: Establishing the Foundations for Teaching and Learning
	Chapter 2: Teaching Diverse Students
	Chapter 3: Managing the Classroom Environment
	Chapter 4: Planning and Organizing Instruction
	Chapter 7: Using Direct Teaching Methods
	Chapter 8: Using Authentic Teaching Methods
	Chapter 9: Using Integrated Teaching Methods
	Chapter 10: Teaching Effective Thinking Strategies

part I

Setting the Stage for Successful Learning

Today you will take the first step on your journey toward becoming an elementary or middle school teacher. As you prepare to enter this prestigious profession, you are invited to ponder these questions: What is the purpose of education? How do societal needs and legislation impact what happens in your classroom? What content knowledge and skills do you need to acquire to address all students' needs in today's increasingly diverse classroom? How can you set the stage for successful learning in your future classroom?

Part I addresses the constantly changing field of education and the skills needed to teach in our increasingly complex society. The purpose of this first section is to help you gain insight into the process of teaching and to establish a cognitive framework that will assist you in preparing to teach.

Chapter 1 delves into the art and science of teaching. Teaching is much more than just a job; it is a challenging profession that requires long hours of work and preparation. How do educators become professionals? Chapter 1 explores how effective teaching skills, accountability, professional standards, and licensure contribute to the professionalization of teachers.

Professionalism is only part of being an effective educator, however. Teachers also establish caring classroom climates conducive to learning. Successful teachers must learn to anticipate, accommodate, and navigate a wide spectrum of student academic and social needs. Chapter 2 explores various ways to address the needs of today's increasingly diverse student population.

Because students cannot learn and teachers cannot teach in chaotic classroom conditions, Chapter 3 investigates multiple ways that teachers can organize their classrooms and establish expectations that help students assume responsibility for their behavioral choices.

Establishing the Foundations for Teaching and Learning

A good teacher can inspire hope, ignite the imagination, and instill a love of learning.

—Brad Henry

Before We Begin

Envision your very favorite elementary or middle school teacher. What personal qualities, knowledge, and skills made that teacher particularly effective? Draw a sketch or create a word collage that captures that person's essence. Be ready to compare your view with classmates.

OVERVIEW

Elementary and middle school teachers invite students to learn by sharing their subject matter expertise through high-interest, motivational lessons. They verify that they are highly qualified teachers by meeting state and national standards and passing rigorous exams for teacher certification and licensure. Teachers do much more than just teach, however. They are also decision makers, mentors, teacher–leaders, action researchers, home-school liaisons, counselors, and social psychologists.

Effective teachers strive to help students reach their academic and personal potential. To maximize student achievement, they consider learning theories plus student needs, differences, and abilities as they carefully plan lessons, create positive classroom environments, use diverse instructional strategies, and exhibit professional behavior.

Many educational, community, and societal factors influence what teachers teach, how they teach, and whom they teach. We will focus our attention, however, on those factors that directly impact the classroom.

OBJECTIVES

After completing your study of Chapter 1, you should be able to

- identify major theoretical influences that have shaped American education,
- describe how **teaching** can be both an art and a science,
- name characteristics and skills associated with effective teaching,
- describe the constructivist approach to learning,
- state the purposes and benefits of school and program accreditation, and
- explain the purpose of the state licensure/certification process.

What makes a *good* teacher, an *effective* teacher, a *successful* teacher? Are there certain identifiable skills that make an exemplary educator? Let's examine how aspiring elementary and middle school teachers establish a foundation of theoretical and pedagogical knowledge and skills so they can set the stage for successful learning experiences in their future classrooms.

TEACHING

What does it mean to teach? Moore (2007) defines teaching as "the actions of someone who is trying to assist others to reach their fullest potential in all aspects of development" (p. 5). The personal characteristics and skills needed to accomplish this noble task have been debated throughout the history of education as educators struggle to determine whether teaching is an art or a science.

Historical Perspective on Teaching

American public schools have always been dedicated to the concept of providing an education to prepare the nation's youth to be productive global citizens. As a reflection of our ever-changing society, schools will continue to change, but if history is a guide, this change will come slowly. A brief overview of the important historical changes in the role of American education can be found on the web-based student study site (**www.sagepub .com/mooreteachingk8**). In the future, some things may remain the same. Because of the Tenth Amendment to the U.S. Constitution, communities will likely continue to make decisions about their local schools. Elementary and middle school teachers will continue to provide instruction to diverse groups of children in self-contained and blended classrooms. However, societal expectations for teachers and students will likely change drastically in the years to come. To meet these challenges, it is imperative that elementary and middle school teachers are highly qualified professionals who embrace teaching as an art and a science.

Teaching as an Art and a Science

Is teaching an art or a science? Do some teachers have better instincts for teaching than others? If so, can these instincts be identified and taught? Some educators argue that teachers are born and not made, and the ability to be an effective teacher cannot be taught. Conversely, other educators argue that teaching is a science with specific laws and principles, which can be taught.

Those who think *teaching is an art* may argue that good teaching is primarily a creative act. That is, teachers spontaneously combine educational theories, content knowledge, and teaching experiences into a new whole that is specially suited for their academic situation. Although these artful educators may recognize the need for a strong educational background, they follow their instincts to put theory into practice. This theory of teaching suggests that there are some who possess a special sense of knowing what to do and when to do it that cannot be taught. Although this idea doesn't provide prospective teachers with tangible options for combining theory, practice, and experience, it does explain a mysterious aspect of teaching that many spend a lifetime seeking. Indeed, this may be the mystery that has motivated so much research in the hope that perfect formulas will be discovered to direct us in our search for best practices and methods in education.

Those who contend that *teaching is a science* believe that good teaching is the result of having a deep knowledge of the subject matter and a solid understanding of the principles of teaching and learning. They believe it is possible to learn and master the skills and strategies needed to be a successful teacher. Decades of research have provided specific information about how learning occurs, what motivates students, and which particular teacher skills produce learning. Promoters of the teaching as a science theory identify specific methods and skills that are attainable for the prospective teacher. They believe that teachers who learn to use these skills will be successful.

Today, most educators agree that there is a scientific basis for the art of teaching. Experienced teachers know it is not simply a matter of sharing what they know with their students. Teaching is a complex and challenging profession. Effective teachers transform knowledge into learning activities that motivate students to learn and translate complicated concepts into student-friendly language. Thus, teaching can be viewed as having both artistic and scientific elements. Essentially, educators accept the viewpoint that aspiring teachers fall somewhere along the continuum shown in Figure 1.1. Furthermore, many agree that specific artistic and scientific elements can be taught to future teachers.

FIGURE 1.1   Teaching as an Art and a Science

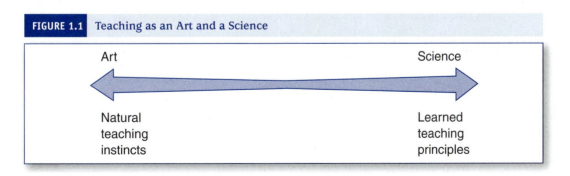

"I can't tell you what a relief it is to relax after a whole year of teaching!"

SOURCE: Created by Ford Button.

THEORIES THAT SHAPED TEACHING

For many years, it was believed that a teacher's personal qualities were the most important attributes for effective teaching. Teachers who were warm and loving were thought to be more effective than those who lacked such attributes. This belief has a measure of truth to it, but it also gives an incomplete picture of effective teaching. Although establishing a caring classroom climate motivates students to learn, effective teachers also need to have the professional and pedagogical knowledge and skills to help *all* students learn each and every school day.

The search for what constitutes effective teaching is ongoing. The overall framework for **thinking** about effective teaching comes mainly from three sources: (1) educational reformers and researchers, (2) research-based teaching strategies and **procedures**, and (3) the wisdom of experienced teachers. Effective teachers begin by focusing upon the students. How do students learn best? Do all students learn in the same way? What instructional

Teaching is both an art and a science.

strategies promote the highest student achievement? Multiple learning theories abound. Because no one theory offers all the answers to effective teaching, this text will address only some of the commonly agreed upon thoughts. Learning about these theories will help you to develop your own philosophy of teaching and to make decisions about classroom teaching and learning.

Jean-Jacques Rousseau

Jean-Jacques Rousseau (1712–1778), a French philosopher, was one of the first to popularize developmental theories. In his book, *Emile* (1792), Rousseau described children's natural characteristics and the type of education appropriate for each age. He believed that children naturally evolve through the processes of maturation. As a humanist, Rousseau believed that educators should provide developmentally appropriate activities that ensure children develop a healthy sense of self-worth and morality. He promoted a natural educational environment that does not restrict children's natural growth and development.

Johann Pestalozzi

Johann Pestalozzi (1746–1827), a Swiss educational reformer, postulated that children learn through their senses and concrete experiences. Instead of teaching through rote memorization and recitation, Pestalozzi believed children should be actively engaged in the learning process. To prepare children for life, Pestalozzi emphasized the use of concrete, or hands-on, instructional materials. Like Rousseau, Pestalozzi advocated sympathetic understanding of children, rather than harsh punishment. He believed that children develop their intellectual powers from within and that schools should provide learning environments conducive to the maximum development of children's natural talents. The primary characteristics of Pestalozzi's teaching methods include recognizing children's potential through careful observation, understanding the importance of teacher–student relationships, strengthening peer relations, and providing opportunities for children to learn through the senses.

Friedrick Froebel

Friedrick Froebel (1782–1852), a German educator, is often referred to as the "father of kindergarten." He believed that through careful observation, educators can provide developmentally appropriate activities to enable children to learn what they were ready to learn when they were ready to learn. According to Froebel, very young children discover their uniqueness and develop their motor skills through play activities. His ideas about the values of play, singing, storytelling, language activities, and circle time experiences are considered essential elements of kindergarten and early childhood education.

John Dewey

John Dewey (1859–1952), a leading reformer during the Progressive Era, was perhaps the most influential American educator in the 20th century. He was instrumental in developing modern educational theory. As a progressive, Dewey believed that because the world is ever-changing, students need to become information seekers who are able to apply what they've learned to current, relevant problems. Students learn through interacting with others, exploring self-selected topics, and applying what they have learned to solve **authentic** problems. Dewey's approach focused upon students' interests rather than subject matter. From this theory comes student-centered **curriculum** and student-centered schools that emphasize learning through experiences. Teachers facilitate students' learning through probing questions, problem-based learning, democratic classrooms, and **metacognitive** activities.

Maria Montessori

Maria Montessori (1870–1952), an Italian physician, greatly influenced instruction in contemporary early childhood and elementary programs. She believed that teachers should carefully observe children so they can create respectful, child-centered classrooms that celebrate the unique nature of each child. The **Montessori method**, a system for educating children and youth, develops children's knowledge and skills through prescribed sets of materials and physical exercises. These materials arouse interest, and the interest motivates children to learn. Children decide whether or not to use the materials. Through highly individualized instruction, children develop self-discipline and self-confidence.

Lev Vygotsky

Lev Vygotsky (1896–1934), a Russian developmental psychologist, emphasized the role of social interaction in students' construction of knowledge. Although children can learn some things independently, Vygotsky suggested that their learning is enhanced and extended by interacting with significant others such as their parents, teachers, siblings, and peers. Vygotsky believed that learning takes place when children are working within their zone of proximal development (ZPD). Tasks within the ZPD are ones that a child cannot yet do alone but could do with the assistance of more competent peers or adults. To facilitate, or scaffold, children's educational efforts, teachers build structured learning environments with plentiful opportunities for modeling and interaction. Vygotsky believed that as a result of teacher–learner collaboration, the learner uses concepts acquired in the collaborative process to solve problems independently of the teacher. His theories laid the foundation for cooperative learning and the basic tenets of constructivism.

Jean Piaget

One of the most complete theoretical statements about critical periods in the intellectual development of the individual was presented by the Swiss psychologist Jean Piaget (1896–1980). According to Piaget, children progress through a sequence of stages of cognitive development (see Table 1.1).

TABLE 1.1 Piaget's Stages of Cognitive Development	
Stage	**Cognitive Skills**
Sensorimotor *(infancy)*	Uses senses to explore world. Egocentric perspective. Recognizes events may be caused by intentional actions. Realizes objects exist even when not present. Focuses on the present.
Preoperational *(toddler/early childhood)*	Uses representational symbols. Rapidly develops language. Less dependence on senses. Classifies objects by a single feature. Believes everything happens for a reason.
Concrete Operational *(elementary/adolescence)*	Thinks logically about objects and events. Classifies objects by several features. Understands numbers. Realizes objects can appear in different forms.
Formal Operations *(adolescence/adulthood)*	Solves complex verbal and hypothetical problems. Thinks through symbols. Able to reason scientifically and logically. Capable of abstract thinking that includes past, present, and future.

Piaget believed that all people pass through the same four stages of cognitive development in the exact same order. Although these stages are generally associated with specific ages, these are only general guidelines for teachers. A classroom of students oftentimes represents multiple stages of cognitive development. Indeed, one particular student might operate at a different cognitive level in different academic content areas! Piaget's theories focused attention on the idea of developmentally appropriate education. Teachers should provide learning environments, curriculum materials, and instruction that correlate with students' stages of cognitive development. They should introduce new concepts with realistic, hands-on activities followed by more abstract learning experiences. Piaget's developmental stages help teachers decide what to teach, how much to teach, and when to teach it.

Piaget also developed the schema theory in which students group similar types of information into schemata (categories) according to similarities and differences. When students encounter new concepts, they either assimilate the information into an existing schema based upon similar characteristics or accommodate by creating a new schema. In view of this theory, effective teachers systematically plan introductory activities that connect new topics with students' existing personal and academic experiences. They also use graphic organizers, such as concept maps, to help students see the interconnectedness of related concepts.

Jerome Bruner

Jerome Bruner (1915–), an American psychologist, emphasized the importance of understanding the essential concepts of a subject, the need for active learning as the basis for true understanding, and the value of inductive reasoning in learning. Because Bruner believed that students must be active in their own learning, he identified three sequential modes of learning: (1) learning by doing, called the *enactive* mode; (2) learning by forming mental images, called *iconic mode*; and (3) learning through a series of abstract symbols or representations, called the *symbolic mode*. As children grow older, they depend less on the enactive mode and more on mental imagery and symbolic operations. Bruner suggested that teachers give students more opportunities to learn on their own. Bruner's ideas laid the foundation for a process that has been called discovery learning (see Chapter 8).

CONSTRUCTIVISM

Based on the work of Dewey, Piaget, and Vygotsky, constructivism has a major influence on the way elementary and middle school teachers teach. Constructivism constitutes a paradigm shift in how teaching is viewed. It echoes the basic premise of this ancient Chinese proverb: "I hear and I forget; I see and I remember; I do and I understand." In this student-centered approach, students are active participants in their own learning; teacher-centered strategies, such as lecturing, are minimized. Students' minds are no longer seen as blank slates or as empty vessels that need to be filled.

Constructivists believe that learners construct their own understanding and knowledge of the world based upon their experiences and reflections. Learning becomes a student-directed search for meaning. Students construct their own meaning by negotiating that meaning with others, making connections with and modifying prior conceptions, and addressing content in a variety of contexts. They demonstrate their knowledge in multiple ways (through the arts, for example), apply what they have learned to real-life situations, and participate in group work and cooperative learning activities. Because students are active creators of their own knowledge, they are encouraged to ask questions, explore, and assess what they know. They use and test ideas and skills through relevant activities or authentic experiences. The purpose of learning is for students to construct their own meaning, not just memorize the "right" answers and regurgitate someone else's meaning.

The constructivist view of learning requires a reconceptualization of elementary and middle school teaching. Elementary and middle school teachers focus on helping students construct understanding of concepts themselves by connecting new learning with prior knowledge and experiences. They use open-ended questions and extensive dialogue to encourage students to analyze, interpret, and predict information. Instead of spending time memorizing material, filling in the blanks on worksheets, and repeating large numbers of similar problems, students learn to solve novel problems, integrate information, and create knowledge for themselves. Teachers facilitate learning by building upon students' preexisting knowledge, urging them to use active techniques (experiments, real-world **problem solving**) to create more knowledge, and then providing time for reflection upon what they have learned. Constructivist teachers encourage students to constantly assess how the learning activity is helping them gain under-standing. By questioning themselves and their strategies, students in the constructivist class-room ideally become "expert learners." This gives them ever-broadening tools to keep learning. With a well-planned classroom environment, students learn "how to learn."

TRADITIONAL MODEL OF TEACHING

Joyce and Weil (1996) and Joyce, Weil, and Calhoun (2003) have identified and described more than 20 major approaches to teaching that are based on traditional perspectives about elementary and middle school teaching and learning. Each model differs in its basic rationale or philosophical base and in the **goals** it is designed to achieve. Obviously, it is unrealistic to ask elementary or middle school teachers to be this prescriptive in classrooms when they must deal with such a wide diversity of students. However, each model shares many effective procedures and strategies, such as the need to motivate, define expectations, and involve students in their own learning. You will learn about many of these procedures and strategies throughout this text and also through the wisdom shared by experienced elementary and middle school teachers.

ELEMENTARY AND MIDDLE SCHOOL CLASSROOM TEACHING

High-quality elementary and middle school teachers know that good teaching is more than simply telling, explaining, and discussing (Kostelnik, Soderman, Whiren, and Contributor, 2010; Powell, 2010). Indeed, teachers must also be able to make decisions about classroom organization, material management, discipline, teaching strategies, **assessment**, and student motivation. How do they accomplish all of this? Valuable insight into **decision making** and the teaching process can be provided by websites such as ProTeacher (www.proteacher.com), MiddleWeb (www.middleweb.com), Teaching Tips (www.teachingtips.com/blog), and Teachers at Risk (www.teachersatrisk.com). The Through the Eyes of an Expert interlude gives an overview of the ProTeacher site.

Through the Eyes of an Expert

ProTeacher Community (www.proteacher.net)

A popular and carefully moderated discussion site for elementary schoolteachers, ProTeacher is host to hundreds of ongoing discussions and tens of thousands of teaching ideas contributed by teachers nationwide.

Professional classroom teachers, specialists, substitute teachers, student teachers, and administrators working in early childhood, elementary, and middle school are invited to participate—and many do. Although ProTeacher has been designed primarily for elementary schoolteachers, the discussions and ideas are often applicable to all grade levels.

Participation is free of charge, and no registration is required. All newcomers, however, should first read their Participation Guidelines page, which contains helpful advice for first-time visitors, as well as established rules and policies. Special rules apply to student teachers.

The ProTeacher motto is "By sharing ideas and being helpful, we're encouraging others to do the same!" With experienced teachers from across the country doing just that, ProTeacher is definitely worth a visit!

Skills of Effective Teachers

Because teaching elementary and middle school is such a complex profession, effective teachers need to have a solid foundation of subject area content knowledge and teaching skills. The National Council for Accreditation of Teacher Education (NCATE), Interstate New Teacher Assessment and Support Consortium (INTASC), No Child Left Behind (NCLB) legislation, state education professional standards boards, and professional organizations have all identified the content knowledge and skills they deem constitute effective teaching. In addition to content area knowledge, most national and state teaching standards address lesson design and implementation, classroom management, collaboration, technological proficiency, assessment, professionalism, and dispositions. Teachers demonstrate their professional competencies by taking national exams developed by organizations such as the Educational Testing Service (ETS) and Pearson. They extend and refine this knowledge through continuous professional growth experiences.

Danielson (2007) created a framework for effective teaching. She believed that effective teachers (1) engage in quality planning and preparation, (2) prepare a positive classroom environment, (3) use proven instructional techniques, and (4) exhibit professional behavior. These skill areas are derived from the work of the ETS in the development of Praxis III: Classroom Performance Assessments, an exam used by some states to assess actual teaching skills and classroom performance. The Danielson skill areas are grounded in the constructivist approach to learning and are based on formal analyses of important tasks required of beginning teachers: reviews of research, analyses of state regulations for teacher licensing, and extensive fieldwork.

Quality Planning and Preparation

Many people assume all that teachers need to be able to do is to know their subject area and be able to tell students what they know. In reality, content knowledge is only part of the instructional process. Effective teachers spend considerable time and energy planning the activities, materials, and evaluation elements associated with teaching the content. They use their knowledge of the subject, student development, and learning theories to identify appropriate instructional goals and **objectives**, to design and teach high-interest, motivational lessons, and to assess students' learning. Quality instruction is centered around appropriate content, materials and methods, interaction patterns, and well-planned lessons. Thoughtfully structured lessons have clear objectives, developmentally appropriate content, preplanned explanations, active student involvement, and plentiful opportunities for all students to demonstrate what they have learned in the way they learn best.

The Classroom Environment

Effective teachers create and maintain a positive, student-focused learning environment. They begin by establishing caring, respectful relationships with their students to create a learning community where students feel free to take risks while exploring new ideas and trying out new skills. Furthermore, effective elementary and middle school teachers organize classroom materials, carefully schedule activities, and address inappropriate student behavior to increase time on task.

Video Link 1.1:
Watch a video about displaying student work.

An inherent part of creating a positive learning environment is exhibiting caring teacher dispositions. NCATE defines dispositions as the values, commitments, and professional ethics that influence behaviors toward students, families, colleagues, and communities and affect student learning, motivation, and development, as well as the educator's own professional growth. Dispositions are guided by beliefs and **attitudes** related to values such as caring, fairness, honesty, responsibility, and social justice. Because students learn how to interact with others by observing significant others in their lives (including teachers), effective educators must be aware of their verbal and nonverbal behaviors to ensure every child feels accepted. Exhibiting these dispositions will build a caring classroom climate and will enhance teachers' professional relationships with colleagues, administrators, and students' parents.

Although every teacher has his or her own personality, there are six common dispositions and attitudes that effective teachers hold. First of all, effective teachers are genuine. Within reason, they share their true selves with students. Second, effective teachers have realistic, yet challenging, expectations for *all* of their students. Third, effective teachers care about their students. They have an attitude of unconditional acceptance, respect, and trust. Fourth, effective teachers are excited about teaching and learning. Fifth, effective teachers value diversity. They treat *all* students equitably and fairly. Finally, effective teachers are willing to collaborate. They see themselves as part of an educational team and community. Great teachers do not just love kids. They facilitate a love of learning in the students they teach.

Classrooms are multidimensional and crowded with people, tasks, and time pressures. Teachers need to be able to manage this multidimensional environment by establishing clear expectations, starting classes on time, organizing materials, and using time effectively. Students learn best when they know what they are expected to accomplish, willingly stay on task, and understand the purpose and importance of assignments. Clear communication with students, parents, and administrators is imperative.

Instructional Techniques

Teachers need to carefully plan instructional activities that will captivate students' interest and motivate them to learn. Techniques include such strategies as questioning, using student ideas and contributions, and reinforcing. Effective teachers establish open classroom communication, clearly articulate their ideas, actively engage students, use a variety of teaching strategies, promote students' critical thinking, provide timely feedback, and spontaneously modify their instruction based upon students' feedback and perceived needs.

Professional Behavior

Teachers have multiple professional responsibilities that extend beyond traditional classroom instruction. Effective teachers embrace these challenges by becoming leaders in their classrooms, schools, and communities. True professional teacher–leaders develop their sense of self as lifelong learners by examining their place in the school and community, reflecting upon their instruction, keeping abreast of current best practices, demonstrating respect for others' perspectives during continuous collegial dialogues, and establishing quality, respectful relationships with colleagues, parents, community members, and students (Lambert, 2003). Furthermore, they are student advocates, change agents, and reflective decision makers who seek continuous professional growth opportunities.

Teachers, like other professionals, must continue to grow professionally. For example, technology for classroom use is evolving at an astonishing rate. Technology is ever-prevalent in all classrooms at all levels, but many experienced teachers and prospective teachers lack the technology skills to make effective use of classroom technology. Former techno-phobic teachers have attended workshops and received training so they can embrace the use of instructional technology. To remain effective, teachers need to continuously hone their skills by attending workshops, seeking training, reading professional literature, and being involved in professional education organizations. Professional teachers are dedicated to continuous learning—both about the subjects they teach and the teaching–learning process.

REFLECTIONS ON TEACHER PRACTICE 1.1: Making Education Meaningful

1. Are elementary and middle schools today setting students up for failure? If so, how must schools change to provide success for all students?

2. What is the attitude of most parents regarding school involvement? How can elementary and middle school teachers involve parents and the community to a greater extent in our schools?

Education should be painless. I believe the education of students should be a partnership between teacher and student, and it is the greatest gift we can give a student.

Students approach education in different ways. Some are easily stimulated and are easily taught. Others are harder to reach. The trick is to balance the teaching approach to benefit each student as an individual. Education should encompass a variety of experiences that add up to a complete entity, the educated person.

Students need encouragement, a stable classroom/school environment, and a chance to succeed. In our modern world of fast-moving images and strong media influence, a student's ability is often taken for granted. Since we are inundated with information, it is easy to assume students are being educated when they are out of the classroom. In most cases, however, this is not the case. Students need a stable classroom environment in which to be the students they are and learn what they need to know.

Students deserve the chance to succeed. By manipulating some situations, it is possible to give each student the satisfaction of being a success.

Effective teachers should be flexible and should be able to wear a lot of different hats. Sometimes these different hats have to be worn at once, so flexibility is paramount. Flexibility allows for trial and error. If one teaching method or strategy isn't working, something new should be tried. A teacher isn't just a teacher anymore, which accounts for the many hats. A teacher has to assume the role of parent, counselor, and disciplinarian. An effective teacher should be able to assimilate these roles into one package. In addition to flexibility and juggling hats, an effective teacher has to be both receptive and perceptive. A receptive teacher is open to new ideas, which is important when trying to teach a variety of different students. A perceptive teacher is able to see the student. By keeping a close watch on students and student performances, you open up opportunities to reach them.

Teachers should involve families and the community in the school. Parents should be seen as partners in the education of students. Parents should be kept informed of progress both good and bad. The old adage, "No news is good news" is outdated. Parents need to be made a part of the education of students. When possible, parents should be used as a classroom resource. Many parents have skills or experiences that can be tapped for classroom use as a speaker or helper.

The community should be welcome in the school. The community supports public schools financially through taxes and fund-raising and should feel a part of the school. In most cases, the school is a central focus in the community. This focus should be a good thing, not a bad one. The community has vast resources for schools both financial and academic. Through programs like "adopt a classroom" and others, the community can be brought into the school for a purpose and both school and community benefit. The education of students should not occur behind closed schoolhouse doors. The community and parents should feel a connection to the school and feel they are part of the education of our children.

—*Rachel, elementary school teacher*

Please visit the Student Study site at **www.sagepub.com/mooreteachingk8** *for additional discussion questions and assignments.*

SOURCE: Reprinted with permission from ProTeacher, a professional community for elementary school teachers (www.proteacher.net).

This completes our introduction to teaching. Table 1.2 summarizes the concepts addressed in this section. Review the summary and complete Reflect and Apply Exercise 1.1.

TABLE 1.2	Teaching Concepts
Concept	**Description**
Teaching as art	Effective teachers have natural instincts for teaching.
Teaching as science	Effective teaching comes from learned laws and principles of teaching.
Organized classroom	Classroom is structured around a businesslike atmosphere and well-planned appropriate lessons.
Transfer	The ability to use information acquired in one situation in new situations.

REFLECT AND APPLY EXERCISE 1.1: The Skills Associated With Elementary and Middle School Teaching

Reflect

- Elementary and middle school teachers have many different responsibilities in today's schools. Do you think elementary and middle school teachers are asked to do too many things? If so, what can be done to improve the working conditions of elementary and/or middle school teachers?

- Brainstorm a list of the roles of elementary or middle school teachers. Do you feel qualified to carry out these roles? Which roles would be your strengths? Do you have any weak areas?

- Understanding and willingness to adapt instructional strategies and responses to students are often suggested as attributes of the successful teacher. Do you possess these attributes? What other attributes do you feel effective teachers must have?

Apply

- Consider how the learning theories presented in this chapter will apply to your future students. Create a two-column chart with these headings—theory, rationale. In the "theory" column, write at least five elements of the various theories that you found the most important. In the "rationale" column, state why each element is important. Be ready to share.

- Are effective elementary and middle school teachers "born," or can an individual be taught to be an effective elementary or middle school teacher?

"Have you had any experience working with children?"

SOURCE: Created by Ford Button.

PROFESSIONAL TEACHING STANDARDS

Research shows that what teachers know, do, and value have a significant influence on the nature, extent, and rate of student learning. Recognition of the impact teachers have on the student–teacher relationship and students' achievement highlights the need to better define and build on what constitutes effective teaching. Professional teaching standards provide a powerful mechanism for achieving this aim.

Challenges in Preparing to Teach

Many recent regulations from local, state, and federal agencies have brought new challenges to teaching. For example, a national mandate that has had a major impact on our schools is the **No Child Left Behind (NCLB) Act** of 2001 (U.S. Department of Education, 2004). Moreover, teachers must be aware of and follow laws that can have an impact on classroom instruction such as the Individuals with Disabilities Education Improvement Act (IDEIA), Section 504 of the Rehabilitation Act, and the Family Educational Rights and Privacy Act (FERPA). A review of NCLB and educational law can be found on the web-based student study site (**www.sagepub.com/mooreteachingk8**).

Video Link 1.2:
Watch a video about teacher preparation.

As you prepare for a career in teaching elementary or middle school students, you will become familiar with rules and policies that govern many aspects of what happens in the classroom: teacher qualifications, allotted time per subject area, curriculum adoption, professional ethics, student assistance, and grading practices. Regulating agencies also require institutions, like the university or college you are attending, to meet rigid standards within teacher education programs that are preparing future teachers for the classroom. Professional educational organizations and state educational professional standards boards have identified teaching standards and benchmarks. Your teacher preparation program is aligned with these standards. This ensures that you are developing the skills and dispositions that you will need to become an effective elementary or middle school teacher.

Although there are a growing number of new requirements guiding the profession, many teachers express satisfaction with the amount of control they have in presenting instruction within their classrooms. The school district where you will be teaching one day will identify *what* you need to teach and possibly *when* you need to teach specific topics. The First Amendment of the U.S. Constitution assures academic freedom, or your right to decide *how* to teach the content. As always, everything you do must be in the best interest of the students.

In our technology-based society, teachers must be technologically literate so they can help their students become technologically proficient. The International Society for Technology in Education (ISTE) has created the National Educational Technology Standards (NETS) for prospective teacher technology literacy and for student technology literacy. Many teacher education programs have adopted the NETS standards for prospective teachers and for students. These standards can be accessed at www.iste.org.

Several national groups and professional associations have invested considerable time, energy, and resources in establishing a rationale for teaching standards. They have worked closely with classroom practitioners to design and test various models and approaches to professionalize teaching. These efforts resulted in the recommendation and establishment of standards and **teacher testing**. Playing a central role in these efforts were NCATE, the National Board for Professional Teaching Standards (NBPTS), INTASC, and ETS. Most teacher preparation programs are specifically aligned with the INTASC standards at the undergraduate level (initial licensure) and with the NBPTS at the graduate level (advanced licensure). In addition, some states require teacher education programs that prepare teachers (early childhood, elementary, English, mathematics, science, special education, etc.) and other school personnel (counselors, principals, superintendents, etc.) to meet specific Specialized Professional Association (SPA) standards. A brief discussion of NCATE, NBPTS, and INTASC can be found on the web-based student study site (**www.sagepub.com/mooreteachingk8**).

ESMERELDA: A REFLECTIVE CASE STUDY

Esmerelda smiled and wiped away a tear after saying good-bye to her fifth grade students the last day of school. She relaxed against the door frame and reflected upon her journey toward this day. Esmerelda furrowed her brow as she remembered how she had struggled to complete her BS in education because of personal, financial, and academic issues. Her eyes twinkled as she envisioned her family's celebration when she'd finally passed the Praxis exams the second time around! Esmerelda's dimples deepened as she reflected upon the caring classroom community she had established her very first year of teaching and the great job she'd done organizing her classroom and designing developmentally appropriate, high-interest lessons. Her students had grown academically and socially. Esmerelda had grown even more. Her thoughts were interrupted when Mr. Gattadue, the principal, walked into the classroom to introduce Albert, who would be joining the faculty next fall. Albert, a former chemist for the local plastics company, would be teaching fourth grade and fifth grade science classes. Mr. Gattadue explained that Albert had earned a degree in chemistry and passed the Praxis exams instead of gaining certification through the traditional route. Esmerelda welcomed her colleague with a warm smile and mixed feelings.

1. If you were Esmerelda, how would you feel? Why?

2. In your opinion, should Albert be allowed to teach with little or no teacher preparation training? Why or why not?

3. Do you see any potential problems with alternative certification for elementary and middle school teachers? Why or why not?

Assessment of Standards

To ensure that the INTASC standards are being met, many states require all teacher candidates to pass a standardized **test** that assesses their content knowledge and their knowledge of teaching and learning. Forty states use the Praxis Series to assess the national standards. Some states developed their own tests to assess whether candidates meet INTASC standards.

The ETS developed the Praxis Series to assist state education agencies in making licensing decisions. The Praxis Series: Professional Assessments for Beginning Teachers is a set of rigorous and carefully validated assessments designed to provide accurate, reliable licensing information. Access www.ets.org/praxis to check Praxis test requirements for your state. The three categories of assessment in the Praxis Series correspond to the three decision points in a teacher preparation program:

- Entry into a teacher training program—Praxis I: Academic Skills Assessments

- Requirement for initial licensure into profession—Praxis II: Subject and Pedagogy Assessments

- Requirement for permanent licensure—Praxis III: Classroom Performance Assessments

Only the Praxis I and II are used extensively by states in their licensure process. The Praxis I: Academic Skills Assessments (Pre-Professional Skills Tests, or PPST) tests candidates' reading, writing, and mathematics abilities. Some teacher education programs use students' ACT or SAT scores to demonstrate their academic proficiency instead. The Praxis II: Subject and Pedagogy Assessments contain two types of tests: Multiple Subjects Assessments and Principles of Learning and Teaching (PLT) Tests.

The Praxis II: Multiple Subjects Assessments tests teacher candidates' subject matter knowledge. Some of these subject area tests include multiple exams, and some include a pedagogy exam. For example, the elementary exam tests students' knowledge in four major content areas: (1) math, (2) science, (3) social studies, and (4) reading/language arts. The social studies and reading/language arts exams consist of two content exams and a pedagogy exam. Most of the exams are 1 or 2 hours in duration.

The Praxis II: PLT Tests are designed to assess pedagogical knowledge in such areas as educational psychology, human growth and development, classroom management, instructional design and delivery techniques, evaluation and assessment, and other preparation. These assessments are divided into early childhood, Grades K to 6, Grades 5 to 9, and Grades 7 to 12 to reflect the different levels of licensure. Each assessment includes 24 multiple-choice questions and four case histories each followed by three short-answer questions about the case. The multiple-choice questions cover candidate knowledge in the following areas:

Students as Learners

Student Development and the Learning Process

Students as Diverse Learners

Student Motivation and the Learning Environment

Instruction and Assessment

    Instructional Strategies

    Planning Instruction

    Assessment Strategies

Communication Techniques

    Basic, effective verbal and nonverbal communication techniques

    Effect of cultural and gender differences on communications in the classroom

    Types of communications and interactions that can stimulate discussion in different ways for particular purposes

Profession and Community

    The Reflective Practitioner

    The Larger Community

Because you will probably be required to demonstrate competency relative to the INTASC standards during your initial teacher preparatory program and perhaps to the NBPTS in an advanced program, we will focus on these standards throughout this text. The Deconstructing the Standards exercises located on the web-based student study site (www.sagepub.com/mooreteachingk8) are designed to assist you. We will also indicate how the text content relates to sections of the Praxis II: PLT Tests.

REFLECTIONS ON TEACHER PRACTICE 1.2: The Standards Movement

1. Why should schools have to meet national and state standards? Do standards really lead to more effective teaching and learning?

2. What benefits and problems do you [associate] with high-stakes testing?

The establishment of standards has changed how most teachers teach. However, one problem with the "standards movement" is that advocates of standards-based classrooms have lost control of their message, as high-stakes state testing advocates have seized the "standards" language—tacking it onto the state accountability system without sufficient thought and certainly regarding the needed major investment in professional development required to make standards a meaningful tool to raise student achievement.

I've had the opportunity to observe standards-based classrooms where teachers are improving teaching and learning through the use of standards. In every case, the standards were developed or modified by the school system, with active teacher participation, and were accompanied by "performance standards" that showed teachers and students what is "good enough." The standards-based initiative was accompanied by lots of professional development that linked standards to teaching practice, classroom assessment, etc. In these classrooms and schools, the decision to measure student progress against standards provoked deep conversations about the quality of lessons and teaching strategies, about the meaning of grades, and about the need to deepen content. Also, in every case, teachers were using all the provided creative teaching strategies.

Even with help, grasping and applying the standards-based approach to teaching and learning is very hard work. But in dozens of interviews with teachers in these schools, I heard over and over again that the standards-based approach to teaching was improving the curriculum, reducing duplicative teaching across grades in every subject area, and causing teachers to ask some difficult but important questions about the value of favorite projects that kids enjoyed but that did little to increase their skills and knowledge.

In many cases, the process of examining lessons from a standards perspective made it possible for teachers to modify those "favorite units," retaining the fun and excitement while strengthening the academic purpose and the learning outcomes. None of this will have an impact unless teachers move beyond the point of simply trying to "match" a list of standards to their existing lesson plans.

I know there are teachers who have experienced the positives of standards-based teaching. However, in some schools, the growing pressure to perform on standardized state tests has actually stymied the move toward standards-based teaching, as principals and teachers have given in (understandably) to pressure from above to drill, drill, drill—to narrow curriculum and make the state test the Alpha and Omega of schooling.

I don't believe excellent teachers are afraid to ask tough questions about their own teaching and the teaching in their schools. That's what standards should be all about. Unfortunately, politicians and other folks who seek to gain an advantage by leveling blanket attacks on educators, without much clue about the realities of school, are turning the standards movement into a bludgeon. That's a dead-end strategy that won't help teachers, schools, or, most important of all, kids.

In closing, I believe it is possible to criticize the negative effects to high-stakes testing, champion constructive teaching, and still support the proposition that standards-based teaching can raise student achievement.

—*John Norton, education writer*

Please visit the Student Study site at **www.sagepub.com/mooreteachingk8** *for additional discussion questions and assignments.*

Licensure/Certification

Licensure/certification is the process by which teachers receive state permission to teach (see Appendix B). Moreover, in some cases, large cities (e.g., New York, Chicago, Buffalo) have their own licensure/certification requirements that must be met.

The licensure of teachers is as old as the nation. Licensing is generally viewed as absolutely essential to ensure the quality of the teaching force. The goal is to have a fully qualified licensed teacher in every classroom. To receive a teaching license, all states require successful completion of an approved teacher education program that culminates with at least a bachelor's degree.

Teacher shortages in some areas and the growing criticism of current traditional teacher education practices have combined to spawn a wide movement toward alternative teacher certification. Every state in the nation has implemented or is now seriously working on the challenge of creating alternatives to the traditional undergraduate college teacher education program route for certifying teachers. These programs are designed for people who already have at least a bachelor's degree in a field other than education and want to become licensed to teach. More information on alternative teacher certification for each state can be obtained at the following sites:

http://teach-now.org/intro.html

www2.ed.gov/admins/tchrqual/recruit/altroutes/index.html

www.ncei.com/Alt-Teacher-Cert.htm

Preparing quality teachers is a complex and challenging process. Professional standards have been implemented to make sure teacher education programs are preparing teachers who can meet the challenges of our rapidly changing and diverse society. Complete Reflect and Apply Exercise 1.2 to check your understanding of this process.

REFLECT AND APPLY EXERCISE 1.2: Professional Standards for Preparing Elementary and Middle School Teachers

Reflect

- Most states now have assessment requirements for elementary and middle school teacher licensure/certification. Many of these states require that prospective elementary and middle school teachers pass licensure/certification exams and/or develop a competency portfolio. Are these good ideas? Why do you support or oppose testing and portfolio requirements for elementary and/or middle school teachers?

Apply

- Go to this site: http://education.uky.edu/AcadServ/content/50-states-certification-requirements. What are the assessment requirements for elementary and middle school teacher candidates to be licensed/certified in your state?

- Does your state require elementary and middle school teacher candidates to pass a test series? Is it a state-developed test or the Praxis Series? To learn more about the Praxis exam requirements, go to www.ets.org and click on The Praxis Series Tests.

- Does your state require a portfolio for licensure/certification? If so, what should be included in a portfolio to demonstrate elementary and/or middle school teacher competency?

- Go to your state's Department of Education site. Does your state offer alternative licensure/certification routes for elementary and middle school teachers? What are the requirements?

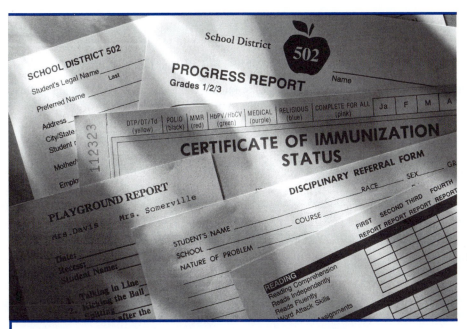

Teachers and school personnel must meet state licensure/certification requirements.

SUMMARY

This chapter introduced you to teaching and professional teaching standards. The main points were as follows:

Teaching

- Educational theorists' perspectives on how students learn establish a foundation for modern schools and teaching.
- Effective teaching is an art as well as a science.

Theories That Shaped Teaching

- Teachers need the professional and pedagogical knowledge and skills to help all students learn.
- Multiple learning theories abound on effective teaching.

Constructivism

- Constructivism focuses on actively involving students in their own learning.
- Constructivists believe students construct their own meanings.

Traditional Model of Teaching

- Educators have identified and described numerous approaches to teaching that are based on traditional perspectives about elementary and middle school teaching and learning.
- It is unrealistic for elementary or middle school teachers to be too prescriptive in their teaching approach when they must deal with such a wide diversity of students.

Elementary and Middle School Classroom Teaching

- Teaching requires a repertoire of skills and the ability to put these skills to use.

- Teachers' effectiveness depends on the subject, students, and environmental conditions.

- Danielson (2007) suggests four skill areas are needed for effective teaching: (1) quality planning and preparation, (2) preparation of a positive classroom environment, (3) use of proven instructional techniques, and (4) professional behavior.

- Teachers in today's schools must be technologically literate.

Professional Teaching Standards

- ETS developed the Praxis Series to assist state education agencies in making licensing decisions.

- Licensure/certification is the process by which teachers receive state permission to teach. Licensure regulations vary a great deal among states.

DISCUSSION QUESTIONS AND ACTIVITIES

1. **Teaching Effectiveness.** Revisit the sketch or word collage you created for the Before We Begin activity. Use that initial vision of teacher effectiveness plus what you've learned in this chapter to create a concept map, or web, that depicts your current thinking about teaching, learning, and teacher effectiveness.

2. **The Challenge.** Think about the grade level you expect to teach. Describe at least two challenges you will face. How will you cope with these challenges?

3. **Teaching Knowledge.** Some teaching knowledge is gained only through experiences and cannot be found in a textbook or in a college course. Do you agree or disagree with this statement? Give some examples to support your opinion.

4. **Personal Dispositions.** Make a list of personal dispositions you possess that will assist you in teaching at your planned grade level. Form pairs with a future elementary teacher and a future middle school teacher. How are the lists the same? Different?

TECH CONNECTION

Teachers must be technological leaders in their classrooms so they can help students develop their technological proficiency. Complete the following two application activities to review the suggested technology skills for teachers and students.

- The ISTE created five broad categories of standards for teacher technological literacy. Access these standards at www.iste.org. Select NETS for Teachers in the Standards heading. Then click NETS for Teachers 2008. Rate your proficiency for each standard using a scale of 1 (low) to 5 (high). Discuss your technology competency levels with classmates.

- Stay on the same page. Click NETS For Students under Standards. Then click on NETS for Students 2007 under Page Links. Review the six standards. Then go back to the previous page and click on 2007 Student Profiles. Examine the specific NETS*S profiles that address the standards for the grade level you plan to teach. Each indicator is followed by numbers within parentheses. These numbers are the standards that the indicators address. According to the student profiles, what types of activities need to be integrated in your teaching for students to meet technology-related standards? Discuss your results with classmates.

CONNECTION WITH THE FIELD

1. **Classroom Observation.** Observe a kindergarten, elementary, or middle school classroom. Document ways the teacher demonstrates effective teaching strategies and professionalism. Be prepared to share this information with your classmates.

2. **Educators' View of Effective Teaching and Learning.** Interview one teacher and one administrator. How do they define effective teaching and learning? How do they know when it has occurred in the classroom? How would they measure effective teaching and learning? How do the teacher/administrator perspectives compare? Which view do you tend to support? Share your interview results with classmates. Are there differences at the elementary and middle school levels?

3. **Evaluation of Effective Teaching and Learning.** Visit at least two local school districts. Do these school districts **evaluate** their teachers? If so, who does the evaluation? What criteria are used? What do teachers think of the evaluative process? What do you think of the criteria? Would you want to be evaluated using the criteria?

4. **Alternative Licensure/Certification.** Many states are now offering alternative and/or fast routes to teacher certification. Interview some public school elementary or middle school teachers and administrators. What do they think of alternative certification?

STUDENT STUDY SITE

Visit the Student Study Site at **www.sagepub.com/mooreteachingk8** for these additional learning tools:

- Video clips
- Web resources
- Self quiz
- E-Flashcards
- Full-text SAGE journal articles
- Portfolio Connection
- Licensing Preparation/Praxis Connection

CHAPTER 2

Teaching Diverse Students

Give me your tired, your poor, Your huddled masses yearning to breathe free, The wretched refuse of your teeming shore. Send these, the homeless, tempest-tost to me, I lift my lamp beside the golden door!

—Emma Lazarus
Inscribed on the base of the Statue of Liberty

Before We Begin

Before We Begin: Describe the cultural composition of an elementary or middle school classroom in your community. How can teachers meet the needs of the diverse cultures represented in these classrooms? Be ready to compare your view with classmates.

OVERVIEW

America's public school system was founded upon the premise that all people, regardless of their cultures or special circumstances, are entitled to a free, quality education so that they can become productive, contributing citizens in our society. Modern-day educators have extended that vision to create global citizens. Education is, in a sense, a "golden door" of opportunity that enables people to transcend social, physical, economic, or cultural barriers to pursue their dreams. Increasingly diverse classrooms provide a venue for children to learn to embrace cultural differences and eliminate the barriers of racism, sexism, and prejudice. If we want all students to enter this golden door of educational opportunity, teachers must be sensitive to their students' cultural and academic differences. They need to create culturally sensitive learning communities, develop positive teacher–student–parent relationships, design lessons that motivate all students to learn, and implement those lessons using differentiated instructional strategies to maximize student learning.

OBJECTIVES

After completing your study of Chapter 2, you should be able to

- explain why teachers need to embrace diversity and establish high expectations for *all* students,
- discuss the changing demographics of American classrooms,
- explain the role communication plays in culturally sensitive classrooms,
- describe ways to enhance home-school communication,
- define and describe the various dimensions of **differentiated instruction** and **learning styles**, and
- explain the concept of **multiple intelligences** and describe Gardner's eight areas of intelligence.

Everything you do in your future classroom will center upon meeting the needs of your diverse student population. Therefore, you must gain an understanding of *all* children's unique academic, emotional, and cultural differences so that you can help them on their academic and life journeys. To support a culturally sensitive learning community, you need to design and implement lessons that address all students' academic needs, learning styles, and multiple intelligences.

Modern classrooms are often highly diverse.

CLASSROOM DIVERSITY

Video Link 2.1:
Watch a video about adapting to diversity.

Historically, America's classrooms were populated by students of mostly European descent. Modern classrooms, however, reflect the nation's increasing cultural diversity. Today, more than 25% of the U.S. population is non-European (Tompkins, 2005). Moreover, because of an influx of immigrants and increased birth rate, Hispanic and Asian American populations have grown by more than 20%, and the African American population has increased by 12%. Another form of diversity that impacts many American classrooms is transiency. Approximately 40 million Americans move each year, causing the student populations in many classrooms to almost totally change between fall and spring (Ornstein, Behar-Horenstein, & Ornstein, 2007). As a result of these trends, more cultures are represented in today's classrooms, and more foreign languages are being spoken in our schools than ever before. Many of these cultures and languages have yet to be represented by the formal curriculum.

During classroom interactions and instruction, teachers must keep the special cultural needs of their diverse student population in mind. Please note, however, that students' cultures include much more than national origin or race. The National Council for Accreditation of Teacher Education (NCATE) now defines diversity as differences among groups of people and individuals based on ethnicity, race, socioeconomic status, gender, exceptionalities, language, religion, sexual orientation, and geographical area. Thus, teachers must be prepared to identify diverse students' strengths, weaknesses, aspirations, limitations, and special needs. Today's classrooms must celebrate diversity.

Most classrooms include students who have documented intellectual, physical, and/or emotional exceptionalities. Under the Individuals With Disabilities Education Improvement Act (IDEIA), children with disabilities must be educated in the least restrictive environment (LRE), or an educational setting that is as similar as possible to the one in which children who do not have a disability are educated. In the past, children with special needs were mainstreamed into general education classrooms on a limited basis for a limited number of subjects. Today, mainstreaming has been replaced by inclusion, as children with special needs are taught full-time in a general education classroom by a regular education teacher and specialists. Some educators believe that *all* children benefit from inclusion because it creates an authentic microcosm of the society students will be participating in once they graduate (Karten, 2010; Rea, McLaughlin, & Walther-Thomas, 2002).

MIGUEL AND JUANITA: A REFLECTIVE CASE STUDY

In the middle of class one sunny September morning, Ms. Ima D. Voss, Smallville Consolidated School District's K–8 principal, interrupts your lesson. She introduces Miguel and Juanita, two new arrivals who would be joining your class. Their family has come to Smallville to assist with harvesting the corn and soybeans. You welcome the twins warmly, find desks and materials for them to use, and continue with your lessons. At the end of the day, you reflect upon Miguel's and Juanita's academic participation and social interactions, review their academic records, and ponder ways you can facilitate their educational efforts.

1. List the special needs that Miguel and Juanita bring to the classroom.
2. How can you address these needs before the harvest ends?
3. How can you make Miguel and Juanita become accepted members of an already-established learning community?

What does a diverse classroom community look like? Please complete Reflect and Apply Exercise 2.1, which will check your understanding of the importance of knowing your students' backgrounds.

REFLECT AND APPLY EXERCISE 2.1: Background Impact

Reflect

- Because of their racial, ethnic, cultural, socioeconomic, and intellectual differences, students bring unique needs to the classroom. Consider the geographic area where you plan to teach. Create a concept map, or web, depicting the various cultures represented by the diverse student population. What can you do to learn more about the cultures that are currently unfamiliar to you?

Apply

- List at least five school and/or community resources you can use to address the diverse needs of your future students.

Teacher Expectations

Teachers must plan very carefully to ensure that *all* students participate in high-interest educational activities that are personally relevant. Failure to recognize and address students' unique backgrounds could result in a large portion of the future adult population of this country who cannot participate successfully as global citizens. Academic experiences and parental perceptions impact students' attitudes toward education. To create enthusiastic, lifelong learners, effective teachers show students that what they are learning in school will equip them with the knowledge, confidence, and skills necessary to have fulfilling lives.

Teachers' expectations have a powerful effect on students' performance. Effective teachers hold high, realistic expectations for themselves and *all* students. They believe in their ability to create a caring classroom climate and in their students' ability to succeed. If teachers act as though they expect their students to be hard working, interested, and successful in class, they are more likely to be so. Researchers have found that students who feel they have supportive, caring teachers are more motivated to engage in academic work than students with unsupportive, uncaring teachers (McCombs, 2001; Newman, 2002).

Teachers communicate their expectations and attitudes toward their students through their actions and words. Students' perceptions of teachers' expectations and attitudes can affect their motivation and self-concept. Oftentimes, teachers show favoritism to high achievers by interacting with them more frequently, giving them more time to answer questions, and increasing the amount of positive feedback given to them. Conversely, low-achieving students are often seated toward the back of the room, have less opportunity to respond to questions, receive more criticism for incorrect responses, and are interrupted more frequently. Generally, teachers tend to be more supportive and positive toward capable students.

Students' academic performance and self-esteem are enhanced when teachers set high expectations and hold them to these expectations. Therefore, teachers need to set realistic expectations for *all* students when making assignments, giving presentations, conducting discussions, and grading examinations. "Realistic" in this context means that the standards are high enough to motivate students to do their best work but not so high that students will inevitably be frustrated in trying to meet those expectations. Teachers should guard against setting too low or too high expectations for students with special needs and too low expectations for gifted students. To develop the drive to achieve, students need to believe that achievement is possible—which means that teachers need to provide plentiful opportunities for success.

Effective teachers help students set achievable goals and encourage them to focus on long-term improvement, not just grades on current assignments. Students learn to evaluate their progress, critique their own work, analyze their strengths, and address their weaknesses.

"What did I learn today? My mother will want to know."

SOURCE: Created by Ford Button.

Most importantly, effective teachers treat all students the same, regardless of their culture, socioeconomic status, or special needs. They continuously express their confidence in students' ability to succeed. This becomes a positive self-fulfilling prophecy because students begin to behave and achieve in accordance with teachers' expectations. Be aware, then, that students perceive teachers' actions as a mirror of themselves, so teachers need to challenge their students and communicate a belief in students' abilities—and mean it.

Teaching Students With Special Needs

Public Law 94-142 (PL 94-142) and its successors require that an individual education plan (IEP) be written for every student with special needs. These IEPs describe the student's abilities, educational and/or socioemotional needs, developmental level, and academic/behavioral expectations. They also identify required instructional modifications and accommodations (Rothstein, Rothstein, & Johnson, 2010). Teachers use this information to differentiate instruction, or customize their instructional delivery to address the needs of all students.

Teachers differentiate instruction by modifying the instructional delivery and assignments. For example, they create outlines, concept maps, and other visual aids for students who have difficulty processing complex concepts. Teachers record step-by-step instructions for students who are struggling in science labs, while using a traditional lab approach with general education students. In language arts classes, teachers use recorded books, leveled readers, or optical readers to share quality literature with challenged readers. During the writing process, students who have motor difficulties record their stories or have scribes. Primary children are encouraged to express themselves through multiple sign systems (pictures, numbers, letters, and pseudo-writing). Emergent and beginning writers create language experience stories with the teacher. In math class, struggling students use hands-on manipulatives to demonstrate mathematical concepts; they can also write math problems, one digit per square, on graph paper. Other examples of lesson modifications include modified worksheets, individualized instruction, specialized software, modified assignments, peer tutors, study guides, oral or hands-on exams, and **assistive technology (AT)**. Some school districts help teachers create differentiated assignments by developing classroom modification plans for school use. Figure 2.1 shows a sample plan with three categories. The teacher checks those items that will apply to a specific student.

Some planning guidelines for working with students who have special needs follow:

1. Gather information about the nature of the exceptional student's difference and how that difference might affect the learning process.

2. Seek assistance from district special education or resource experts.

3. Use specialized equipment (typewriters, computers, DVD player, print enlarger, Braille material, etc.) to allow students to function at an optimum level.

4. Individualize the curriculum by adapting materials and teaching strategies to better meet the needs of the exceptional students.

5. Remove physical and psychological barriers that limit exceptional students' ability to succeed in your classroom.

Response to Intervention

Response to intervention (RTI) is a relatively new approach to identifying students with academic needs that has gained increasing interest. RTI, which emphasizes "student outcomes instead of student deficits," provides early and more immediate support for students' academic needs by screening students as early as kindergarten (Kavale, Holdnack, & Mostert, 2005; Vaughn & Fuchs, 2003). This strategy is used to identify and provide early intervention activities so that students who are struggling academically can participate and progress in general education curriculum. Students who are not responding to traditional instruction are provided additional academic support through individualized and small-group instruction provided by teachers who use research-based strategies. If students

| FIGURE 2.1 | Classroom Modification Plan |

Student: _____   Teacher: _____

School: _____   Grade/Course: _____

A. Exam Modification

____ 1. Reduce the number of exams to _____
____ 2. Open-book exams
____ 3. Allow more time for regular exam
____ 4. Reduce the length of the regular exam
____ 5. Use more objective items (fewer essay items)
____ 6. Give some exam orally
____ 7. Write down test items for students
____ 8. Read test items to student
____ 9. Substitute assignment for test
____ 10. Enlarge test item print
____ 11. Allow use of computer
____ 12. Other   (specify) _____

B. Assignment Modification

____ 1. Provide more detailed directions
____ 2. Repeat instructions
____ 3. Give instructions through several channels (oral, written, etc.)
____ 4. Provide materials that are programmed/self-checking
____ 5. Brief student on major points before starting an assignment
____ 6. Allow more time for regular assignments
____ 7. Reduce length of regular assignments
____ 8. Break assignment into a series of smaller assignments
____ 9. Reduce reading level of the regular assignment (edit, reword)
____ 10. Change format of the instructional materials
____ 11. Use different format materials to teach the same content
____ 12. Provide study aids (hints, cue cards, guides, calculators, computers)
____ 13. Provide hands-on activities/physical assignments
____ 14. Allow oral presentations/reports/projects/games, etc.
____ 15. Other (specify) _____

C. Content Alternatives

____ 1. Make cassette or CD or DVD recordings of lectures for individual playback
____ 2. Allow teacher aide/volunteer to take notes for student
____ 3. Allow classroom peers to make carbon copies of classwork for the student
____ 4. Use visual (DVDs, charts, pictures, etc.) and/or audio materials (CDs, tapes, records)
____ 5. Use individualized learning contract or learning centers
____ 6. Use computer learning packages
____ 7. Provide hands-on/learning by discovery experiences
____ 8. Use self-checking materials
____ 9. Other (specify) _____

continue to struggle, they receive even more individualized instruction targeting the area of academic need. Then, students who still exhibit academic difficulties are referred for special diagnostic testing and possible special education services.

Assistive Technology

AT enables *all* students to be successful in the general education classroom. Through the use of specialized technology such as closed circuit monitors, Braille readers, voice activated software, TTY telephones, and motorized wheelchairs, students are able to participate in educational activities that might have been difficult or impossible otherwise. Indeed, the latest amendments to the Individuals With Disabilities Education Improvement Act of 2004 (IDEIA) encourage implementation and development of technology to enhance instruction in regular classrooms. In effect, Congress suggests the effective use of technology reduces and/or eliminates many of the barriers that block instruction and improves teachers' ability to better address the needs of *all* students.

Effective teachers develop learning materials and activities commensurate with the abilities of students with special needs, much as they adapt lessons to the individual differences of all students. In doing so, they work closely with available resource teachers, specialists, and other support personnel.

Limited English Proficiency

A major challenge facing many school districts in many areas of the country is teaching students a second language: English. During this past decade alone, approximately 4.4 million children were **English language learners (ELL)** (Hancock, 2007). In many communities today, it is not uncommon for more than half the students to come from homes where the first language is not English. In the Los Angeles Unified School District, for example, more than 81 languages are spoken in the homes. Big city school districts in New York City, Miami, and Houston, as well as many smaller districts, now have populations of ethnic minorities that equal or exceed nonminority students. Nationwide, the number of students whose first language is not English is expected to increase during the next couple of decades. By 2026, it is projected that about one fourth of all students will come from homes in which the primary language is not English. Yet Standard English will continue to be a necessity for success in school and society.

Limited English students who are learning to communicate reasonably well in English need encouragement and help. The terms **limited English proficiency (LEP)** and *ELL* are used for students who have not yet attained an adequate level of English to succeed in an English-only program. Students who are learning **English as a second language (ESL)** may attend special classes for ELL. Some schools use a pullout system, in which part of the student's day is spent in special bilingual classes or individualized tutoring sessions and part in the general education classroom. This instruction enables them to learn the major concepts being taught in the general education classroom while they learn English. Other schools place students in sheltered classes consisting of specific cultural groups where the teacher is specially trained to work with LEP students. School districts who have a high percentage of ESL students often hire bilingual teachers to teach English and ELL students in one classroom.

Whatever system is used, teaching students who have limited proficiency in English should include the use of plentiful visual displays, demonstrations, dual language texts, bilingual software programs, physical education activities, hands-on activities, group work, artwork, and cooperative learning (see Chapter 9). Teachers should attempt to communicate with LEP students through gestures, pictures, and any words they know from the students' native language. Take time to teach English-speaking students some key words, phrases, or gestures so they can build peer relationships as well. Encourage other students to include LEP students in their activities, explaining that they can make the new students comfortable by helping them learn the standard procedures and popular activities. Always maintain a positive attitude, even though attempting to communicate with LEP students may be challenging.

Gifted and Talented

Most general education classrooms will also have some **gifted and talented (G/T) students** (Davis, Rimm, & Siegle, 2010). Teachers should vary the academic content, instructional process, or student products to challenge these G/T students. For example, G/T students can develop their own hypotheses and experiments in science, create faux interviews or scripts in language arts, and apply mathematical concepts to solve real-life problems. Help G/T children develop their critical thinking skills using strategies described in Chapter 10.

REFLECTIONS ON TEACHER PRACTICE 2.1 Working With Parents

1. What benefit would be gained from extending the school year and student time in school?

2. How are parents unrealistic about the function of schools and what schools can accomplish?

As an educator, I am familiar with the old "boredom" tale from parents. I listen politely without comment. Then I ask them nicely what I can do to make my class more interesting for their child. Usually, they don't have an answer. The real problem is that in this age of instant results, many parents today expect their child's entire education to occur within the 6-hour school day. And they expect it to be individually tailored to their child. Whereas teachers should consider individual needs, it is unrealistic to individualize instruction for all students. I think many parents and educators have lost sight of the original intent of public education in the United States. Public education was set up to provide students with a foundation of skills and opportunities for education. It was assumed that truly interested students would continue learning at home. Now, with most parents working to make ends meet, I believe they have an absolute right to expect more from their child's school. But because most kids are only in school for about 1,200 hours per year, it is unrealistic to expect schools to work miracles. So much has changed in society, but our country's educational system has not yet caught up.

Perhaps we need to restructure our country's educational system to better address the needs of today's parents, who, just trying to survive, are often spread too thin to educate their children at home. If individualized instruction is what we need to have, then perhaps all students should be designated for "special education," with smaller classes of students working toward individual goals. After all, every student has his or her own special needs. As our system works now, only certain "identified" students are having their "special" needs met. Is that really fair?

Perhaps students should be in school for more hours. I feel like I have so much to "cover" for standardized tests that my students don't get the opportunity to practice newly learned skills as much as research says they need to. Of course, changes in our educational system will not happen until teachers are seen (and ultimately paid) as the highly specialized professionals that we are.

—*Mary, elementary school teacher*

Please visit the Student Study site at **www.sagepub.com/mooreteachingk8** *for additional discussion questions and assignments.*

SOURCE: Reprinted with permission from ProTeacher, a professional community for elementary school teachers (www.proteacher.net).

This completes our study of some of the challenges presented by a diverse student population. Complete Reflect and Apply Exercise 2.2 to explore the impact of racial and ethnic differences on the classroom and to further explore your diversity awareness.

REFLECT AND APPLY EXERCISE 2.2: Diversity Awareness

Reflect

- Effective teachers learn about students' backgrounds and needs, respect all students, avoid using stereotypes, use culture-fair and gender-fair language, and integrate diverse perspectives throughout the curriculum. What qualities and experiences do you possess or lack that might affect your ability to be a teacher who embraces a diverse student population?

- How will diversity awareness affect your ability to better work with students, parents, and professional colleagues?

Apply

- How will diversity and cultural differences affect your teaching and students' learning?

- How can you use racial, ethnic, and linguistic differences to enhance your classroom community and curriculum?

- How can you adjust your teaching strategies and curricula to better meet the needs of all students in your future classroom?

MULTICULTURALLY SENSITIVE COMMUNICATION

Of all the knowledge and skills teachers possess, being able to effectively communicate is perhaps the most significant and the most useful. Through communication, teachers teach, colleagues collaborate, and students learn. Without communication, teaching does not occur, children do not learn, and schools do not function.

Children learn both verbal and nonverbal communication strategies through imitating the significant others in their lives—their parents and teachers. At home, most American parents only converse with their children approximately 38 minutes per week. Yet, elementary and middle school teachers communicate with children up to 7 hours per school day (Hansen, 1999). So who has the most potential impact on how children learn to communicate? Teachers do!

Most teacher preparatory programs place a great deal of emphasis on future teachers' ability to read and write with little emphasis given to speaking and the ability to listen. These programs often only require one public speaking course and entirely overlook the importance of nonverbal communication. The most persuasive teachers do not rely exclusively on reading and writing; they talk, they observe, and they listen.

Teachers, therefore, need to become proficient verbal and nonverbal communicators to interact effectively with *all* students and *all* families. Establishing quality teacher–student–parent communication doesn't just happen; it requires special skills and dispositions such as good listening techniques, tact, kindness, consideration, empathy, enthusiasm, an understanding of parent–child relationships, and an awareness and knowledge of cultural factors that affect communication.

Communication With Parents

At the outset of each school year, teachers need to invest time getting to know students and their families. These activities will set a positive, professional tone and form a friendly foundation for ongoing home–school communication throughout the school year. Many teachers make home visits, sometimes accompanied by a translator or professional colleague, depending upon the situation. During the visit, they get to know the family, introduce themselves, share their curricular goals and classroom expectations, and answer the family's questions. Other teachers prefer to send a letter of introduction or e-mail to parents that includes classroom expectations, curricular goals, a personal introduction, an invitation for parental involvement, and professional contact information (see Figure 2.2). If possible, personalize the letter with the parents' or guardians' actual names and translate it in the family's native language if they are non-English speaking. Be sure to have several colleagues check for accurate language, spelling, grammar, and punctuation! Send the letter through the traditional mail or e-mail rather than via the black holes of students' backpacks and lockers. Continue the conversation through positive phone calls, e-mails, notes, newsletters, and invitations for parental involvement throughout the semester or year. Complete Application Activity 2.1, which will give you the opportunity to draft an introductory letter to the parents of your future students.

APPLICATION ACTIVITY 2.1 Introductory Letter to Parents

Prepare an introductory letter that you might send to parents at the start of the school year (see Figure 2.2). Share it with your instructor and classmates.

LANGUAGE AND CULTURE

Language and culture tend to bind us to others, but they also can separate us from those who do not share the same cultural norms (Kabagarama, 1996; Nolan, 1999). Verbal and nonverbal communication often can be a challenge in a culturally diverse classroom. In many instances, language cannot be directly translated (word for word) because meanings can be different. Therefore, it is essential that you understand much more than just the language of your students.

Most Americans are unaware of the important role their nonverbal behaviors play in communicating their feelings and attitudes toward others. This lack of self-knowledge interferes with their ability to build student, parent, and professional relationships, especially with people whose cultures differ from their own. Therefore, American children and teachers need to learn the meaning of the gestures indigenous to their own culture and become cognizant of cross-cultural nonverbal behaviors. With this knowledge of nonverbal behaviors, they will be able to communicate more effectively with members of their local and global communities (Hansen, 1999).

FIGURE 2.2	Sample Letter to Parents

Jones Elementary School
2004 Elementary School Road
Wichita, KS

September 5, 2011

John and Mary Miller
5555 Springdale Drive
Wichita, KS

Dear Mr. and Mrs. Miller:

I am Larry's new [fourth grade] teacher. I am excited about this year and look forward to working with you to accomplish your child's academic needs. I will use several methods to give feedback to you and your child about his progress. Please note that I use the following:

1. quarterly grade reports that will give your child's progress to date

2. graded homework assignments weekly

3. graded quizzes and tests

4. our [fourth grade] Internet school site

I hope you will ask Larry about his homework and weekly grades. Please have him share his work with you. I do schedule parent conferences as needed. If you wish to schedule an appointment with me, please call 471-1234. I am available before and immediately after school. Those hours are 7:30 a.m. to 8:00 a.m. and 3:00 p.m. to 4:00 p.m.

So you will be able to talk with your child about his work this first 9 weeks, the objectives we will cover include

•

•

•

I look forward to meeting you at the open house on September 11 at 7:00 p.m.
My room number is 28, and I am located in the north wing.

I look forward to the opportunity of working with you and your child this year. Together we will make a terrific team.

Sincerely,
Jane Zimmerman
Teacher

Different cultural norms affect students' perception of time (e.g., punctuality), group work, importance of education, authority, or competition. Likewise, nonverbal messages expressed through facial expressions, eye contact, voice tone, touch, gestures, and personal space can have different meanings in different cultures. Because we acquire our culture's nonverbal and verbal language simultaneously, it is very difficult to manipulate our own nonverbal behaviors. Cultural differences between the uses of nonverbal signals can easily lead to confusion and problems over intentions and reactions. If someone displays what we feel to be inappropriate nonverbal behavior, we dismiss them as rude or disrespectful. Instead, we need to understand they might be acting in accordance with their cultural norms. For example, Japanese tend to be straight-faced when happy and smile to mask unpleasant feelings such as anger or sadness. Because the left hand is considered unclean in Islamic cultures, it is offensive to use it to offer something to someone. Arabians prefer to stand extremely close to the speaker. Southeast Asians use two fingers, instead of one, to point.

Cultural practices may greatly influence how students communicate in school. For example, in some cultures, children avoid eye contact with an authority figure as a way of showing respect, and others view looking away when someone is speaking as demonstrating attentiveness. Some students consider interruptions as rude, while others have been encouraged to speak over each other to show that they are actively involved in the conversation. Being aware of, and sensitive to, such differences will help you better relate to students and families whose culture is different from your own.

When communicating with students and parents from other cultures, you must try to be more aware of your own automatic responses and nonverbal behaviors so that you don't send an unintentional message. Remember always to give your students and parents the benefit of the doubt and assume that their intentions are not unkind. You should learn to gauge people's communication reactions to you and be prepared to adapt your approach.

DEALING WITH DIFFICULT PARENTS

Sometime during your teaching career, you will have to deal with difficult parents. To prepare for that eventuality, become familiar with your school's and district's policies for dealing with parent conflict. What steps should you take if you cannot resolve the problem? Are there policies addressing specific situations (e.g., contesting student grades, censorship)? If or when conflict arises, confer with your administrator to ensure you follow the district's policies, guidelines, and procedures.

Each school district that receives Title I, Part A funds develops a written parental involvement policy that provides opportunities for participation of parents whose children are ELL, disabled, economically disadvantaged, or members of a racial or ethnic minority group. District teams of parents, teachers, administrators, and community representatives cooperatively design, implement, and reflect upon programs, activities, and procedures that promote parental involvement. The plan is updated periodically to meet the changing needs of parents and schools. It must also be written in a format and language readily understood by parents and school personnel. According to the plan, schools must

1. hold an annual meeting to inform parents of the school's involvement in Title I, explain Title I requirements, and explain parents' rights to be involved;

2. offer, whenever practical, a number of meetings;

3. involve parents in an organized, ongoing, and timely way, in the planning, review, and improvement of the parent involvement plan;

4. invite parents to attend informational sessions regarding the curriculum, forms of assessment used in the school, and student proficiency level expectations; and

5. give parents opportunities to make suggestions and to participate as appropriate in decisions relating to the education of their children.

As more and more school districts across the United States implement site-based management, teachers, administrators, community leaders, and parents share the authority to make decisions about the school's educational mission, expenditures, hiring practices, curriculum, and instructional approaches. Site-based management decentralizes control from the central district office to individual schools as a way to give school constituents—principals, teachers, parents, and community members—more control over what happens in their neighborhood schools.

Ultimately, educators must find ways to open and support culturally responsive communication between parents and schools. Too often, low income and minority families face sustained isolation from the school culture. Such isolation can result in an "us" versus "them" mentality. Teachers then often blame parents for student academic failures. Keep in mind, however, that because of changes in modern families (e.g., non-English speaking, single-parent families, decreasing family size, both parents working, and increased poverty), it often takes a whole community to educate our young people.

This concludes the discussion of communication in the multicultural classroom. In the next section, we will consider another very important topic related to working with diverse students: student differences. However, before we address student differences, complete Reflect and Apply Exercise 2.3, which will give you the opportunity to evaluate your own communication skills.

REFLECT AND APPLY EXERCISE 2.3: Identify Good Approaches to Communication

Reflect

- What are your own communication strengths and weaknesses? What might you do to improve them? How does your ability to speak and listen affect your view of the world? To refine your communication and listening skills, go to the web-based student study site (**www.sagepub.com/mooreteachingk8**).

Apply

- What are some barriers to effective communication in a multicultural classroom?
- What are some important aspects of nonverbal communication in a multicultural classroom?

Through the Eyes of an Expert

Home-School Partnership

It is important to have a strong partnership between home and school. Research and experience have shown that parents usually spend more time with their children than teachers. As such, it is imperative that children have a stable home environment so that their educational goals will be the central focus when in the school setting. Most parents really care about their children and have important perspectives about their goals.

Good communication between teachers and parents doesn't just happen. Teachers must ensure that there are open lines of communication between parents/guardians, students, and teacher. In this era of almost instant communication, electronic mail (e-mail), web sites, newsletters, phone calls, conferences, and notes are common forms of communication. When parents/guardians feel welcome and important in the schools, it makes for a great partnership in getting them involved with activities held at the school.

At Martin Luther King, Jr. Elementary School in Hopkinsville, Kentucky, we are very fortunate to have both a Family Resource Center (FRC) as well as the Kentucky Parent Information Resource Center (KYPIRC) housed in the building. The FRC and KPIRC helps to connect parents and school by providing programs that encourage and promote relationships between the families and staff. Doughnuts for Dads, Muffins for Moms, Male to Male, and Female to Female night are programs that give parents and students a time to bond while being in the school setting. The KYPIRC offers trainings on how to ensure children are successful in school. Seminars/trainings are held in the community so that everyone has the opportunity to attend. Family Reading and Math Nights are wonderful ways to get parents into the schools while at the same time informing them of various ways that they can improve the education of their children in those areas.

SOURCE: Veronica Russell, 2nd grade teacher, Murray State University Distinguished Practitioner, Martin Luther King Jr. Elementary School, Hopkinsville, Kentucky. Used with permission.

STUDENT DIFFERENCES

Video Link 2.2:
Watch a video about cultural proficiency.

Historically, teachers used a one-size-fits-all approach to deliver instruction. Every child heard and did the exact same thing. They hadn't yet realized the importance of customizing their instruction to address the full spectrum of students' abilities, interests, and cultures. Today's classrooms are becoming increasingly diversified through the assimilation of immigrant populations and the inclusion of students with special needs. Furthermore, in this information age, students need to be able to use information as independent, reflective decision makers and problem solvers. Therefore, the traditional, teacher-centered direct instructional approach no longer meets today's students' needs.

Effective teachers adjust the curriculum to address student differences rather than expect students to modify themselves for the curriculum. They use a variety of instructional techniques suitable for diverse learners, such as peer group learning, cooperative learning, peer tutoring, community problem solving, and self-directed learning. When appropriate, they employ AT to facilitate students' efforts to accomplish instructional goals. Above all, effective elementary and middle school teachers help students make personal connections between their current cultural and academic experiences and the world

REFLECTIONS ON TEACHER PRACTICE 2.2: Teacher Teams

1. Is the establishment of "school building teams" a good idea? If at all, how should they be used?

2. How should "school building teams" be involved in school and/or district policy decisions?

One of the most important aspects of "school building teams" is continual communication with the team leaders from the administration of the building. There has to be an open trust and the administration has to be willing to listen to all, while the team leaders have to be willing to provide solutions and suggestions along with their "venting."

Three years ago, we made the conscious decision to look to our team leaders as instructional leaders, and we modeled for them at our team leader meetings open dialogue around instructional issues, not business issues. We then asked them to do this twice a week with their teams. We provided them support by listening, giving them training, and listening some more. We also shared this expectation with all the team members. It seemed to work, and our school now uses e-mail for MOST of the "business conversations."

The downside of a team is when a group of teachers form a team of friends, but not a team of professionals. Then, they seem to band together around petty issues, instead of the real issues. When we have this happen, we struggle with whether to disband the team or teams that are doing this.

—Michelle, middle-level teacher

Please visit the Student Study site at **www.sagepub.com/mooreteachingk8** *for additional discussion questions and assignments.*

SOURCE: www.middleweb.com. Reprinted with permission.

Students are different and often have unique needs.

outside the classroom. Lifestyle, gender, religious, language, and socioeconomic status differences should be discussed and respected in an intellectually honest way. Teachers need to individually and collectively value all students and challenge them to reach their highest potential.

Differentiated Instruction

Differentiated instruction involves providing students with alternate avenues to acquire content, process information, and demonstrate what they have learned (Gregory & Kuzmich, 2010; Kryza, Duncan, & Stephens, 2010). Teachers begin by creating a safe and nurturing learning environment where students feel accepted, safe, and willing to take personal and academic risks. Teachers designate quiet work areas, set clear guidelines for independent work, provide materials that reflect students' academic and personal backgrounds, work with students to identify performance criteria, and help students discover their unique learning styles. Because differentiated instruction generates active student involvement, teachers need to be able to tolerate some movement and noise, particularly with learning centers. Active monitoring and awareness of what is going on in the room at all times (withitness) is a must!

Once a nurturing learning environment has been established, teachers maximize student achievement by designing lessons that meet students where they are in the learning process and move them along as quickly and as far as possible in the context of a mixed-ability classroom (Tomlinson, 1995). This is accomplished by varying the content, process, and product based upon the students' readiness, interests, or learning profiles.

1. *Content.* This is what the student needs to learn or how the student will access the information. Teachers use reading materials at varying readability levels; record texts; present ideas through both auditory and visual means; provide learning packets or task cards, and create small, similar-ability groups to reteach ideas to struggling students or to extend the thinking skills of advanced learners. After initial instruction to provide a common foundation of information, students conduct additional research on related topics of their choice.

2. *Process.* These are activities in which the students engage to make sense of or master the content. Teachers create various activities with different levels of support, challenge, or complexity; offer manipulatives, graphic organizers, or hands-on activities; use a mixture of independent, whole-class, small-group activities; and vary the length of time students may take to complete an activity. Students are given the opportunity to select their own resources. Teachers create learning centers representing multiple learning styles and levels of ability. When prepared properly, the materials will accommodate different rates of learning and different learning styles.

3. *Products.* These are culminating projects that ask the students to rehearse, apply, and extend what they have learned in a unit. Students are given several choices on how to demonstrate what they have learned such as simulated journal entries, puppet shows, dioramas, peer projects, or multimedia presentations. Teachers use rubrics to assess students' efforts, allow students to work alone or in small groups on projects, and encourage students to choose how they want to demonstrate what they have learned.

G/T students also benefit from differentiated instruction because it addresses their unique needs, abilities, and interests. Developing curriculum that is sufficiently rigorous, challenging, and coherent for students who are gifted can be a challenging task, however. A class is *not* differentiated when assignments are the same for all learners and the adjustments consist of varying the level of difficulty of questions for certain students, grading some students harder than others, requiring gifted students to tutor their peers, or letting students who finish early play games for enrichment. It is *not* appropriate to have more advanced learners do extra math problems, extra book reports, or work on extension assignments after completing their "regular" work. Karnes and Bean (2000) suggest several ways in which the learning environment should be modified for gifted students:

- Create a learner-centered environment that allows for student choice, flexibility, and independence.

- Focus on complexity rather than simplicity.

- Provide for high mobility within the classroom and various grouping arrangements.

- Express openness to innovation and exploration.

Differentiated instructional practices increase student achievement and motivate students because they are being taught in ways that are responsive to their readiness levels, interests, and learning profiles. There is no recipe for differentiation. Rather, it is a way of thinking about teaching and learning that values the individual and can be translated into classroom practice in many ways.

Learning Styles

Judith C. Reiff once wrote "Students' ways of learning are as different as the colors of a rainbow." Students learn more and retain it longer when they have an opportunity to learn and to demonstrate what they've learned using their preferred learning style. Visual learners learn best by seeing, auditory learners learn best by hearing, and physical learners learn best through hands-on activities. Some students learn quickly; others learn rather slowly. Some require substantial teacher help; others are able to learn independently. Most students exhibit each of these learning styles at one time or another, depending on the circumstances; however, they tend to favor one style over another. Differences in students' learning styles are often due in part to differences in their **cognitive style**—that is, differences in how they respond to the environment and process information (Green, 1999; Riding & Rayner, 1998).

Video Link 2.3:
Watch a video about learning styles.

Researchers have produced vital information for teachers regarding the relationship between learning and learner characteristics. Dunn and Dunn (1993) describe learning styles as a person's preference in four main aspects of the learning situation:

1. *Environmental:* preferences in lighting, sound, temperature, and physical room arrangement

2. *Emotional:* preference in level of student responsibility and persistence, structure, and supervision

3. *Sociological:* preference for a large or small group, for being alone, or for adult assistance

4. *Physical:* sensory mode preference (e.g., visual, auditory, tactile, and kinesthetic) in learning plus the need for movement, food intake, and a specific time of day

Factors in these four areas have a major impact on student learning. For example, some students prefer dim lighting, whereas others prefer brightly lit environments. Frequently, room temperature and noise level are the first learning style preferences communicated by students. Teachers who are unaware of the environmental effects on learning may interpret this communication as simple complaining. Informed teachers realize that this is just a manifestation that students learn in unique ways.

Sensitive teachers can sometimes identify the learning preferences of students through careful observations. They might, however, have difficulty identifying students' learning styles accurately without some type of instrumentation. Some characteristics simply are not observable—even to the experienced teacher. Moreover, teachers can misinterpret students' behaviors and misunderstand their symptoms. A learning styles record form, such as the four-category form shown in Figure 2.3 on page 46, can assist their efforts. Interviews are an excellent way to have students talk about their experiences as learners

"It's not easy getting all your homework done between dinner time and prime time."

SOURCE: Created by Martha Campbell.

and preferred learning styles. An instrument often used to determine learning style that has high reliability and validity is the Dunn, Dunn, and Price Learning Style Inventory (LSI), with subtests for students in Grades 3 to 12. Teachers can have students take the LSI and receive a formal report on their styles. According to Dunn (Shaughnessy, 1998), the LSI does the following:

1. Allows students to identify how they prefer to learn

2. Recommends a classroom environment that will complement students' learning styles

3. Identifies the group arrangement in which each student is likely to learn most effectively (e.g., alone, with two or more classmates of similar interests or talents, with a teacher, or a combination of venues)

4. Tells which students need direction and high structure and which students should be given options and alternatives

5. Sequences and then reinforces the perceptual strengths individuals use to begin studying new and difficult information

6. Tells how each student should study and do homework

7. Outlines methods through which individuals are most likely to achieve (e.g., programmed learning, contracts, tactual manipulatives, multisensory resources, kinesthetic games, or any combination of these)

8. Tells which children are conforming and which are nonconforming and explains how to work with both types

9. Specifies the time of day each student learns best, thus showing how to group students for instruction in difficult subjects based on their natural learning-styles energy-highs

10. Indicates whether movement or snacks will enhance students' learning

11. Identifies if students prefer analytical or global instructional approaches

Some student differences in learning styles can be accommodated; others are more problematic. The number of different learning styles often is too varied to make it practical for teachers to accommodate every student's learning style. As much as possible, however, they should see that students' learning needs are met. If sound is needed, allow students to use iPods or CDs. Encourage students to use personalized computer software packages and Internet sites to supplement classroom resources. If verbal interaction is important, block off a portion of the room for conversation. If complete silence is needed, provide noise filters. Provide individualized attention and encourage unmotivated students; check in periodically on motivated students as they work independently. Finally, work with the administration and specialists to schedule students' toughest classes when they are in their prime. Some students will be morning learners, while others will learn better in the late afternoon. Teacher flexibility and willingness to experiment with different techniques will provide opportunities to maximize learning.

FIGURE 2.3 Sample Learning Styles Record Form

Learning Styles Record Form

Directions: For each student, record your observations regarding the following items related to the student's preferred style of learning.

Student's name: _____

Learning Style Attribute		Findings (check when applicable)	
		No	Yes
1. Style of working:	Prefers to work alone	_____	_____
	Prefers to work with others	_____	_____
2. Learning modality:	Listening	_____	_____
	Reading	_____	_____
	Watching	_____	_____
	Writing	_____	_____
	Discussing	_____	_____
	Touching	_____	_____
	Moving	_____	_____
3. Need for structure:	Low	_____	_____
	High	_____	_____
4. Details versus generalities		_____	_____

Multiple Intelligences

Intelligence is usually defined as the ability to answer items on a traditional IQ test. Teachers need to be aware that students are able to exhibit their intelligence in multiple ways. Howard Gardner showed insight and compassion in developing a multiple intelligence theory (Armstrong, 1994; Checkley, 1997). Gardner has argued that humans have at least eight distinct intelligences relating to their abilities: (1) linguistic, (2) logical–mathematical, (3) spatial, (4) bodily–kinesthetic, (5) musical, (6) interpersonal, (7) intrapersonal, and (8) naturalist (see Figure 2.4). Gardner (2003) also is investigating whether a spiritual or existential intelligence may satisfy his criteria for individual intelligences.

Gardner's multiple intelligences theory gives classroom teachers two extremely valuable tools that make learning more focused on individual abilities. First, it helps teachers to identify students' innate strengths and abilities. Second, it enables teachers to design classroom activities that will give students an opportunity to experience working in different areas of intelligence. This will help students discover talents that may otherwise have gone unnoticed or untapped. Because K–8 children are experiencing rapid developmental changes, teachers need to use Gardner's multiple intelligences approach to help students embrace who they are, develop a sense of self, recognize their strengths, and capitalize on talents that will strengthen their self-esteem.

FIGURE 2.4	Gardner's Eight Areas of Intelligence

Intelligence	Core Components	Teaching Activities
Linguistic	Ability to use language, either oral or written. Sensitivity to the sounds, structure, meanings, and functions of words and language.	Activities related to word games, e-mail discussions, choral reading, card games, journal writing, Internet searches, etc.
Logical-mathematical	Ability to use mathematics and numbers. Sensitivity to and capacity to discern logical or numerical patterns; ability to handle long chains of reasoning.	Activities related to problem solving, mental calculations, classification, number games, critical thinking, solve puzzles, etc.
Spatial	Ability to perceive the spatial world. Capacity to perceive the visual-spatial world accurately and to perform transformations on one's initial perceptions.	Visual activities related to graphic art, mind mapping, visualization, maps, pictures, imagination games, models, etc.
Bodily-kinesthetic	Ability to use one's body movement. Ability to control one's body movements and to handle objects skillfully.	Hands-on activities, drama, pantomime, dance, sports that teach, tactile activities, etc.
Musical	Ability to undertake musical endeavors. Ability to produce and appreciate rhythm, pitch, and timbre; appreciation of the forms of musical expressiveness.	Songs that teach, rapping, learn tunes, create rhymes, superlearning, enhance ability to learn, etc.
Interpersonal	Ability to understand other people. Capacity to discern and respond appropriately to the moods, temperaments, motivations, and desires of other people.	Cooperative learning activities, lead discussions, community involvement, dramatic activities, social activities, simulations, etc.
Intrapersonal	Ability to understand oneself. Access to one's own feelings and the ability to discriminate among one's emotions; knowledge of one's own strengths and weaknesses.	Individual instruction, read books, journal writing, independent study, self-esteem activities, play activities, cooperative groups, etc.
Naturalist	Ability to understand nature. Ability to make distinctions in the natural world; capacity to recognize flora and fauna.	Activities related to the natural world and the biological sciences, exploration of nature, find origins, study nature objects, etc.

Traditionally, schools have reinforced a learning profile emphasizing verbal/linguistic and logical–mathematical abilities and de-emphasizing or excluding the other multiple intelligences. With creative thinking and careful planning, however, teachers can address all of the multiple intelligences in their instruction. Gardner emphasized learning in meaningful contexts. For example, when learning about ecosystems, students can gather pond specimens, create terrariums, visit an indoor jungle, write haikus, or calculate the spread of kudzu. Students can learn about community history through interviews, reenactments, local architecture, field trips to local museums, research, films, cemetery strolls, and guest speakers. To ensure all students have an opportunity to learn the way they learn best, teachers need to systematically design their units of instruction, or series of lessons on a particular topic, using activities that address all eight intelligences. Table 2.1 offers example teaching strategies that focus on Gardner's eight areas of intelligence.

TABLE 2.1   Teaching Strategies to Address the Multiple Intelligences

VISUAL/SPATIAL These children use charts, graphs, and visual representations.	VERBAL/LINGUISTIC These children learn through reading, writing, and speaking.
• Use graphic organizers (Venn diagrams, webs). • Include visual projects(dioramas, posters, artwork). • Use manipulatives to teach math/science concepts. • Include art projects in each instructional unit. • Have students visualize specific situations. • Create a colorful classroom atmosphere. • Use videos and YouTube clips. • Have students use sketch journals. • Provide a computer center with graphic design software. • Use video demonstrations.	• Use quality literature throughout the curriculum. • Read aloud to your students. • Have independent reading time each day. • Use cooperative group activities to promote speaking. • Encourage students to make presentations. • Have students write regularly. • Display students' creative use of language. • Add a variety of books to the class library. • Incorporate playful language during your instruction. • Use choral reading and poetry.
MUSICAL/RHYTHMIC These children learn through songs and rhythms.	BODILY/KINESTHETIC These children enjoy physical activities.
• Include music activities in each instructional unit. • Play background music during independent work time. • Use wind chimes as an attention-getting signal. • Use music to open and close lessons. • Have students write songs, raps, poems, or jingles. • Provide time to dance, sing, listen, and move to music. • Share the music of other cultures. • Create listening and music centers. • Make homemade instruments. • Use songs or raps to help students memorize facts.	• Physically demonstrate the lesson objective. • Make human equations. • Include role play activities. • Have students record responses on the whiteboard. • Take students on field trips. • Intersperse movement during long lessons. • Use exploration activities involving feeling and touch. • Incorporate plentiful hands-on experiences. • Include physical games into each theme. • Celebrate classroom successes with physical hurrahs.

LOGICAL/MATHEMATICAL	NATURALIST
These children enjoy numbers, logic, and problem solving.	These children are in tune with nature.
• Use hands-on materials to teach new concepts. • Provide outlines and agendas to structure your lessons. • Use mnemonic devices to memorize patterns. • Share instructional goals and objectives. • Challenge children through critical thinking activities. • Provide problem-solving activities. • Use graphic organizers. • Encourage pattern awareness. • Provide mind puzzles and games. • Use math and science learning centers.	• Explore what it means to be "green." • Have students care for classroom pets and plants. • Integrate nature themes into each instructional unit. • Create a student recycling center. • Hold some class sessions outdoors. • Discuss conversation of natural resources. • Keep a weather chart. • Write nature-focused poems. • Design environmental posters and commercials. • Interview park rangers or environmentalists.
INTRAPERSONAL	INTERPERSONAL
These children ponder their feelings and ideas.	These children enjoy interacting with others.
• Invite students to keep personal journals. • Allow wait-time for serious reflection. • Use open-ended questions that invite students' opinions. • Individualize instruction matched to students' interests. • Create a quiet area in the room for reflection. • Display posters with motivational sayings. • Provide multiple opportunities to reflect. • Use goal-setting. • Conduct surveys. • Provide opportunities for student choice.	• Create a classroom learning community. • Take time for "class talks" about current issues. • Use cooperative learning activities. • Engage in class discussions. • Arrange desks in small groups. • Teach students different group roles. • Create learning centers so they can work with peers. • Teach social and conflict resolution skills. • Create group problem-solving activities. • Use peer tutoring, study groups, and share pairs.

This completes our look at making modifications for student differences. However, before we leave this section, complete Reflect and Apply Exercise 2.4, which will let you further explore the strategies for making modifications for student differences.

REFLECT AND APPLY EXERCISE 2.4: Student Learning Differences

Reflect

• Some educators suggest that teachers match instruction to individual learning styles and individual intelligences. Would this be beneficial to all students? Why or why not?

Apply

• What strategies will you use to address the learning styles in your future classroom?

• Choose a topic you might teach one day. Describe how you could teach that topic using all eight multiple intelligences.

• How can you arrange your classroom setting and schedule to meet all students' needs?

SUMMARY

This chapter focused on the diverse student populations in our classrooms. The main points were as follows:

- Teachers must be culturally sensitive to the diverse populations in our schools.

Classroom Diversity

- Children have changed and more foreign languages are being spoken in our schools. Teachers must be sensitive to the changes in our schools.

- Teachers must plan to meet the needs of diverse school populations.

- Hold high but realistic expectations for *all* students.

- Modify plans for special students and G/T students.

- LEP is a major challenge in some parts of the country. In some schools, more than half the students have a first language other than English.

Multiculturally Sensitive Communication

- Teachers need to develop better communication and listening skills.

- Effective teachers communicate with parents, school administrators, and community leaders.

- Language and cultural differences tend to make accurate communication with students and parents difficult at times.

Student Differences

- Teachers must be sensitive to and accommodate students' learning styles.

- Gardner suggests that humans have eight different intelligences: (1) linguistic, (2) logical–mathematical, (3) spatial, (4) bodily–kinesthetic, (5) musical, (6) interpersonal, (7) intrapersonal, and (8) naturalist. Teachers need to focus instruction on these different abilities.

DISCUSSION QUESTIONS AND ACTIVITIES

1. **Teaching All Students.** Remember that a teachers' job is to teach all students and assume an attitude that all students can learn. Research techniques and strategies that can be used to accomplish this task. Sources of information include the library, the Internet, current journals, and recent books.

2. **Diversity.** What other elements of diversity will you find in your students that have not been discussed in the chapter? How will you be sensitive to these differences?

TECH CONNECTION

Technology can be an effective support and resource when planning for students with special needs. Complete the following two application activities that use technology as a resource in planning for students with special needs.

- Use one of the Internet search engines to search for "sample individualized education plans." Review sample IEPs that would be appropriate for the grade level you expect to teach. Form groups of four or five and discuss how all students could benefit from receiving the type of feedback present in an IEP. Share your finding with classmates.

- Access lesson plans on sites such as www.lessonplanet.com (Lesson Planet), http:// atozteacherstuff.com (A to Z Teacher Stuff), or a site of your choice. Select a lesson plan to addresses at least two different multiple intelligences. Work with your classmates to identify related activities that would address the remaining intelligences.

CONNECTION WITH THE FIELD

1. **Classroom Observation.** Complete several observations at the grade level you expect to teach. Collect data related to the following:
   a. The student differences
   b. The effectiveness of the communication process
   c. The teacher's nonverbal behaviors
   d. The teachers' listening skills

2. **Parent and Community Involvement.** Interview several teachers from local schools about how they foster parent and community involvement. Try to visit with a kindergarten teacher, an elementary teacher, and a middle school teacher. Are they successful in promoting parent involvement? How do these teachers work with parents who resist involvement? Summarize your discoveries.

STUDENT STUDY SITE

Visit the Student Study Site at **www.sagepub.com/mooreteachingk8** for these additional learning tools:

- Video clips
- Web resources
- Self quizzes
- E-Flashcards
- Full-text SAGE journal articles
- Portfolio Connection
- Licensing Preparation/Praxis Connection

CHAPTER 3

Managing the Classroom Environment

The greatest sign of success for a teacher . . . is to be able to say, "The children are now working as if I did not exist."

—Maria Montessori

Before We Begin

What are some responsibilities that today's children have in the classroom and at home? What additional responsibilities will they have as adults? How can teachers prepare them for these responsibilities? Be ready to compare your view with classmates.

OVERVIEW

Every day we hear about the importance of leaving no child behind, yet, unfortunately, we are leaving American teachers behind! Did you know that up to 50% of American teachers leave their classrooms behind within the first 5 years of entering the profession? One of the major reasons has been the teachers' frustration with their lack of preparation to effectively manage their classrooms (Latham & Vogt, 2007).

This chapter will focus on classroom management. Students cannot learn and teachers cannot teach in a chaotic environment. Therefore, teachers must deal effectively with students' misbehavior and promote student self-control so everyone can meet their emotional needs and academic goals. All teachers have management challenges. How they deal with students' behavioral choices depends on their educational philosophy and their preferred management approach. To prepare you for that venue, we will examine the principles of three current approaches to classroom management.

Next we will explore such issues as beginning the school year on a positive note, establishing classroom guidelines and rules, monitoring students' behavior, identifying causes of misbehavior, and administering appropriate consequences. Finally, you will learn teacher-tested ideas for structuring the classroom environment and for conducting daily classroom business.

OBJECTIVES

After completing your study of Chapter 3, you should be able to

- define *classroom management*, and identify its various aspects;
- describe the **self-discipline approach**, **instructional approach**, and **desist approach** to classroom management;
- specify causes of classroom misbehavior;
- describe organizational techniques that lead to effective classroom management;
- summarize teacher-tested techniques for proactively preventing classroom management problems; and
- discuss the use of appropriate consequences.

Many beginning teachers harbor concerns about their abilities to manage students' behavior. These concerns might be well-founded because teachers, administrators, parents, and students report that misbehavior often interferes with the ability of a teacher to teach and with the ability of students to learn (Charles, 2002; Evertson, Emmer, & Worsham, 2003; Gallup & Elam, 1988). Although such reports suggest that there are serious management and **discipline** problems in the public schools, it would be a mistake to assume that students are out of control. Let's explore how effective elementary and middle school teachers use classroom management techniques to encourage students to assume responsibility for their own behaviors.

THE ROLE OF CLASSROOM MANAGEMENT

Classroom management is the process of organizing and conducting the business of the classroom. Many perceive it as the preservation of order through teacher control. Classroom management is much more than that, however! It also involves the establishment and maintenance of the classroom environment so that educational goals can be accomplished (Savage & Savage, 2010).

Effective classroom managers create orderly, safe environments where students feel valued and comfortable, thus setting the stage for teaching and learning. To achieve that, they strategically arrange classroom space to support a variety of independent, small and large group activities (Crane, 2001). Elementary teachers also designate a large area of floor space where students can gather for read-alouds, demonstrations, and class meetings. In all classrooms, there should be no "blind" areas in the room where students can be out of view. To structure "traffic flow" and minimize disruption, teachers separate high-traffic areas such as group work areas, learning centers, students' desks, the teacher's desk, the pencil sharpener, bookshelves, computer stations, and storage areas. Teachers ensure plentiful room for student movement, especially for students who have physical handicaps. Furthermore, they decide how to store classroom materials, including students' personal items, textbooks, resource books, instructional materials, frequently used materials, and equipment. Finally, they decide what materials will be accessible by students and which areas are designated for teacher use only.

Although not its sole component, discipline is another highly important aspect of classroom management. Discipline is a systematic way of teaching students to assume responsibility for their behavioral choices; punishment focuses upon negative consequences for misbehavior. This chapter will focus on discipline rather than punishment even though your success as a classroom teacher will depend on your adequacy in making sound decisions in both of these areas.

Effective elementary and middle school teachers create optimal learning environments by establishing and enforcing rules, creating caring teacher–student relationships, addressing problem behaviors, and using quality communication. Students of all ages may have behavioral, attitudinal, and social issues. Older students' problems, however, are more long standing and thus more difficult to address. Many middle school students resist authority and place greater importance on peer norms. Furthermore, because most middle school students have more advanced reasoning skills than younger students, they generally demand more elaborate and logical explanation of rules and discipline. Keep these differences between elementary and middle school students in mind as we explore effective classroom management strategies.

There are a number of classroom management strategies available to teachers. Let's begin by taking a look at three management approaches. These three approaches to classroom management form a continuum, from the self-discipline approach at one extreme, to the instructional approach, to the desist approach at the opposite extreme.

The Self-Discipline Approach

The self-discipline approach is built on the premise that students can be trusted to reflect upon and regulate their behaviors to benefit themselves and others. Advocates for this democratic view of classroom management argue that teachers need to exhibit the dispositions of respect, realness, trust, acceptance, and empathy toward students so they can build and establish working teacher-student relationships. Different variations of this management approach include William Glasser's (1965, 1977, 1986) **reality therapy**, Thomas Gordon's (1974) **teacher effectiveness training (TET)**, Barbara Coloroso's (2002) **inner discipline**, and Alfie Kohn's (1996) **beyond discipline**.

The Instructional Approach

Teachers who use the instructional approach to classroom management prevent most management problems by actively engaging students in high-interest lessons geared to meet their interests, needs, and abilities. Thus, students are motivated to attend class, positively participate in activities, and manage their own behavior. Jacob Kounin (1970) and Frederick Jones (1979) advocate the instructional approach to classroom management.

REFLECTIONS ON TEACHER PRACTICE 3.1: Getting Students Motivated

1. What evidence suggests that many adolescents are self-centered?

2. If adolescents are self-centered, how would you use this characteristic to make your teaching more effective?

Always keep one fact in mind when working with adolescents: developmentally, adolescents ARE self-centered. This is the time they are trying to figure out who they are and how they fit in the world around them. They want to be unique, but they want to fit in. Rather than trying to work against that developmental characteristic, we'd do better to use it to our advantage.

Relevance is a huge issue regardless of what subject or grade level we teach. Most of us have at some point in our lives asked, "Why do I have to learn this?" (I cried it almost daily while taking Geometry in high school; I didn't see relevance until I took Trigonometry.)

I think the key is to NOT water down the curriculum, but, rather, look for ways to bring the curriculum into our kids' real lives. It is a task that really forces us to think outside the box and to get to know our kids and their interests well. For example, when teaching point of view—specifically the concept of, "How would the story change if this other character told the story?"—I have to start with something they already know, usually what they call "He say—she say" stories. Every time I have skipped that step, they continue to change all the events of the story instead of merely telling it as that other person has interpreted it. Point of view now gets a nod because it makes sense in their own lives.

I think the real key with adolescents is to start with them and move the concept outward. It's not always easy, but my kids are always more successful when I figure out a way to do this.

—*Ellen, middle-level teacher*

Please visit the Student Study site at **www.sagepub.com/mooreteachingk8** *for additional discussion questions and assignments.*

SOURCE: www.middleweb.com. Reprinted with permission.

The Desist Approach

The desist approach to classroom management gives the teacher full responsibility for regulating the classroom. The teacher establishes and enforces a set of specific rules to control student behavior in the classroom. Because the desist approach models of classroom management give teachers power to deal forcefully and quickly with misbehavior, they can be viewed as power systems. This approach probably is the most widely used classroom management strategy in today's schools. The desist approach is advocated by Lee and Marlene Canter (1976) in their **assertive discipline** model and by B. F. Skinner (1968, 1971) in his research on **behavior modification**.

"I'd like to overwhelm them with instructional excellence, but I'm not above winning through intimidation."

SOURCE: Created by Martha Campbell.

The three management approaches are summarized in Table 3.1. To help you determine your own modus operandi, or managerial style, please study the additional information provided on the web-based student study site (www.sagepub.com/mooreteachingk8). How you respond to management problems will depend on which classroom management approach best fits your educational philosophy and your perception of the cause of the students' misbehavior.

TABLE 3.1 Management Approaches

Approach	Description
Self-discipline approach	View that students can evaluate and change to appropriate behavior
Instructional approach	View that well-planned and well-implemented instruction will prevent classroom problems
Desist approach	View that the teacher should have full regulatory power in the classroom

Let's now look at some of the reasons students misbehave. But first review the approach summary and complete Reflect and Apply Exercise 3.1.

REFLECT AND APPLY EXERCISE 3.1: Approaches to Classroom Management

Reflect

- What classroom management approaches have your past teachers used? Were they successful? If not, how would you change them?

- Compare and contrast effective classroom management at the elementary and middle school levels. Which classroom management approach would be the most effective at the grade level you expect to teach?

Apply

- Describe how you will arrange your classroom space to promote student self-regulation and to provide a safe, orderly learning environment.

- Conduct additional research on one of these approaches to classroom management: Reality Therapy, TET, Inner Discipline, Beyond Discipline, Instructional Approach, Assertive Discipline, Discipline with Dignity, CHAMPS, Achieve, or Boys/Girls Town Social Skills Programs. Be ready to share.

CAUSES OF MISBEHAVIOR

Teachers who are ineffective classroom managers spend much of their time frantically putting out small "fires." They need to learn a lesson from professional firefighters—the best way to deal with a fire is to prevent it from happening in the first place. Proactive classroom managers create "fireproof" classroom environments by addressing causes of misbehavior that might fuel emotional explosions. Some misbehaviors are sparked by conditions that are not readily obvious. According to Maslow, once their physiological needs are met, students are motivated by the need to be physically and emotionally safe, loved and accepted, admired and respected, and personally fulfilled. A careful examination of students' classroom behaviors, desirable as well as undesirable, can reveal that they are influenced by forces and pressures inside and outside the classroom. Identifying and addressing these issues will proactively prevent future behavioral conflagrations (Belvel, 2010).

Home Environment

Students do not leave their concerns and confusion about family situations at the classroom door. Parents are students' first teachers. Not all parents teach their children to

Video Link 3.1: Watch a video about principles of cultural proficiency.

respect themselves and others, to respond to authority figures, and to follow the golden rule. Parents' attitudes toward the importance of education are often mirrored by their children. If parents do not see the purpose of studying hard to prepare for a future career, their children will balk at school work, too.

Lack of supervision in the home is a common problem in our society. Many students come from single-parent homes or from homes where both parents are too busy with their own lives to be concerned with the children. Therefore, you may have students who stay up too late or who watch television past midnight. Other students may live on junk food or come to school without breakfast. These students sometimes lack the energy to carry out assignments or even to pay attention. You need to counsel these students, and perhaps the parents, on the importance of rest and proper diet. Enlist the assistance of the school nurse, counselor, and principal if you suspect deeper home issues such as sexual abuse, neglect, or drug abuse.

ALEX: A REFLECTIVE CASE STUDY

Alex was having a no good, very bad day. His mother and her friends had partied all night long. Alex had given the last of the Raisin Bran to his little brother and sister before getting them dressed and walking them to their bus stop. He'd earned a one-legged A on his essay—evidently Ms. Wright didn't think he'd written it right. When Mr. Data handed out a pop quiz in algebra, Alex threw his books onto the floor, slumped in his chair, and let out a loud moan.

1. How might an ineffective teacher deal with Alex's disruption?

2. Describe how an effective classroom manager might handle the disruption.

The Teacher

Effective classroom managers provide a structured, caring environment that meets students' personal and academic needs. Such teachers are perceived as authority figures in the classroom. They share high behavioral expectations, design/implement developmentally appropriate lessons, and establish and enforce behavioral guidelines. Because effective teachers respect students as individuals with rights, values, and feelings, they carefully choose their words and actions to protect students' dignity. They actively engage students in meaningful, challenging educational experiences and provide plentiful positive feedback. In short, they set their students (and themselves) up for success.

Ineffective teachers are poor planners. They do not start class on time; become sidetracked easily; use limited, low-interest teaching strategies; create a disorganized environment; and hold unclear academic and behavioral expectations. Furthermore, they abdicate responsibility for helping students to make good behavioral choices by trying to be the students' friend instead of their teacher. When that approach generates misbehaviors, ineffective teachers use ridicule, sarcasm, and put-downs to "put students in their place." Students' disrespect for these teachers is evidenced through increasingly frequent classroom disruptions and exceedingly poor behavioral choices.

Once you have formulated your personal philosophy of classroom management, you are poised to proactively address potential problems by removing the causes that kindle misbehavior and by immediately addressing misbehaviors with consistent consequences. This cannot be accomplished by smoke and mirrors; it takes reflective thought and careful strategizing. You need to have a plan in place to extinguish the flame before it becomes a classroom-wide behavioral forest fire.

REFLECTIONS ON TEACHER PRACTICE 3.2: Managing the Classroom

1. Why is classroom management a major problem for many teachers?

2. Can teachers really treat all students equally?

I believe the selection of a classroom management strategy has to be based on the teacher's personality and the characteristics of the class being managed. To use a system that doesn't fit you will create unnecessary stress and you won't use it well. If it doesn't suit the students, it will not work either. So, I suggest that you study as many strategies as you can and evaluate them in terms of your personality.

My biggest suggestion is, whatever strategy you choose, do not attempt to teach until it is working. If you begin the year insisting on proper discipline and behavior, it will become a habit that will continue through the rest of the year. If you let things slide at the beginning, the students will expect it to last till the end. This doesn't mean that you have to be an ogre until Thanksgiving. It does mean that you must find a way to create the atmosphere you want before you do any serious amount of teaching.

As for respect, the students will respect you when you are consistent. Students, as a group, don't like surprises. There can be few, if any, exceptions to rules and procedures. If any exceptions should become necessary, you should explain to the students why an exception has been made. The other side of respect is to respect students in return. Whatever forms of respect you demand from your students you should extend to them as well.

—*John Vose, elementary school teacher*

 Please visit the Student Study site at **www.sagepub.com/mooreteachingk8** *for additional discussion questions and assignments.*

SOURCE: Reprinted with permission from ProTeacher, a professional community for elementary school teachers (www.proteacher.net).

ORGANIZING FOR EFFECTIVE MANAGEMENT

When you are forming your personal philosophy of classroom management, please note that the three approaches to classroom management have their advantages and limitations. You do not have to select one approach over another. Effective classroom managers often blend together the best parts of different approaches. Be sure your classroom management plan enables you to build trusting relations with students, prevent misbehavior, redirect minor misbehavior, stop major disruptive behavior, and teach self-control. Let's now look at some other key classroom problem prevention areas.

Through the Eyes of an Expert

School Safety

Passing by the office on the way to your kindergarten classroom you hear loud voices and you see the back of a male visitor who seems agitated. Quickly, you stand at the classroom door as the students come back from music. A few of them stop to sing a piece of a song they learned. You rush them into the room as the noise from the office spills out into the hall. The principal and two other teachers are following a crazed man who has just withdrawn a two-foot machete from under his trench coat. The principal jumps the man in front of your door but he is able to get into your classroom, still brandishing the machete. What would you do? Could this really happen? It already has, February 2001 in Red Lion, Pennsylvania. The principal and two teachers were severely wounded and 11 kindergarteners sustained injuries.

Because schools are dealing with more challenges than ever before, they must proactively prepare to respond to a wide range of emergency situations ranging from natural disasters to threats of violence. Effective school safety planning is developed in collaboration with community partners, school staff, and students. These school specific plans should be reviewed regularly and tested in order to ensure that all affected persons are aware of their role in an emergency. Effective school safety planning involves four phases of emergency management:

- Mitigation/Prevention
  - Mitigation is the action schools and districts take to eliminate or reduce the loss of life and property damage related to an event that cannot be prevented.
  - Prevention is the action schools and districts take to decrease the likelihood that an event or crisis will occur.

- Preparedness
  - Preparedness is the process of deciding what you will do in the event of an emergency before the emergency actually occurs.

- Response
  - Response is the process of implementing appropriate actions while an emergency situation is unfolding. In short, responding means "doing what you planned to do."

- Recovery
  - Recovery is the process of assisting people with the physical, psychological, and emotional trauma associated with experiencing tragic events.

Locate and familiarize yourself with your school's emergency plan. Within your classroom assure easy access to the response protocols, evacuation procedures, and your emergency supplies. The plan is a living document that needs to be updated, reviewed, practiced, and revised regularly. Schools need to be ready to respond to any type of crisis before returning to the serious business of learning and teaching as quickly as possible.

Visit these websites to learn more about emergency planning:

- Kentucky Center for School Safety: http://www.kycss.org/clear/EMGpage.html

- Practical Information on Crisis Planning—U.S. Department of Education: http://www2.ed.gov/admins/lead/safety/crisisplanning.html

SOURCE: Karen McCuiston, Kentucky Center for School Safety, Murray, Kentucky. Used with permission.

Effective planning is often the key to a smooth-running classroom.

Planning

Effective teachers plan carefully to maximize learning time and minimize behavioral problems. They know exactly how they will teach the lesson and have all the necessary instructional materials in place. They carefully plan every moment of instructional time, maintain a brisk, appropriate instructional pace, and ready additional extension/enrichment activities in case their original lesson doesn't take as much time as anticipated.

Effective teachers consider the school calendar when planning. For instance, the day before a major holiday, the day of an afternoon assembly or special school event, and the weeks before Christmas or spring break are apt to require special attention and preparation. At such times, it is essential that students be involved in highly motivating, fast-paced, and interesting activities that will compete successfully with other, external events.

Establishing Routines

Many school and classroom activities are basically routine—for example, taking attendance, issuing hall passes, and collecting papers. The school establishes some routines; individual teachers establish others. When you first begin teaching, familiarize yourself with the school routines by consulting the school handbook and talking with your principal and colleagues. Honoring established routines creates an orderly environment, minimizes student uncertainty, and decreases discipline problems.

Take time the first few days of school to establish simple classroom routines. Teaching routines and procedures saves time and prevents stress because the students know what

Student busing often impacts what teachers can do in the classroom.

to do and you do not have to nag students or repeat expectations. For example, kindergarten teachers can save time by teaching students to take turns at the drinking fountain, on the playground, and at the pencil sharpener. Other common classroom routines and procedures include lining up, sharpening pencils, starting class, checking attendance, taking lunch count, distributing materials, and collecting and checking homework. Devise ways to save time. For example, have students line up by small groups instead of individually, and use seating diagrams to take attendance. Provide meaningful bellringer activities for students to complete independently while you're taking care of routine duties. Elementary students might complete a penmanship practice page, daily oral language grammar activity, or set of math problems. Middle school students could journal to a provided prompt, check homework, or have sustained silent reading.

Because unnecessary amounts of time spent on routine tasks often lead to student misbehavior, teachers need to streamline the collection and distribution of papers and materials. Instead of handing each individual a paper, distribute a set of materials to each row or group. During group activities, one team member can collect the necessary resources. For major projects, lay out the materials in a central location and call up one group at a time to select the materials they need. Whenever possible, empower students by having them assist in the distribution or collection process.

Taking care of excused absences is another time-consuming and challenging administrative chore. Elementary teachers can label one large manila envelope for each absent student. Place missing assignments inside the envelope; write student-friendly directions on the outside. When necessary, have a parent, peer tutor, or teacher's aide assist the student with missed content. Middle school students should get notes from at least two classmates. Teachers can also create a bulletin board featuring a monthly calendar (see Figure 3.1) plus a container or clip with handouts from missed classes. Students know what classroom activities and assignments were completed on a given day. The calendar also gives stronger students the opportunity to work ahead so they can work on other individual projects. Teachers can use computers to generate personalized calendars that feature classroom announcements, student accomplishments, and birthdays.

FIGURE 3.1   **Monthly Calendar**

S	M	T	W	T	F	S
1 Welcome back to class, Jesse.	**2** Text pages 450–451. Do practice 1–10. Do pages 452-453: Apply section.	**3** Text pages 454–455. Do practice work 1–10. Persevere! you can do it!	**4** Text pages 456–457. Do all practice work.	**5** Text pages 458–459. Do all practice work. This one is a "piece of cake."	**6** Spelling test. All assignments must be in baskets today!	**7** Birthdays this month are Kevin, Kendra, Thomas, Alison, Jennifer, and Hope!
8 Failing notices go out Friday. Don't be caught off balance. Turn in all work NOW.	**9** Spelling. Text pages 462–463. Do all practice work.	**10** Text pages 464–465. Do all practice work. Stretch your neck out and try Part C.**	**11** Text pages 468–469. Do A&B.	**12** Text pages 470–471. Do all practice work.	**13** NO SCHOOL TODAY!	**14** ALCOHOL IS A DRUG.
15 Welcome back to class, Carlos.	**16** Tune into Spelling! 50 words this week for the spelling spin-off on Friday.	**17** Text pages 472–475. Do all practice work. Challenge** Try the Apply*	**18** Film today on preparing speeches!	**19** TIME FOR TALK. DISCUSS TOPIC FOR SPEECHES TODAY.	**20** SPELLING SPIN-OFF** Today!	**21** Character Comes from the Heart! Students Persevere** **************
22 "Write On" with Learning. Essay winners this month are Jay and Natalie****	**23** Library to begin research.	**24** Library work. Bibliography due end of class today. See page 339.	**25** Library work. Topic outlines due today!! See page 340 for help.	**26** Library work. Rough drafts due today. See page 343 for help.	**27** Library work. Final drafts due today. See pages 347–349 for help.	**28** Remember to say "NO" to drugs.
29 Don't forget to vote this month for the most improved student in your class.	**30** Text pages 502–504. Do all practice work.					

Students with special needs respond favorably to an environment that is structured, predictable, and orderly. These students may have difficulty transitioning from one activity to another. Teachers need to give students with special needs private 5-minute, 2-minute, and 1-minute warnings that an activity is about to end and another activity will begin to help them successfully transition to the next activity.

You should never become a slave to routine; however, when routines will expedite classroom business efficiently, they should be used. Determine and use the routines and procedures that are appropriate for your particular classroom.

Establishing Limits

Effective classroom managers create emotionally safe, orderly environments by establishing limits specifying acceptable and forbidden classroom behaviors. Creating limits helps teachers maintain classroom order so more teaching and learning can take place. Teachers who avoid setting limits and imposing necessary structure will often find that chaos results. However, take care not to have too many rules, unenforceable rules, and unnecessary rules; concentrate on the essentials.

Elementary teachers can use quality literature such as *Miss Nelson Is Missing!* (Allard, 1977) to introduce the importance of having classroom rules. Middle school teachers can host a class discussion about how classroom rules contribute to a learning community. Ask elementary or middle school student teams to generate lists of proposed classroom rules. Emphasize that rules should always reinforce the basic idea that students are in school to study and learn. Record all ideas on the whiteboard. Impeach ridiculous or unnecessary rules. It is often better to have a few general rules that cover a wide range of desirable behaviors rather than to list all the specifics. Write the rules in student-friendly talk. Use positive wording—tell students what to do instead of what they should not do. Clarify and combine ideas until no more than five rules remain. Elementary students respond well to these general rules:

1. *Keep your hands and feet to yourself.*

2. *Always use nice words.*

3. *Follow directions.*

4. *Raise your hand to get attention.*

5. *Respect others.*

Examples of appropriate middle school general rules and rationales might include the following:

1. *Be prepared with books, paper, pencil, and so on when you come to class.* You should discuss exactly what is to be brought to class.

2. *Be in your seat and ready to work when the bell rings.* You may want students to begin working on a warm-up activity that is written on the overhead, you may require that they have homework ready to be checked, or you may ask that they have notebooks open and ready to take notes when the bell rings.

3. *Take care of your classroom, and respect other people's property.* This means school, teacher, and fellow student property is to be left alone.

4. *Be polite and respectful.* This conduct covers verbal abuse, fighting, talking back, and general conduct.

5. *Obtain permission before speaking or leaving your seat.* Address exceptions to this rule, such as when to sharpen pencils, where to dispose of trash, and how to seek assistance.

After students generate rationales for each rule, they can create a classroom poster depicting the rules using pictures and words. Have all students sign the poster as their "behavioral contract." Then they copy the rules to share with their families. Requiring signatures ensures students and parents understand the rules.

Considering Consequences

As soon the rules are established, you must decide on the consequences for breaking a rule. It is often rather difficult to make this decision at the time the rule is broken. The appropriate response is often to have the student "right the wrong." For example, messes can be cleaned up, incomplete papers can be finished or redone, and broken property can be replaced.

To cover unforeseen situations, you will need to create some generic consequences as well. Be sure to create consequences you are comfortable with enforcing. The key is consistency. A sequence of consequences might be verbal warning (remind student of the rule and the desired behavior), time-out, phone call home (students make the call first and then you get on the phone), separate seating for one day (choice of designated desks), principal intervention, in-school suspension, and expulsion.

When you have established the rules for your classroom and the consequences for breaking the rules, you have taken the first step in making students aware of what will and will not be tolerated in the classroom. You must now think about managing the classroom on a daily basis.

MANAGING THE CLASS

Effective classroom managers ensure their students get off to a positive start and then work daily to keep the class moving smoothly toward established goals. How can you meet this challenge your first year of teaching?

Getting Started

Wong and Wong (1998) contend that the first days—or even the first few minutes—of school or a class will determine your success or failure for the rest of the school year. During these initial days, it is essential that you establish your credibility as a classroom manager and effective teacher worthy of students' respect.

"First, you have to get their attention."

SOURCE: Created by Martha Campbell.

Initially, you should focus upon establishing a caring classroom climate conducive to learning. Teach classroom routines and procedures, share expectations, and work with students to create classroom rules. By following the established rules and procedures, more learning will occur. Furthermore the likelihood of finding time to have fun learning through group activities and special events will increase if time isn't wasted dealing with misbehavior. Use plentiful, specific praise while students are learning and practicing the new behaviors and procedures. Create a positive classroom environment, and establish a supportive learning community.

Involve students in meaningful, motivational activities from the very first day. Thoroughly plan high-interest lessons using differentiated instruction to teach authentic content. Clearly communicate high academic expectations, and establish an atmosphere of free exchange. Involve students as much as possible in the learning process. Finally, monitor student behavior closely, and deal with misbehavior quickly, fairly, and firmly.

Using time productively on the first day is especially critical. Here are some things to consider when planning:

Elementary teachers might use these activities on the first day:

1. *Preparation.* For kindergartners' very first day of school, arrange tables and chairs, place carousels of supplies in the centers of tables, ready cubbies for students' personal items, and set up learning stations. Before older students' first day of school, match up the various-sized desks and chairs, tape on name labels and penmanship strips, stack textbooks atop the desks, and lay out basic school supplies (if provided by your school district). Prepare colorful bulletin boards, designate a common classroom meeting area, and post a list of student names outside the doors.

2. *Greeting.* Stand by the door to greet students as they enter. Help them locate the right-sized desk, and show them where to stow their book bags, lunch boxes, and coats.

3. *Morning Routine.* Teach the morning routine (line up outside door; enter room quietly; put away personal items; indicate lunch preference; sharpen pencil; sit down; complete bellringer activity). Practice, practice, practice! Take attendance and lunch count once they've learned the routine.

4. *Introductions.* Share a me-box full of a few items that represent you. Have students do a mixer activity to identify classmates with similar interests.

5. *Rules.* Cooperatively establish classroom rules and consequences using the procedures discussed earlier in this chapter.

6. *Classes.* Teach content areas according to the normal schedule. When possible, preassess students' content knowledge using various games and activities.

7. *Routines and Procedures.* Concurrently teach classroom routines and procedures as they naturally occur. For example, before going to the lunch for the first time, teach students how to line up properly; right before recess, teach them safety procedures. Practice, practice, practice for the next several days.

8. *Closing.* Teach students the end-of-the-day routine (writing in the class daily journal, cleaning floor area, clearing off desk, stacking chair).

Middle school teachers would have a different sequence of events because they are teaching a different age of students and are teaching multiple classes in one day. They might consider using these activities:

1. *Seating Slips.* Pass out seating slips, and have students sign them. Collect them in order, separating each row with a paper clip. It is often wise to count and inspect the slips as they are collected so you don't find slips signed by "Snow White" or not signed at all.

2. *Introductions.* Introduce yourself. Share appropriate information that will make you a "real" person; express your vision for the semester or school year. Begin building a learning community by having students participate in a mixer activity.

3. *Books.* Assign books to students, keeping an accurate record of assigned book numbers. Remember, you or the student will replace any lost, stolen, or destroyed book. Have a short activity for students to do as you distribute books.

4. *Class Rules.* Cooperatively create class rules according to the procedures discussed earlier in this section.

5. *Assignment Sheet.* Distribute and explain an assignment sheet representing at least one week's work. Make your first assignment short, interesting, engaging, and not dependent on the textbook.

6. *Class Discussion.* Discuss unique contributions of your subject that make it important and relevant to them.

7. *Homework*. Discuss the assigned homework topic. Pose some provocative questions.

8. *Marking System*. Give a brief explanation of your policies and procedures for grading, homework, testing, and so on.

9. *Dismissal*. Save some time at the end of the period for needed cleanup and for giving assignments. When—and only when—you are ready, you should dismiss the class. Don't let the bell dismiss (or start) the class. This should be understood from the first day.

Completing all of these tasks will be difficult on the first day, but accomplishing a great deal the first day may serve you well. Be sure to review procedures and rules multiple times over the next few days until they become a habit. Students will be impressed with your organization and businesslike manner, and first impressions are important (and lasting).

Complete Application Activity 3.1 to generate ideas for starting the school year at the grade level you expect to teach.

APPLICATION ACTIVITY 3.1 Getting Started

The first few weeks of school are critical to a smooth-running classroom. What do you need to do before the students enter the door? Using the elementary/middle school first day lists as a guide, ponder how you would conduct first-day activities for your preferred grade level. How would you communicate your expectations to students? How would you make sure they understood your expectations? Share your thoughts with classmates.

Managing Technology

In today's "wired" classrooms, effective classroom managers need to organize, manage, and monitor student use of in-class technology. Some teachers have in-class computer labs, Internet access, DVD players, SMART Boards, and televisions. Others have school-wide labs and technology carts (with computers, printers, and monitors) available on a checkout basis. Thoughtful scheduling, rotating, and monitoring will ensure equitable access to available technology. See the web-based student study site (**www.sagepub.com/mooreteachingk8**) to learn more about managing classroom technology.

Establishing Rules

Lax enforcement makes already-established rules worthless. Students will test your limits to see if you will consistently enforce the rules. When this happens, quickly, firmly, and calmly apply the consequence. If a student tries you—and one always will—you cannot ignore the infraction because the behavior will ripple to other students, and they will also want to test you. Conversely, if you are firm but fair when a student tests you, this action, too, will ripple out to other students, and they will be less likely to test you in the future. The use of the **ripple effect** is especially effective with high-status students. Consequently, you should be firm with these students, and other students will give you fewer problems.

Be consistent and fair in your enforcement of the rules. Treat all students the same, but be humane. Sometimes you must consider the reasons for misbehavior and make exceptions with regard to punishment. Remember, fair is what is right for the individual, not necessarily the masses.

Monitoring the Classroom

When left unsupervised, some students make poor behavioral choices. Therefore, you need to be aware of what is going on in the classroom at all times. This is not an easy task. You need to arrange your classroom so that you can see students at all times from any vantage point. When a potential problem arises, a simple pause in conjunction with eye contact (a teacher look) usually curbs the misbehavior. A well-designed floor plan also allows you to move quickly from place to place so you can address potential problems through proximity. Therefore, when arranging your room, eliminate barriers that may keep you from seeing or readily accessing all areas of the room.

Through the Eyes of an Expert

Bullying

The word bullying conjures images of one student being victimized repeatedly by classmates. However, here are a few facts that might surprise you:

- 80% of adolescents reported being bullied during their school years.

- 90% of 4th through 8th graders report being victims of bullying.

- 15% of students bully regularly or are victims of bullies. Up to 7% of 8th graders stay home at least once a month because of bullies.

- Students reported that 71% of the teachers or other adults in the classroom ignored bullying incidents.

- Bullying most often occurs at school where there is minimal or no supervision (e.g., playground, hallways, cafeteria).

- Most bullying is verbal. (Maine Project Against Bullying, http://lincoln.midcoast .com/~wps/against/bullying.html)

Bullying can be physical, verbal, or emotional and is usually repeated over time. New teachers need to be able to recognize potential bullying and be willing to collaborate with other teachers, staff members, school counselors and administers to develop an approach that both controls the behavior when it happens and works toward prevention. When students complain or report that other students have offended them either verbally or through unwanted physical contact, teachers should immediately address and document the suspected bullying and complaint. With so many students reporting bullying behavior, many schools have

(Continued)

(Continued)

implemented a broad definition as to what constitutes bullying type behavior. In fact, many schools have a zero tolerance bullying policy. New teachers need to become familiar with local school board policies, the student code of conduct, and state laws on bullying and harassment. The following may indicate that a child is being bullied:

- Loss of interest in school or play activities

- Appears sad or moody most of the time

- Afraid to ride the school bus or walk to/from school

- Frequently complains of headaches, stomachaches, or other ailments

- Experiences a loss of appetite

- Suffers from low self-esteem

- Seems uneasy around certain groups or individuals

- Plays or stays alone during free time

- Has visible cuts or bruises

In this digital age, we also have to address online or cyberbullying. Cyberbullying is any harassment that occurs via the Internet. Vicious forum posts, name calling in chat rooms, posting fake profiles on web sites, and mean or cruel email messages are all forms of cyberbullying.

It is the teacher's responsibility to eliminate bullying in the classroom. The school counselor is a resource for developing a classroom plan. Working toward a school-wide program to combat bullying is the most effective approach. This type of all inclusive blanketing of the environment provides for a cohesive management system. For more information on bullying, visit these sites:

- Stop Bullying Now http://www.stopbullyingnow.hrsa.gov/adult/indexAdult.asp

- PACER Kids Against Bullying http://www.pacerkidsagainstbullying.org/

- Kentucky Center for School Safety http://www.kysafeschools.org/index.html

Schools have a collective responsibility to protect students and to provide a nurturing learning environment; therefore, bullying should not be taken lightly. It continues to be an extremely serious school problem.

SOURCE: Karen McCuiston, Kentucky Center for School Safety, Murray, Kentucky. Used with permission.

Applying Consequences

Sooner or later, no matter how well you plan to prevent problems, student misbehavior is going to demand that you administer punishment. Some student behavior will be so severe that some kind of adverse stimulus must be employed to decrease the occurrence of the behavior. You must be aware, however, that what is considered punishment by one individual might not be considered punishment by another; in fact, it may even be considered rewarding. Also, when applying adverse consequences for misbehavior, be sure that you communicate to students that by choosing to misbehave, they have also chosen the consequences.

Video Link 3.2:
Watch a video about managing classroom diversity.

The most common consequence used for curbing disruptive behavior is a verbal reprimand, or "warning." Describe the misbehavior, and then identify the desired behavior and its correlating rationale. Beware: Too many verbal reprimands become nagging. Older students want to be treated as adults, not nagged or criticized—especially in front of their peers. Choose your words carefully because criticism, sarcasm, and ridicule may provoke student hostility or outbursts, resulting in a power struggle between the student and teacher, which can escalate the frequency and volatility of the behavior problem.

To protect student's dignity and avoid a confrontation, administer the reprimand privately rather than publicly. When a student "saves face," there is no need to engage in a power struggle. Use active listening strategies to build a closer personal relationship with the misbehaving student. If private interactions fail to solve the problem, more severe consequences must be administered. Such consequences might include loss of privileges, a visit with an administrator, detention, in-school suspension, and out-of-school suspension.

Loss of privileges is a common and effective form of punishment. Depending upon the age of the students, they may lose their choice of playground equipment, eat lunch alone in a supervised setting, sit away from their peers, lose computer time, or remain in the classroom while everyone else attends a special event. Unfortunately, the problem with this form of punishment is the lack of privileges commonly available for use in most classrooms and, consequently, the shortage of privilege to be denied.

Detention is another common form of punishment. After a private verbal reprimand and a reminder that students chose to misbehave, elementary students oftentimes put their heads down on their desks for a specified amount of time, usually no more than 1 minute per year of age. During this time they still can listen to, but not participate, in the class activities. After the time is up, the teacher privately visits with them about how they can choose an alternate behavior in the future, checks for understanding, and praises them for cooperating. Then they proceed with the daily activities. It is important to have an immediate time-out so that elementary students connect behavioral choices and consequences.

At the middle school level, detention generally comes in two forms. One type requires that all students serving detention report to a detention hall at a specified time (e.g., Monday after school or Saturday morning). The other kind requires that the students report back to the teacher's classroom after or before school. But because many students ride buses, many teachers have students return to the classroom during a break during the day (e.g., part of their lunch break). When using detention as a punishment option, the student should be required to complete a serious academic task. Moreover, the teacher should avoid engaging in conversation with students serving detention. Conversation with the teacher may be perceived as enjoyable, and, hence, the misbehavior might be repeated for more of the "enjoyable" detention.

On occasion, misbehavior becomes so serious or persistent that you must solicit outside assistance from the school administration (e.g., the vice principal or principal) and parents. When a student is sent to the principal's office, you should phone or send a message to the office, reporting that a student is being sent and why. A call to parents about a behavior problem usually yields positive results. Most parents are concerned about the behavior and progress of their children and are willing to work cooperatively in correcting any misbehavior. There are exceptions; some parents feel that taking care of school misbehavior is your job.

In-school suspension is becoming very common at the middle school level; it is used occasionally at the elementary level, too. This technique involves removing misbehaving students from a class and placing them in a special area where they do their schoolwork. They generally are placed in a bare room, furnished with only a table and chair. They report to this room at the beginning of the school day and remain until the end of the day. Meals are sent in, and teachers send in the class work for the day. If the in-school suspension does not correct the misbehavior, out-of-school suspension usually follows. However, out-of-school suspension should be used with extreme cases and as a last resort.

Teachers should not assign extra work or deduct from academic grades for misbehavior. Associating grades and subject work with punishment only creates a dislike for school. It is often good policy, however, to request that students redo sloppy or incorrect work. Indeed, accepting sloppy work or incorrect work only encourages more of the same.

Punishment of the whole class for the misbehavior of one or two students has negative repercussions. Although this approach may curb the inappropriate behavior temporarily, other students may perceive it as unfair and, as a result, develop a negative attitude toward that teacher. On the other hand, if the teacher is well-respected and viewed as fair, the use of peer pressure, especially at the middle school level, can be an effective approach to discipline. Proximal praise, or praising the actions of students who are behaving appropriately in close proximity to the misbehaving student, works well at the elementary level.

To this point, we have not mentioned the use of corporal punishment as an option. It is illegal in most states for teachers to administer corporal punishment. Moreover, corporal punishment often fails to address the long-term problem. In short, corporal punishment has proven to be ineffective and can lead to allegations of brutality and legal difficulties. The other disciplinary techniques presented in this chapter result in students' assuming responsibility for their own actions.

When used, the consequence should be administered immediately after the misbehavior, and it should be fair—the punishment should fit the crime. Certainly, the same consequence should not be administered for constant talking as for harming other students. Of course, you must deal with all misbehavior. Therefore, keep your emotions under control, and deal with problems consistently, fairly, and professionally. When you do use punishment, make it swift, fair, and impressive.

When administered appropriately, punishment can be an effective deterrent to misbehavior. Punishment should only be used, however, when no other alternatives are available. If the misbehavior is not severe, a warning should first be issued. State the misbehavior and possible consequence if the student chooses to continue to misbehave. If a warning does not work, consider punishment.

Table 3.2 summarizes the control aspect of classroom management. Review the summary and complete Reflect and Apply Exercise 3.2

TABLE 3.2	Control Techniques

Element	Description
Routines	Classroom activities that are repetitive and follow a common procedure
Limits	The accepted and nonaccepted actions in the classroom
Monitoring	Being aware of what is taking place in the classroom
Punishment	The application of a negative stimulus or removal of a positive stimulus for inappropriate behavior

REFLECT AND APPLY EXERCISE 3.2: Techniques for Effective Classroom Management

Reflect

- What are some problem behaviors your future students might exhibit? In view of your own current skills, how prepared are you for dealing with these problem behaviors?

- Based on your personal experiences and classroom observations, how will you manage your future elementary or middle school classroom? What standards of "good" behavior will be nonnegotiable? Will you be flexible about some things? Explain.

Apply

- How can you establish an effective learning environment?

- What strategies will you use to start off the year on a positive, productive note?

- Describe how you will deal with serious discipline problems.

SUMMARY

This chapter focused on classroom management. The main points were as follows:

- A classroom must be organized and orderly for learning to take place. Student motivation and positive management strategies are essential to effective teaching and learning.

The Role of Classroom Management

- Three common classroom management methods are the self-discipline approach, the instructional approach, and the desist approach.

- Principles of the self-discipline approach to classroom management are supported by the Glasser reality therapy model, the Gordon TET model, the Coloroso inner discipline model, and the Kohn beyond discipline model.

- Principles of the instructional approach to classroom management are emphasized by the Kounin model and the Jones model.

- Principles of the desist approach to classroom management are integral components of the Canter assertive discipline model and Skinner's research on behavioral modification.

Causes of Misbehavior

- Misbehavior sometimes can be precipitated by teacher actions, student attributes, home environments, or community events.

Organizing for Effective Management

- Effective classroom managers organize the classroom space, plan well, establish routines, and set limits.

Managing a Class

- Teachers must establish credibility at the beginning of the year—and then keep it. They must be fair, firm, and consistent with students. They must monitor their classrooms and apply consequences for misbehavior.

- Teachers should use punishment only as a last resort. They should establish a positive classroom atmosphere, where students have an opportunity to develop a sense of self-discipline.

DISCUSSION QUESTIONS AND ACTIVITIES

1. **Discipline Approaches.** Conduct additional research about the three approaches to classroom management on the accompanying website and through the Internet. Identify some basic concepts that all three approaches have in common. Which approach, if any, do you prefer? Combine elements of the different approaches to develop an eclectic model that would work for you. Be ready to share.

2. **Causes of Misbehavior.** Reflect upon disciplinary incidents you have witnessed in classrooms. Identify the misbehaviors and possible causes. Were any of the misbehaviors caused by the teachers' words, actions, or inaction? How might knowledge of the causes of these incidents influence a teacher's actions?

3. **Rules and Consequences.** Prepare a list of rules and rationales for a classroom at the grade level you expect to teach. Create a list of consequences for breaking these rules.

4. **Maintaining Control.** What procedures will you use to maintain control throughout the year? What measures will you take for severe misbehavior problems?

TECH CONNECTION

The Internet offers numerous resource sites that will assist teachers in managing a multidimensional classroom. Completing these application activities will help you identify ideas that will make managing the classroom easier.

- Access these websites: www.theteachersguide.com/ClassManagement.htm and www.pacificnet.net/ ~ mandel/ClassroomManagement.html. Analyze the ideas presented on organizing a classroom. Form small groups to discuss which ideas will be most useful to you at the grade level you expect to teach.

- Access www.disciplinehelp.com. The site gives a list of 117 problem behaviors and suggestions for handling the problems. Select five problems that you think will cause you concern at the grade level you expect to teach. Analyze the website's advice for the five problems. Present your five problems and analyses to classmates.

CONNECTION WITH THE FIELD

1. **Behavior Observation.** Complete several observations in various classrooms at different grade levels. Analyze the effectiveness of the classroom management approaches using the following prompts:
   a. What are the classroom rules?
   b. How are these rules enforced?
   c. Do students appear to assume responsibility for their own behaviors? How do you know?
   d. How do teachers' words and actions impact students' behavioral choices?
2. **Teacher Interviews.** Interview several teachers at different grade levels. Do they have management problems? If so, how do they handle these problems? Do they support the self-discipline, instructional, or desist approach to classroom management? Make a list of ideas you can use when you become a teacher.
3. **Interview Counselors.** Interview school counselors at elementary and middle schools. Ask them to describe the discipline policies at their schools and how well they work. Could you support any or all of the policies?
4. **Student Handbooks.** Examine and compare several student handbooks from different school districts. What are the school procedures and behavioral guidelines? Discuss similarities and differences with your classmates.

STUDENT STUDY SITE

Visit the Student Study Site at **www.sagepub.com/mooreteachingk8** for these additional learning tools:

- Video clips
- Web resources
- Self quizzes
- E-Flashcards
- Full-text SAGE journal articles
- Portfolio Connection
- Licensing Preparation/Praxis Connection
- Part I View from the Classroom
- Part I Public View of Education

part II

Sequencing and Organizing Instruction

The ultimate goal of effective teaching is to help students on their academic journeys toward becoming lifelong learners. To reach that educational destination, teachers must plan well. Part II focuses upon how teachers prepare to teach by identifying goals, collecting resources, selecting appropriate teaching strategies, and planning student assessment. A major purpose of this section is to assist you in becoming a better instructional planner. To do so, you must identify your educational "destination," facilitate students' academic journeys, and evaluate whether the destination has been reached.

Chapter 4 investigates how effective educators decide what to teach within the parameters of the established school curriculum. A well-designed curriculum addresses the perceived needs of students, society, and various disciplines. Curricular goals and objectives must be aligned with district, state, and national standards. Teachers consider all of these factors as they determine and organize intended educational goals and specific objectives to meet the needs of all students.

With these goals and objectives in mind, teachers design and implement curriculum and plan long-term, weekly, and daily educational events. Chapter 5 centers on how teachers create series of interrelated lessons, or instructional units, to guide students toward achieving intended goals and objectives. We will explore various lesson plan formats that organize instruction to achieve the stated objectives, teach the required content, and develop students' critical thinking skills.

Chapter 6 focuses on how teachers assess student learning throughout the instructional process. We will address different forms of authentic assessment, evaluation systems, measurement accuracy, and information sources. Finally, because assessment provides data for grading decisions, we will present various grading techniques and systems.

CHAPTER 4

Planning and Organizing Instruction

To be prepared is half the victory.

—Miguel de Cervantes Saavedra

Before We Begin

Think about the personal and societal issues that today's students will face in tomorrow's world. What are three things students need to learn to prepare them for their future roles as global citizens? Be ready to compare your view with classmates.

OVERVIEW

Because the primary purpose of schooling is to equip students with the knowledge and skills they'll need to become successful adults, a curriculum must be selected with care. Furthermore, every moment of classroom time is precious. Therefore, effective teachers increase student achievement by identifying essential academic goals and planning instruction to maximize available classroom time. Following a seven-step cyclic teaching model facilitates this important planning process.

As the classroom teacher, you will decide exactly what you will teach. In some cases, curriculum committees, curriculum specialists, or district mandates will influence your decision making. In most cases, however, you alone will make the final curriculum decisions.

Selecting the curriculum is only the first step in instructional planning. You must also clarify your purpose and your instructional intent by determining exactly what you want students to learn, how they will learn it, and how you will know they have learned it. Generally, these three steps occur simultaneously when you make decisions about the time, objectives, materials, and methods of instruction.

OBJECTIVES

After completing your study of Chapter 4, you should be able to

- describe the seven steps to teaching excellence;
- define *curriculum*, and describe the backward design model for curriculum design;
- list and explain the areas that must be addressed in curriculum planning;
- compare and contrast the purposes and characteristics of educational goals, informational objectives, and instructional objectives;
- describe the four elements of a properly written instructional objective; and
- write educational goals and objectives representing different levels of the cognitive, affective, and psychomotor domains.

As an effective educator, you will create a learning community, establish positive student–teacher relationships, design motivational lessons, assess students' achievement, form home-school partnerships, outreach to the community, serve on educational committees, and continue your education. How can you accomplish all of this? By being organized! Organization is central to effective teaching. How can you learn to be organized? Let's begin by looking at a model for good teaching.

A MODEL OF TEACHING

Good teaching requires that you make a constant series of professional decisions to increase the probability that all students will learn. Basically, good teaching is a seven-step cyclic quest to help students achieve mastery of a subject.

1. Select curriculum
2. Identify topics
3. Plan instruction
4. Teach lessons
5. Evaluate learning
6. Analyze outcomes
7. Provide follow-up

This sequential, cyclical teaching process is illustrated in Figure 4.1.

FIGURE 4.1   A Model of Teaching

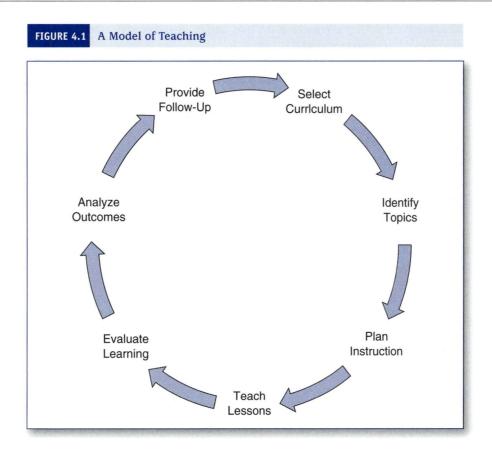

Step 1 involves selecting the curriculum. In addition to prescribed national, state, and district standards, you must consider the needs of students, the needs of society, and the subject. Begin by comparing students' current content knowledge with established standards and perceived needs. Then determine which concepts you need to teach, reteach, or extend.

Video Link 4.1: Watch a video about conceptual lens.

Once you have diagnosed the teaching and learning context, you are ready to outline exactly what will be taught (Step 2). What topics will you address? How will you sequence the topics? How much time will you need to teach each topic?

In Step 3, write objectives delineating exactly what you want students to know. Then select instructional strategies and create lesson activities that will help students achieve the objectives. With these plans in place, you are ready to actually teach the lessons (Step 4). You guide the students through the planned sequence of activities, using your knowledge of students, learning theory, and effective teaching techniques.

In Step 5, determine whether students have achieved the lesson objectives through examinations, presentations, or projects. The results of the evaluation tell you what to do next. If students show mastery, start the next planning cycle (Step 1). If mastery is not demonstrated, follow up with additional instruction.

To become an effective teacher, you need to be a reflective decision maker. Once the lesson has been taught, you reflect upon its success (Step 6), analyze available information, identify any reteaching or enrichment needs, and make decisions accordingly. Then revise the lesson if it is to be taught again.

During the follow-up stage (Step 7), use new approaches to teach additional lessons addressing learning gaps or to extend what students have learned. The extent of your teaching or reteaching will depend upon the achievement results and analysis. Once you are sure all students have the required knowledge, begin the entire teaching process anew!

As you can see, achieving teaching excellence is a major undertaking. We will teach you how to apply this model of good teaching throughout subsequent chapters.

THE CURRICULUM

What exactly is a typical elementary or middle school curriculum? Although specialists have suggested several different definitions for the term *curriculum* (Armstrong, 2002; Oliva, 2000; Wiles & Bondi, 2010), they agree that the curriculum, student body, and teaching strategies of a school reflect the values, attitudes, beliefs, and goals of the surrounding community. For our purposes, let us define *curriculum* as all the planned and unplanned learning experiences that students undergo while in a school setting.

The teacher's responsibility involves selecting which curriculum to teach, both on a long-term and short-term basis. To accomplish this task, the teacher must consult a variety of sources, including established academic standards, state curriculum frameworks, district curriculum guides, school guidelines, and relevant adopted textbooks. These curricular decisions become the blueprint for instruction.

Curriculum Mapping

The gap between district curriculum guidelines and what teachers actually teach presents a challenge to personnel trying to improve the curriculum in a district. They cannot make valid curricular decisions unless they know what is really being taught. Curriculum mapping can help.

Curriculum mapping is a technique for gathering data on what is actually being taught throughout an academic year (Jacobs, 1997). To create a school curriculum map, all teachers enter information about their classroom curricula into a computer database. Teachers note major activities related to three types of data: (1) content, (2) specific skills, and (3) assessments. The process does not judge teachers' styles, techniques, and materials. By carefully analyzing the maps, schools can detect and address curriculum gaps, eliminate repetitions in the curriculum, and refine scope and sequence connections. The school can also identify potential areas for curriculum integration, better align their assessments with state and district standards, and even consider ways to upgrade teaching strategies and materials.

Backward Curriculum Design

Wiggins and McTighe (2005) offer an alternative approach to curriculum design that is particularly well-suited for the academic community. The backward design model is a three-stage approach that identifies the desired results first and then "works backward" to determine assessment criteria before developing instruction to achieve the desired results (see Figure 4.2).

FIGURE 4.2 Backward Design Model

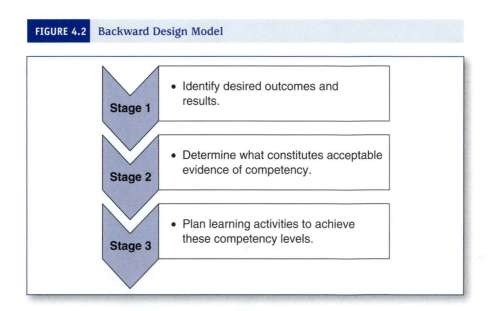

Stage 1
• Identify desired outcomes and results.

Stage 2
• Determine what constitutes acceptable evidence of competency.

Stage 3
• Plan learning activities to achieve these competency levels.

Stage 1. Identify Desired Results

In Stage 1, teachers identify desired results in the form of enduring understandings, or long-term learning. Examples of enduring understandings might include an understanding of community helpers by first graders, an understanding of the digestive system by fifth graders, or an understanding of the role of technology in people's lives by seventh graders. Instead of starting with a textbook, the teacher starts with the desired end results (goals, standards, or benchmarks). District, state, and national standards often identify enduring understandings.

Next, teachers develop essential questions that correlate with the enduring understandings. Good essential questions should

Video Link 4.2: Watch a video about improving curriculum.

- be open-ended with no simple or single right answer;
- be deliberately thought-provoking, counterintuitive, and/or controversial;
- require students to draw upon content knowledge and personal experience;
- pique and sustain student interest;
- engage students in evolving dialogue and debate; and
- lead to other essential questions posed by students.

Essential questions focus on the key knowledge (what students will know) and skills (what students will be able to do). These questions can be created by turning national or state standards and benchmarks into question form. Possible examples are "Is there enough water to go around?" or "How do food choices affect our bodies?"

Stage 2. Assessment

During the second stage, teachers define what forms of assessment will demonstrate that students have acquired the desired knowledge, enduring understanding, or skill. Multiple types of assessment might include performance task (an authentic task of understanding), criteria-referenced assessment (quiz, test), unprompted assessment (observations, dialogues), and self-assessment (journal, checklist).

Stage 3. Plan Learning Experience and Instruction

Next, teachers determine what sequence of instructional activities will lead students to develop and demonstrate the desired understanding. To facilitate all students' learning, teachers employ a large repertoire of research-based, direct and indirect instructional strategies.

Clearly the backward design is a better fit for the reality of the classroom. An abridged illustrative example of the design for a 4-week sixth grade nutrition unit is outlined in Figure 4.3. We will discuss unit planning in detail in Chapter 5.

A more enriching classroom curriculum is one that supplements the textbook content with issues related to student interests.

FIGURE 4.3	Abridged Illustrative Backward Unit Design

Stage 1. The established goals (usually national or local standards). Students will understand essential nutrition concepts.

- Students will understand elements of a balanced diet.

- Students will analyze their own eating patterns and ways in which these patterns may be improved.

- Students will plan a balanced diet for themselves and others.

Essential questions

- What is a balanced diet?

- How can I improve my eating habits?

Stage 2. Acceptable evidence of learning. How students demonstrate understanding.

- Use a KWL (know, want, learned) chart to preassess students' knowledge of what constitutes a balanced diet. Before instruction, students independently complete the *K* column by listing what they think they already *know* about balanced diets. They write questions about what they *want* to learn in the *W* column.

- Teacher observes students' daily work and participation in group activities. Teacher takes notes (anecdotal records) of student misunderstandings and gaps of knowledge that need to be addressed and plans additional instruction accordingly.

- Students create brochures or posters depicting healthful eating habits. These are evaluated using a rubric.

- Students keep an eating log for 3 days. They analyze that log to determine if their diet is balanced. What food groups are in place? What changes could they make?

- Students periodically revisit the KWL chart during the unit. They star items in the *K* column that are accurate and cross out inaccurate information. They answer the questions in the *W* column by writing what they've *learned* in the *L* column. They write more questions in the *W* column before progressing to the next set of activities.

- Teacher administers an end-of-the-unit test.

Stage 3. Planning learning experiences and instruction. The instructional strategies to be implemented.

- Unit activities and cooperative learning group work related to the different food groups and the types of foods found in each group.

- Cooperative construction of a food pyramid

- Jigsaw research activity exploring human nutrition needs for carbohydrates, protein, sugar, fat, salt, vitamins, and minerals; minimum daily requirements for nutritional elements; various health problems that arise from poor nutrition; groups and individuals use nutrition pamphlet from USDA; preapproved Internet sites; and health textbook as resources

- Direct instruction relative to nutrition concepts

- A nutrition video or Internet video clip. Read and interpret the nutrition fact labels on foods, learn about portion size, and plan healthy menus.

- A nutritionist from a local hospital to talk about diet, health, and planning healthy menus

"Yes, your findings are correct. No, I don't believe
you should publish your findings."

Most teachers undertake course planning on their own. We will look at procedures for accomplishing this task in the next section. Before we proceed, complete Reflect and Apply Exercise 4.1.

REFLECT AND APPLY EXERCISE 4.1: Curriculum Decisions

Reflect

- Many factors affect curricula decisions in schools. Think of the K–12 school system in your hometown or where you hope to teach one day. What student needs, societal needs, and academic mandates might impact the curricula in that school district?

- Many experienced teachers use the backward curriculum model. What rationale can you see for this decision?

Apply

- Think about how you will make curriculum decisions for your classroom. What resources will you use to assist your decision-making efforts?

CURRICULUM PLANNING

All teachers are responsible for the instructional emphasis within their classrooms. What they emphasize is determined, in part, by mandated academic competencies to be demonstrated by learners. These standards, skills, outcomes, or benchmarks represent what all students, pre-kindergarten through 12th grade, should know and be able to do at various grade levels. For example, the state of Oklahoma has established learning outcomes for students completing all grades and subjects, whereas Arkansas has established benchmarks for all subjects and grades. Some state standards are being replaced by the Common Core State Standards Initiative. Governors and state commissioners of education have worked with teachers, administrators, college and university professors, and other educational professionals to cooperatively create national English/language arts and mathematics standards. These are now being use in 48 states, two territories, and the District of Columbia. For more information, go to www.corestandards.org/.

EMILIO: A REFLECTIVE CASE STUDY

Emilio was excitedly planning for his first year teaching eighth grade social studies. During a curriculum mapping session with his middle school team, he mentioned that he wanted to expand the coverage of Hispanic American's societal contributions during the past century. Carrie, a colleague, said he needed to focus on what's on THE state test and ONLY the test. Emilio asked how that would meet the needs of the high Hispanic student population in their school.

1. What should Emilio do? Why?
2. Is it possible to teach creatively and still address state standards? Give an example.
3. What is an "extra" topic you'd like to expand upon in your future classroom? How could you persuade your colleagues to support your curricular decision?

National textbook companies and local school districts align their curricular efforts with these educational mandates. The procedures for identifying the content for a complete school program (K–12) can be quite sophisticated. Essentially, the district's curriculum specialists and curriculum committees (with community, administrative, and teacher representatives) select textbooks or other curricular materials based upon the perceived student needs, district goals, and needs of their community. They cooperatively create a suggested scope and sequence of instructional topics. Teachers further individualize their courses to meet the needs of their specific student populations.

Course Planning

Frequently, your first task as a teacher will be to plan instruction for the school year (Posner & Rudnitsky, 2000). Organize course instruction so that students achieve mastery of the state-mandated and district-designated curricula. To ensure that you will address all of the required content within the semester or school year, you must carefully plan your instruction for each subject you teach. Keep in mind, however, that curricular mandates don't necessarily include everything necessary to prepare well-rounded students to be successful global citizens. There also are "generic" and worthy "enrichment" activities that are equally important. Therefore, seek input from experienced teachers who teach the same grade level and/or subjects to help you make decisions about the time, personnel, energy, and resources allocated to each of these important components of the curriculum.

Many states now rank their schools on how well students master the state-mandated curricula. For example, Florida grades its schools using an A to F grading scale, while Texas rates its schools as Exemplary, Recognized, Academically Acceptable/Acceptable, and Academically Unacceptable/Low Performing. Kentucky publishes a "School Report Card" sharing test results. Furthermore, schools who do not make "adequate yearly progress" receive specialized assistance to improve students' achievement. The ranking of schools is spreading across the nation.

Technology Planning

Whenever possible, teachers integrate technology throughout the curriculum, both as an instructional resource and as a learning tool. Technology can be used in many ways, including assessing students' knowledge, accommodating students' special needs, motivating students to learn more about the topic, providing practice opportunities, extending students' knowledge, and teaching students new skills. Regardless of how technology is used, teachers and/or technology planning committees should consider the needs and interests of their unique student populations, national and district technology standards, and available resources as they plan technology integration.

This completes our study of the curriculum and curriculum planning. Let's now direct our attention toward determining lesson learning intent.

REFLECTIONS ON TEACHER PRACTICE 4.1: The Curriculum

1. How can teachers emphasize both breadth and depth when teaching the required school curriculum? Why is both breadth and depth needed for understanding?

2. How can teachers planning and teaching as a team result in more effective teaching? How would such teaming make schools more of a challenge for students?

I find it very difficult to "cover" my curriculum by myself, but with the cooperation of other teachers (not just core teachers), I am able to cover and practice much more. We often think of related arts classes as being nonacademic, but they are only nonacademic if we teach them that way.

The science teacher on my team has partnered with the FACS teacher on the human body, hygiene, and rocks/fossils/minerals content very successfully. Likewise, the science teacher on my team is having her students reply to response-like questions in the same way I have been requiring them to answer in my classroom. We are already making plans for next year's first quarter to be sure our students are able to take notes and present research effectively as well as other overlapping skills.

We need more time to plan together as well as the openness of others to include/hook into each others' subject concepts. It takes time to see the connections, but it is vital if we are ever to live up to the grand expectations of those who write our curriculum.

Breadth is wonderful, but not if it is at the expense of understanding and deep knowledge.

—*Ellen, middle school teacher*

Please visit the Student Study site at **www.sagepub.com/mooreteachingk8** *for additional discussion questions and assignments.*

Source: www.middleweb.com. Reprinted with permission.

Complete Application Activity 4.1, which will let you further your understanding of the curriculum you will be teaching.

APPLICATION ACTIVITY 4.1 The Curriculum

Think about your K–12 experiences. Did your school district do an adequate job of addressing the needs of the community, students, and society? How effective was the curriculum in meeting your needs? How will you determine what curriculum to teach in your future classroom? Explain.

RATIONALE FOR OBJECTIVES

Almost anything that happens in a classroom results in some type of learning. To produce desirable learning, however, your lesson must have direction and purpose and must align with state and district curricular mandates. For example, your state and school district might want to focus on developing students' ability to write answers to open-response questions according to prescribed guidelines. Thus, even though writing is a broad and basic skill, you would integrate open-response activities into instructional content and related specific objectives. Viewed in this context, your objective can be defined as a clear and unambiguous description of instructional intent. It is finite and measurable. Its accomplishment can be verified.

An objective is *not* a statement of what you plan to do; it is a statement of what your *students* should be able to do after instruction. For example, if the purpose of instruction is to foster student understanding of the conditions that precipitated American space exploration, the objective would *not* be "The *teacher will present* information about the NASA space program." Remember, the focus should be on what the students learn. Therefore, the objective should be "The *student will identify* three world conditions that launched the American space program." Objectives, then, are student-centered; they emphasize *student* outcomes or performance.

Well-written objectives establish a framework for instruction by suggesting teaching strategies, lesson activities, and evaluation procedures. For example, if your objective is the instant recall of multiplication facts, your activities must include practice in memorizing those facts. If, on the other hand, the objective is to teach students how to become proficient problem solvers, you must provide students with an opportunity to practice problem-solving procedures. Objectives also prescribe exactly what skills and knowledge students must manifest as a result of instruction, thus inferring how students' efforts will be evaluated.

Course planning is essential to effective teaching.

Let's now look at determining instructional intent in greater detail. However, before we do so, complete Reflect and Apply Exercise 4.2, which will further explore the concepts in the section.

REFLECT AND APPLY EXERCISE 4.2: Curriculum Decisions

Reflect

- Should we have a national and/or state agenda that shapes our school goals and instructional objectives? Explain.

- Do you think teachers should be held accountable for the academic progress of their students? Why or why not?

Apply

- Think of a recent college class you attended. What were the objectives of the lesson? How were they related to class activities? How were you evaluated?

EDUCATIONAL GOALS

When designing a lesson or **instructional unit**, teachers develop educational goals, **informational objectives**, and **instructional objectives**. These three levels vary in specificity. Whereas goals are usually broad statements describing the purposes of schooling or the purposes of a course, objectives are narrower statements of the intended student learning resulting from a specific lesson. Goals are written for a school course or unit; informational and instructional objectives are written for specific lessons within the unit. Examples of these three levels of specificity are shown in Table 4.2. Note that although the levels of specificity differ, educational goals, informational objectives, and instructional objectives are all interrelated.

Because educational goals are broad, they often take an extended period of time to be accomplished. Note how the goal in Table 4.1 is helping students become computer literate. The informational and instructional objectives support that goal by specifying how students will demonstrate their computer literacy. Following are other examples of educational goals:

1. Students will develop a command of Standard English.

2. Students will embrace diversity.

3. Students will develop good health habits.

Educational goals give us general direction in deciding what to teach. Therefore, they are usually concerned with covert (nonobservable), internal changes, which are not readily

TABLE 4.1	Examples of Educational Goal and Objective Specificity
Type	**Example**
Educational goal	The student will develop computer literacy.
Informational objective	The student will be able to use a word-processing software program.
Instructional objective	Given a set of specific requirements, the student will be able to use a word-processing program to write a one-page paper with no errors.

measurable or observable. Some verbs that should prove helpful in writing educational goals are listed in Table 4.2. Notice that many of the verbs used in writing educational goals are rather vague and open to interpretation. This allows teachers to use a variety of learning activities to attain each educational goal.

TABLE 4.2	Some Illustrative Verbs for Writing Goals	
A apply appreciate **B** believe **C** comprehend cope **D** demonstrate develop	**E** enjoy **F** familiarize fully appreciate **G** grasp **I** imagine **K** know	**L** like **R** realize recognize **T** think **U** understand **V** value

Once the educational goals are in place, we must now decide more precisely what students should know and, consequently, do to demonstrate that they have accomplished these goals. These decisions are stated in informational and instructional objectives. Complete Application Activity 4.2 to further explore educational goals.

APPLICATION ACTIVITY 4.2 Educational Goals

Access the Department of Education website for the state in which you hope to teach one day. What are the goals for the grade level you expect to teach? Study the content standards and one content area for one grade level. What are some topics you might teach someday soon? How does that list of topics compare with what you remember learning at that grade level?

STATING OBJECTIVES

Like educational goals, objectives are focused upon student learning as a result of instruction. Because objectives are more specific, however, you should be able to observe or measure what the students have learned. Therefore, to ensure students learn what you intend, informational and instructional objectives must be clearly stated, observable, and measurable. Table 4.3 suggests some verbs that are appropriate for informational and instructional objectives. Note the difference in clarity of language between the verbs listed in Tables 4.2 and 4.3.

TABLE 4.3 Illustrative Verbs for Writing Informational and Instructional Objectives

A	E	P
add	evaluate	pick
adjust	explain	plan
analyze		point
appraise	**G**	pronounce
arrange	graph	
assess		**Q**
	I	question
B	identify	
build	infer	**R**
	inspect	read
C		recite
calculate	**J**	run
chart	judge	
choose	justify	**S**
circle		select
cite	**L**	sing
classify	label	sort
compare	list	state
construct	locate	support
contrast		
critique	**M**	**U**
	make	underline
D	manage	use
define	measure	
describe		**V**
diagnose	**N**	validate
draw	name	
		W
	O	write
	operate	
	order	
	organize	

Elements of Instructional Objectives

There are a number of approaches to writing objectives. While there are advantages and disadvantages to each approach, this text will focus on Mager's (1997) version, because it is the most widely used and perhaps the most inclusive.

Instructional objectives precisely communicate learning intent. Mager (1997) suggests three components of instructional intent: (1) behavior, (2) conditions, and (3) criterion. This book, however, recommends that an expression of instructional intent comprise these *four* elements:

1. Identify the student *performance* that will demonstrate the intent has been achieved.

2. Specify the *product* that is the result of student actions.

3. Describe the *conditions* under which the students will demonstrate what they have learned.

4. State the *criteria* of acceptable performance. How well do you want the students to perform?

At times, not all of these elements are necessary. The object is to clearly communicate your intent. Thus, sometimes informational objectives (addressed later in this chapter) will suffice and sometimes not.

Element 1: The Performance

When writing an instructional objective, first you need to specify exactly what you expect students to be able to do after they receive instruction. Because you will need to observe or measure students' performance, you must carefully select a verb that is clear, specific, and unambiguous. You, interested colleagues, your principal, and your students must interpret the same meaning from each verb used in your objectives. Instead of using subjective, vague terms, such as *know*, *realize*, and *understand*, use terms such as *list*, *identify*, and *sing*, which denote observable (overt) actions or behaviors. The action associated with the verb should describe a specific, measurable performance that demonstrates the students' attainment of the intended outcome. Go back and review Table 4.3 for further examples of appropriate verbs for writing instructional objectives.

Element 2: The Product

The second element of an instructional objective specifies the result of the students' performance. You will evaluate this student product to determine whether the objective has been mastered. Students should be given a choice of ways to demonstrate what they have learned. They could, for example, produce a one-page book report, a list of correctly spelled words, a PowerPoint biography of a famous black American, a diorama depicting an animal in its habitat, or a model of the solar system.

Element 3: The Conditions

The instructional objective also establishes the conditions under which the learner will perform the prescribed action. Conditional elements can refer to restrictions in time and space or to materials, information, or special equipment that will or will not be available during the assessment event. We've emphasized the conditional element in this example:

Given the formula, the student will be able to calculate the area of an isosceles triangle. This condition tells students that they will not need to memorize the formula; they should simply know how to use it. Here are other examples of conditions that might be included in an instructional objective:

Given a list of verbs . . .

After reading Chapter 10 . . .

With a ruler, protractor, and compass . . .

From memory . . .

Given the necessary materials . . .

With the use of a calculator . . .

During a 5-minute interval . . .

Although conditions are usually written as the first component in the objective, their placement can be anywhere in the objective. For example, notice the location of the emphasized conditional element in this objective: The student will compute 20 long division problems, *without the use of a calculator,* with 100% accuracy.

Element 4: The Criteria

The fourth, and last element of an instructional objective is the level of acceptable student performance. How well do students need to perform to show mastery? The level of mastery can be specified in terms of time limits, percentage of correct answers, an acceptable tolerance, and other observable operations. Criteria are reflected on evaluation instruments such as rubrics, rating scales, checklists, or through scores on homework assignments, paper or project, etc. Students need to know the exact standards, or criteria, used in judging their performance. Examples include

. . . at least three reasons

. . . 9 of the 10 cases

. . . with no spelling errors

. . . with 80% accuracy

. . . within plus or minus 10%

. . . in less than 5 minutes

Each of these criterion levels represents well-defined standards toward which students can strive. Usually, such standards are selected rather arbitrarily on the basis of past experiences and class expectations. Be sure to set reasonable levels of performance that challenge but don't overwhelm your students.

Now that you know the four elements of an instructional objective, you are ready to differentiate between informational and instructional objectives.

Informational Objectives

Frequently, you will want 100% of the class to attain 100% of the objective—that is, 100% mastery. Furthermore, objectives often have no special conditions. In these cases, informational objectives will meet your instructional needs.

Informational objectives are abbreviated instructional objectives. Whereas instructional objectives contain four elements, informational objectives specify only the student performance and the product. Consider, for example, the following instructional and informational objectives written for the same instructional intent.

> Instructional Objective: Given the voltage and resistance, the student will be able to calculate the current in a series and parallel circuit with 100% accuracy.

> Informational Objective: The student will be able to compute the current in a series or parallel circuit.

Notice that the informational objective is an abbreviation of the instructional objective in that it omits the conditions ("given the voltage and resistance") and the criterion for judging minimum mastery ("100% accuracy"). The informational objective contains only the performance ("to calculate") and the product ("the current in a series or parallel circuit"). Frequently, the conditions are implied. The informational objective implies that students must know the necessary information to calculate the current. Moreover, it infers that 100% accuracy is desired.

Informational objectives are often adequate when you share your instructional intent with students. If you feel more information is needed to communicate the exact intent, however, you should write instructional objectives, or perhaps informational objectives, with the conditions or the criterion added. Let's now look at how you can communicate your objectives to your students.

REFLECTIONS ON TEACHER PRACTICE 4.2: Establishing Objectives

1. What advantages do you see in having students involved in determining educational intent?

2. What impact will student attitudes have on the desire to learn?

My fifth-grade class goes to a physical education teacher once a week. The physical education teacher was complaining about the performance of my students during their once-a-week physical education class. My first response was, "What do you expect me to do?" Yet, I began noticing student attitudes toward their physical education class were very negative and getting progressively worse. Some were bringing notes from home asking that they be excused from physical education for various reasons.

I decided to schedule additional physical education time into our daily schedule in an effort to find out what was going on. I perceived that my students needed to somehow develop a deeper appreciation for physical activity so I decided to take them out to play kick ball and see for myself what was going on. I selected kick ball because it is the simplest, physical game I know. It has simple rules, requires little or no setup time, and the only materials I needed was a ball for them to kick and bases. I required everyone to participate while I observed.

(Continued)

(Continued)

On our first day of kick ball, there was much arguing, intentional cheating by some, disgruntled players, reluctant/discouraged players, and a few (two or three) eager students. The attitudes were awful! Even the eager students had no sense of fair play or team spirit. Some of the students were unable to kick the ball without falling down. Several couldn't run. I mean they really didn't know how to run or even where to run. Some didn't know the correct base order to tag bases. Two students didn't speak English. Furthermore, name calling and negative remarks were the general basis for communication. Indeed, the frustration level for the group was extremely high. Obviously, they were finding very little satisfaction from their learning time. Of course the big question was, "Are they learning anything?" I certainly learned a lot from them. First, I learned that when students do not have explicit objectives for their activities, they tend to devise their own. I asked my group what our objectives should be to justify our time outside each day. Each of them had different ideas about the goals and objectives of physical education time. No wonder they seemed to be going in 20 different directions.

With the help of my class, we made a list of objectives that would address our immediate needs in an effort to focus the group. We made a list of skills needed to be successful at kick ball. The list of objectives gave the group a focus and gave me a tool for evaluation of each student's progress. Students began to focus less on winning and losing and more on skills needed for the game to run smoothly. Certainly, there is nothing wrong with focusing on winning as long as prerequisite skills are not neglected.

The result of having specific objectives focused everyone and the assessment was built into the accomplishment of the objectives. The results were astounding! I've never been more pleased. First, I learned that many of my students honestly didn't know how to run. I guess I thought that was something that just came naturally to children. I learned many of my students rarely played outside. As a result of this, I began communicating more with parents to find out more about my students. My teaching became more personable and I began to realize the connection between what my students could learn and what was going on in their personal lives. I watched each student become more and more proficient with the physical skills needed for their physical education class. Their attitudes about themselves and each other improved dramatically. Many students expressed pride in their accomplishments and began to talk about how they now liked physical education. Getting to know my students on a personal level along with the use of specific, obtainable objectives made a huge difference.

—Susan Moore, 5th grade, Pike Elementary School, Fort Smith, Arkansas

Please visit the Student Study site at **www.sagepub.com/mooreteachingk8** *for additional discussion questions and assignments.*

SOURCE: Courtesy of Susan Moore, Van Buren, Arkansas. Used with permission.

COMMUNICATION OF OBJECTIVES

Sharing objectives in student-friendly terms establishes a purpose for learning, motivates students to excel, and provides a framework for learning activities. Students respond favorably if they know what they need to know or be able to do at the end of

"Recess is my most important subject. I'm going to be a congressman."

SOURCE: Created by Martha Campbell.

the lesson or unit. During the opening section of each lesson, communicate your precise instructional intent orally or in writing, using "kid-friendly" language and "you" instead of "the student will."

This concludes our formal discussion of goals and objectives. Let's now direct our attention to the three domains of learning.

TAXONOMIES OF OBJECTIVES

Objectives can be classified into three primary categories, or domains of learning, based upon their instructional focus: (1) cognitive (thinking), (2) affective (attitudes or feelings), and (3) psychomotor (physical skills). Please note that domains do not occur in isolation. Whereas some behaviors are easily classifiable into one of the three domains, others will overlap a great deal (see Figure 4.4). A good example of this overlap is seen when students are required to write personal narratives. In so doing, they must recall information and think (cognitive), they incorporate emotional elements in the task (affective), and they use fine motor skills to make the necessary writing movements (psychomotor).

FIGURE 4.4 The Three Domains

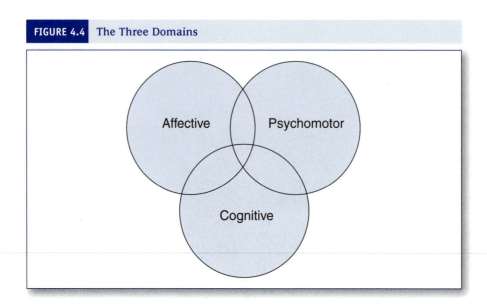

The three domains for objectives were designed to form hierarchical taxonomies of student learning—from simple to complex—with each level building on the behaviors addressed in the preceding level. The levels do not imply, however, that behaviors must be mastered sequentially from the lowest level to the highest level. Indeed, instruction can be directed toward any level of complexity.

Don't write objectives at specific taxonomy levels just to have objectives at all levels. Although it is possible to write objectives at any of the taxonomy levels of the three domains of learning, Mager (1997) suggested that once you have made a suitable analysis of your instructional intent, you will know what you want your students to learn and you will automatically write your objectives at the intended levels. Furthermore, you must guard against falling into the habit of writing objectives only for the lower levels of learning within a particular domain because writing higher level learning objectives is more difficult. Use your knowledge of the taxonomies to formulate the best possible objectives for your teaching intent, representing varying levels of complexity for all three domains.

Cognitive Domain

Objectives in the cognitive domain are concerned with students' thinking and reasoning abilities. Because the ability to think can range from simple recall of information to more complex thinking behaviors, Benjamin Bloom (1956) developed a hierarchical classification system, or taxonomy, to help teachers gain a better perspective on the behaviors to be emphasized in instructional planning.

Bloom's (1956) *Taxonomy of Educational Objectives* classifies cognitive ability into six categories, ranging from the fairly simple recall of information to the complex assimilation of information and evaluation. These six levels, along with verbs commonly used to express the required behaviors, are listed in Table 4.4.

1. *Knowledge.* The simple recall or recognition of previously learned materials.

   Informational Objective: The student will be able to name the food groups represented on the food pyramid.

2. *Comprehension.* Extending beyond the memorization of previously learned material to change its form or make simple interpretations. This is the first level of understanding.

   Informational Objective: The student will be able to describe how vitamins and minerals help the body remain healthy.

3. *Application.* Putting learned information to use in reaching a solution or accomplishing a task.

   Instructional Objective: Given a list of various food items, the student will be able to categorize the items according to their food groups with 90% accuracy.

4. *Analysis.* Breaking down complex material into its component parts so it can be better explained.

   Instructional Objective: Given the menu from a fast-food restaurant, the student will be able to identify the nutritious elements (if any) of a fast-food meal.

5. *Synthesis.* Combining available elements to form a new whole with a new and unique form.

   Instructional Objective: Given an imaginary budget, the student will plan 1 week's menu of nutritious meals aligned with the food pyramid guidelines.

TABLE 4.4	Bloom's Taxonomy and Illustrative Action Verbs
Level	**Student Action**
Knowledge	Identify, define, list, match, state, name, label, describe, select
Comprehension	Translate, convert, generalize, paraphrase, rewrite, summarize, distinguish, infer, alter, explain
Application	Use, operate, produce, change, solve, show, compute, prepare, determine
Analysis	Discriminate, select, distinguish, separate, subdivide, identify, break down, analyze, compare
Synthesis	Design, plan, compile, compose, organize, conclude, arrange, construct, devise
Evaluation	Appraise, compare, justify, criticize, explain, interpret, conclude, summarize, evaluate

6. *Evaluation.* Making a judgment as to the value of materials or ideas. Criteria or standards must be given or determined.

Informational Objective: The student will write a persuasive letter to the school principal to precipitate a change in the cafeteria menu.

Lorin Anderson, a former student of Bloom, worked with a group of educators to revise Bloom's *Taxonomy* (Bloom, 1956) to represent current learning theories and to make it more relevant for today's students and teachers (Anderson & Krathwohl, 2001). Basically, the revision changed the six major categories from noun to verb form and changed the structure of the taxonomy with the addition of a knowledge product dimension. The revised categories, along with student actions associated with each category, are presented in Table 4.5. Some educators suggest the revised taxonomy provides a better tool for alignment between standards and educational goals, objectives, products, and activities.

TABLE 4.5 Revised Bloom's *Taxonomy* and Category Definitions

Level	Student Action
Remembering	Retrieve, recognize, and recall relevant knowledge
Understanding	Construct meaning from oral, written, and graphic messages through interpreting, exemplifying, classifying, summarizing, inferring, comparing, and explaining
Applying	Carry out or use a procedure through executing or implementing
Analyzing	Break material into constituent parts; determine how the parts relate to one another and to an overall structure or purpose through differentiating, organizing, and attributing
Evaluating	Make judgments based on criteria and standards through checking and critiquing
Creating	Put elements together to form a coherent or functional whole; reorganize elements into a new pattern or structure through generating, planning, or producing

The body of work by Arons (1988); Beyer (1984); Haller, Child, and Walberg (1988); Nickerson (1985); Orlich et al. (1990); and Wittrock (1986) led to a novel interpretation of how the cognitive taxonomy may operate. Instead of the six major categories viewed as a ladder (Figure 4.5) that must be climbed one level at a time, a three-dimensional model (Figure 4.6) is offered. This model is analogous to an apple. The outward peel represents knowledge, the first level. The meat of the apple symbolizes the comprehension (understanding) level, and the higher levels of thinking represent the core of all understanding. This model views the cognitive categories as interactive, with the comprehension level being the key to unlocking the other levels. That is, once you truly understand the information, you can branch into any of the remaining four categories— (1) application, (2) analysis, (3) synthesis, or (4) evaluation. Instead of moving through the categories sequentially, students can move from comprehension to evaluation, from comprehension to analysis, from comprehension to synthesis, or from comprehension to application.

Traditional Model of Cognitive Taxonomy as a Ladder

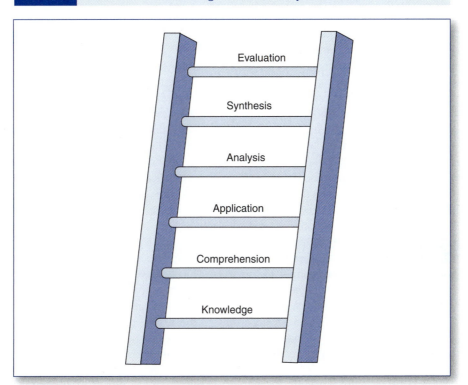

Three-Dimensional Model of the Cognitive Taxonomy

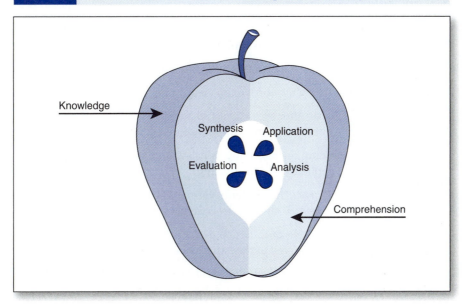

Affective Domain

Objectives in the **affective domain** are concerned with the development of students' attitudes, feelings, and emotions. They can vary according to the degree of internalization of the attitude, feeling, or emotion.

Clearly, because teachers must be concerned with the total development of students, not just development in the cognitive domain, writing affective objectives should be an integral part of the planning process. Affective domain objectives are often difficult to write because attitudes, feelings, and emotions are difficult to translate into overt, observable behaviors. For example, the affective objective "The student will value the need for rules" is not properly written. The behavior "value" is not observable or measurable. The verb *value* must be replaced with an action that shows observable behavior: "The student will support the school rules during class discussions on class rules." This affective objective would be one of many possible indicators that the student "values" the need for rules.

Behaviors related to the affective domain must take place in a "free-choice" situation in order to be true indicators of students' attitudes, likes and dislikes, and feelings. Otherwise, students may exhibit the desired behaviors for a reward or because they want to please you. For example, students who attend class every day might be doing so because attendance impacts their grade, not because they like coming to your class. The objective "The student will eagerly participate in class discussions" specifies one possible indicator that the student likes the class.

Krathwohl, Bloom, and Masia (1964) developed a classification system for categorizing affective responses into five levels, according to the degree to which an attitude, feeling, value, or emotion has become part of the individual. The taxonomy levels and some illustrative verbs commonly used for revealing the extent of internalization are given in Table 4.6.

1. *Receiving.* Being aware of and willing to attend freely to stimuli and messages in the environment (listen and look).

   Informational Objective: The student will demonstrate awareness that there is a class pet (hamster) in the classroom.

2. *Responding.* Freely attending to stimuli and voluntarily reacting to those stimuli.

   Informational Objective: The student will volunteer to clean the hamster's cage.

3. *Valuing.* Voluntarily giving worth to an idea, a phenomenon, or a stimulus.

   Instructional Objective: After seeing a classmate poke items in the hamster's cage, the student will state three reasons why the hamster is entitled to a safe, peaceful existence.

4. *Organization.* Building an internally consistent value system. A set of criteria is established and applied in choice-making.

   Informational Objective: The student will conduct and share additional research about how class pets help children learn to care for themselves and others.

5. *Characterization by a Value or Value Complex.* Consistently acting according to a value and being firmly committed to the experience.

   Informational Objective: The student will organize a fund-raising effort to earn money to buy class pets for all of the school's classrooms.

TABLE 4.6	Affective Domain Taxonomy and Illustrative Action Verbs
Level	**Student Action**
Receiving	Follow, select, rely, choose, point to, ask, hold, give, locate, attend.
Responding	Read, conform, help, answer, practice, present, report, greet, tell, perform, assist, recite.
Valuing	Initiate, ask, invite, share, join, follow, propose, read, study, work, accept, do, argue.
Organization	Defend, alter, integrate, synthesize, listen, influence, adhere, modify, relate, combine.
Characterization by a value or value complex	Adhere, relate, act, serve, use, verify, question, confirm, propose, solve, influence, display.

Psychomotor Domain

Objectives in the **psychomotor domain** relate to the development of muscular abilities that range from simple reflex movements to precision and creativity in performing a skill. The psychomotor domain is especially relevant in physical education, music, drama, art, and vocational courses, but all subjects will relate to this domain to some degree (see Table 4.7). The four-level system presented here is adapted from the work of Harrow (1972) and Jewett and Mullan (1977). Let's now take a brief look at the taxonomy levels.

1. *Fundamental Movement.* Movements that form the basic building blocks for the higher level movements.

   Informational Objective: The student will be able to stand on a stationary skateboard without falling off.

2. *Generic Movement.* Carrying out the basic rudiments of a skill when given directions and under supervision.

   Instructional Objective: Under supervision, the student will be able to propel the skateboard without stopping for at least 5 minutes.

3. *Ordinative Movement.* Competence in performing a skill ably and independently.

   Informational Objective: The student will be able to perform a kickflip without pausing to think.

4. *Creative Movement.* Ability to produce and compose motor options that serve the personal purposes of the performer.

   Instructional Objective: Using proper safety equipment, the student will be able to perform a skateboard routine using multiple surfaces, three tricks, and some personal razzle-dazzle.

TABLE 4.7	Psychomotor Domain Taxonomy and Illustrative Action Verbs

Level	Student Action
Fundamental movement	Track, crawl, hear, react, move, grasp, walk, climb, jump, grip, stand, run
Generic movement	Drill, construct, dismantle, change, hop, clean, manipulate, follow, use, march
Ordinative movement	Play, connect, fasten, make, sketch, weigh, wrap, manipulate, play, swim, repair, write
Creative movement	Create, invent, construct, manipulate, play, build, pantomime, perform, make, compose

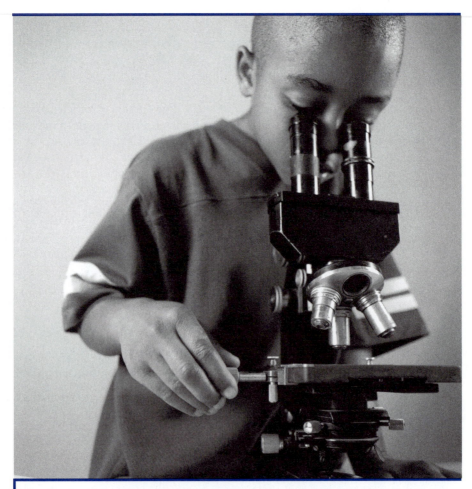

The development of motor skills is an essential part of the learning intent in many classrooms.

Although instruction and learning in the classroom frequently contain elements of all three domains, your objectives for a particular unit will probably place primary emphasis on the cognitive, affective, or psychomotor domain. Don't become a slave to the taxonomies; instead, base your objectives on the needs of your class and use the taxonomies as a guide. Finally, strive to incorporate the higher levels of the taxonomies in your students' learning experiences.

This concludes our discussion of the three learning domains and their respective taxonomies and our study of goals and objectives. Take a few minutes to complete Reflect and Apply Exercise 4.3, which will check your understanding of the concepts presented in this section.

REFLECT AND APPLY EXERCISE 4.3: Goals and Objectives

Reflect

- What goals should be generic to all students and schools? Should goals be different for different students? Should goals be different for elementary and middle schools? Should teachers write enduring understandings instead of goals and objectives? Why or why not?

- How important are instructional objectives? Should teachers be required to write objectives for each and every lesson they teach? Should they write objectives in the three domains? Why or why not?

Apply

- How will you communicate your objectives to students?

- List at least two enduring understandings that should be taught at the grade level you expect to teach.

- Choose one topic. Write an instructional goal related to that topic. Create an informational objective representing *each* of the domains—cognitive, affective, and psychomotor. Convert these informational objectives into instructional objectives. Be ready to share.

SUMMARY

This chapter focused on school curriculum and planning instruction. The main points were as follows:

A Model of Teaching

- Effective teachers must diagnose the teaching and learning context, plan the course, plan instruction, guide planned activities, evaluate, reflect, and, when necessary, follow up.

- Poor planning results in lost instructional time.

The Curriculum

- The curriculum of a school consists of all the planned and unplanned experiences students undergo in the school setting.

- Curriculum mapping can be used to identify gaps in the curriculum being taught.

- The backward design model offers an alternative approach to curriculum design.

Curriculum Planning

- Chapter topics are often combined into units that are then sequenced to form a timeline for instruction.

- A course plan should remain flexible so modifications can be made during the year.

- When integrating technology into classroom activities, teachers need to consider their students' interests, technology standards, and available technology resources.

Rationale for Objectives

- Objectives express your instructional intent to students and specify how students will demonstrate their learning in observable, measurable ways.

- Objectives set the framework for your instructional approach and the evaluation of student learning.

- Objectives hold students and teachers accountable for student learning.

Educational Goals

- The specificity of instructional intent varies from broad educational goals to very narrow specific objectives.

- The three levels of learning intent, in order of specificity, are (1) educational goals, (2) informational objectives, and (3) instructional objectives.

Stating Objectives

- The actions called for by educational goals are overt, nonquantifiable behaviors, whereas the actions called for by informational and instructional objectives are overt and measurable.

- Instructional objectives consist of four elements: (1) the performance, (2) the product, (3) the conditions, and (4) the criterion.

- Informational objectives specify only the performance and the product; the conditions and criterion are usually not specified.

Communication of Objectives

- Objectives should always be communicated to students using student-friendly language.

Taxonomies of Objectives

- Objectives can be written at any of the levels within the three domains of learning: (1) cognitive, (2) affective, and (3) psychomotor. Each domain is arranged in hierarchical order from simple to complex.

DISCUSSION QUESTIONS AND ACTIVITIES

1. **The Curriculum.** Obtain a state and district curriculum guide for elementary or middle school education. How would you improve the curriculum at the level you plan to teach? Should teachers be free to determine what they will teach? What forces commonly influence the school curriculum?

2. **Planning a Course.** Select a basic textbook from your area of specialization. Using the selected textbook, plan a series of instructional units. Select the topics (chapters) to be covered, supplement the textbook where needed, combine the topics (chapters) into appropriate units of study, and make unit time allotments.

3. **Analysis of Textbook Objectives.** Review the teacher's edition of a school textbook from the grade level and/or subject you expect to teach that lists the unit and/or chapter objectives. Address the following questions in your review.
   a. Are informational objectives given for the chapters? Are instructional objectives? Are the objectives the same for all students?
   b. Are objectives written for all three domains of learning?
   c. Are the objectives written at the different taxonomy levels within each of the learning domains?

4. **Writing Goals and Objectives.** Consider your planned teaching grade level and/or subject, and write a broad educational goal that you feel should be addressed at the identified level. Now write at least three different informational and instructional objectives that tell what students should do to show you that the goal has been accomplished.

5. **Writing Cognitive, Affective, and Psychomotor Domain Objectives.** Write 10 cognitive and psychomotor domain objectives for a topic from your area. Make the objectives at various taxonomy levels of complexity. Now write five affective domain objectives at various taxonomy levels for the same class. Let your classmates review and critique your objectives.

6. **Backward Design.** Write an enduring understanding for an area you expect to teach. Write guiding essential questions that cover the enduring understanding.

TECH CONNECTION

The Internet offers numerous resource sites that will assist teachers in planning instruction. Completing the following two application activities will help you identify resource ideas that will make instructional planning easier.

- Access this website: http://teachers.net. Review the various site resources and explore the Just Posted on Teachers.Net options. How useful would this site and similar sites be to you as a teacher? Share your thoughts and conclusions with your classmates.

- Use one or more of the available search engines to explore the web for technological tools such as lesson planning software, words sheets and puzzle tools, poster and bulletin board production tools, and time management tools that will assist you in planning. Form groups of four or five. Share, discuss, and develop a list of your findings. Present your analysis and findings to the class.

CONNECTION WITH THE FIELD

1. **The Teaching Model.** Visit several schoolteachers. Discuss their planning. Do they follow the seven-step planning model presented in this chapter or a modification of the model? Do they use the backward design model? Describe the models used by the teachers.

2. **Teacher Interviews.** Interview several teachers. Are they required to write objectives? Do they write the same objectives for all students? Do they write objectives representing different levels within each of the three learning domains?

3. **Principals' View of Objectives.** Interview two elementary and two middle school principals. What is their view of objectives? Are their views similar to that of the teachers? Are objectives a district requirement?

STUDENT STUDY SITE

Visit the Student Study Site at **www.sagepub.com/mooreteachingk8** for these additional learning tools:

- Video clips
- Web resources
- Self quizzes
- E-Flashcards
- Full-text SAGE journal articles
- Portfolio Connection
- Licensing Preparation/Praxis Connection

CHAPTER 5

Developing Unit and Daily Lesson Plans

First comes thought; then organization of that thought into ideas and plans; then transformation of those plans into reality. The beginning, as you will observe, is in your imagination.

—Napoleon Hill

Before We Begin

Consider an important event in your life that required careful planning. What steps did you undertake to guarantee the event was a success? How will careful planning ensure success in the classroom? Be ready to compare your view with classmates.

OVERVIEW

One memorable life event is going away to college. First, the person envisions a future career that requires a quality college education. Then she searches for a college that is a perfect fit for her academically, financially, socially, and geographically. Next, she applies for admission and arranges for housing. Finally, she packs everything she thinks she'll need and embarks on her academic adventure. It is only through careful planning that the dream of a positive college experience can become a reality.

Creating ideal classroom learning experiences requires careful planning, also, so that every moment is spent teaching and learning. Careful planning is an integral part of effective and efficient teaching. Proactive planning precipitates positive learning experiences and predicates higher student achievement.

This chapter will focus on techniques for effective planning. After reviewing current thoughts about the processes of planning and decision making, we will explore a variety of planning outlines and formats. Next, we will consider the different levels of planning.

Finally, we will focus attention on the basic components of unit and daily lesson planning. Our examination will include a rather detailed explanation of specific planning procedures and several different lesson formats.

OBJECTIVES

After completing your study of Chapter 5, you should be able to

- describe the importance of each of the four levels of planning;
- identify and describe the key components of units and daily lesson plans;
- differentiate between the strategies used during teacher-centered and student-centered instruction;
- define instructional strategy, and name its two components;
- describe four variables that should be considered when selecting an appropriate instructional method;
- discuss the importance of being a teacher who is a reflective decision maker; and
- develop a curriculum map, unit plan, and daily lesson plans for a given area within your area of specialization.

No two teachers teach in the same way; similarly, no two teachers plan in exactly the same way. Effective teachers plan carefully so that they can ready relevant instructional materials and ensure all students are being taught what they need to learn in the way they learn best. Because these teachers have mastered the lesson content and related teaching skills, their lesson delivery often appears to be spontaneous. In reality, however, they have planned—formally or informally—each daily lesson with great care.

PLANNING INSTRUCTION

As shown in Figure 5.1, effective teachers engage in four levels of planning. Curriculum maps and unit plans provide a global framework within which weekly and daily instructional activities take place. At each level of planning, teachers make decisions regarding the coordination of instructional content, teaching materials, and students' special needs.

Teachers do not make these decisions autonomously, however. In response to the public's and government's demands for academic accountability, many states have connected state-endorsed instructional outcomes (standards, essential skills, competencies, or benchmarks) to state-mandated assessments. Effective teachers align their instructional efforts with these mandates.

Students as well as teachers can be engaged in the planning process. Giving students a choice and voice in what they learn is a powerful, motivating way to differentiate instruction and to meet all students' needs. A teacher–student planning approach promotes joint "ownership" of the curriculum. The extent to which students participate in the planning of their own learning activities varies greatly depending upon the students' age and the teacher's educational philosophy.

FIGURE 5.1   Levels of Planning

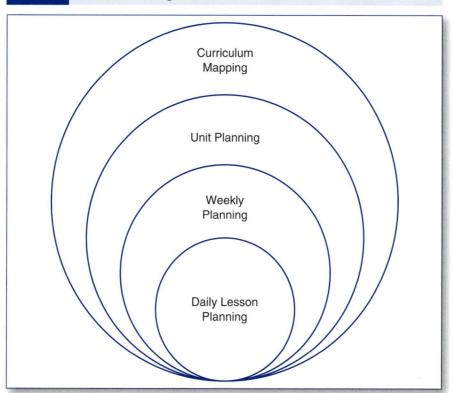

"What homework? These are hall passes, insurance forms, attendance reports, competency updates, and my grocery list."

SOURCE: Created by Ford Button.

To explore your state's curricular mandates and the concept of teacher–student planning, complete Reflect and Apply Exercise 5.1.

REFLECT AND APPLY EXERCISE 5.1: The Planning Process

Reflect

- What role do state mandates have in the planning process? Should the state have extensive decision-making power in school planning? Why or why not?

- Do you support giving students a voice in the planning process? Why or why not?

Apply

- Access www.academicbenchmarks.com and click on the Standards Search tab to review the outcomes (standards, competencies, skills, or benchmarks) for your state. Analyze the outcomes at the grade level you expect to teach. How does your state hold schools, teachers, and students accountable for reaching those outcomes?

- How much student involvement in the planning process do you feel is feasible at the grade level you expect to teach?

Curriculum Mapping

The most general type of planning classroom teachers perform is curriculum mapping (Posner & Rudnitsky, 2000). Teachers or teaching teams create curriculum maps by considering the standards-based knowledge, skills, and concepts students need to attain by the end of the semester or the academic year. In this sense, curriculum mapping supports the backward design approach discussed in Chapter 4. Curriculum maps identify the overarching instructional goals, state-mandated outcomes, methods of assessment, and instructional resources teachers plan to use to attain the desired educational results. These long-term plans are then subdivided into monthly or unit plans.

Although in most cases the textbook forms the basic structure for long-range plans, it should not be the main focus of instruction. Beginning teachers use state and district curriculum suggestions and their textbooks as instructional guides and integrate relevant supplementary material. Seasoned teachers, however, structure their instruction on the basis of experience and use state curriculum suggestions and the textbook to supplement their experience base.

Unit Planning

Classroom instruction is usually divided into a sequence of instructional units that represent discrete segments of the year's work. Standards-based units provide a framework for a series of related learning activities and experiences, unified around a theme or cluster of related concepts, focused upon specific academic standards. For example, first grade teachers might create a unit entitled "Community Helpers" and eighth grade teachers might teach a unit entitled "Systems of the Human Body." Most units focus upon a single content area; however, thematic units integrate instruction across multiple content areas.

REFLECTIONS ON TEACHER PRACTICE 5.1: Rethinking Unit Planning

1. How does unit planning result in more effective teaching?

2. Should students be given long-term class projects to complete or shorter projects? Why?

I teach middle school and have been rethinking the whole way I do units.

In the past few years, I have been writing units that span nearly a full quarter. Each unit included many learning objectives, smaller assignments that helped students learn content along the way, and a large, final assessment at the end of the quarter. I have been pretty proud of my units because of the time and practice allotted to my students to master concepts before formal assessment. If you had asked me a month ago, I would have told you I would never teach another way. But the thing about teaching I have found is to never say never. Faced with only 5 weeks to complete my fairy tale unit, I had to revamp the unit to fit into the smaller space of time.

In 5 weeks, my students completed two projects. One was to work with a partner to identify five characteristics of fairy tales, develop a definition of a fairy tale, and present using PowerPoint.

While the results for some were poor (largely because of off task behavior), the overall motivation, attitude, and thoughtfulness of my students increased dramatically. No one was asking me "What PowerPoint presentation?" like other students had asked me "What magazine article?" in the previous unit. It seemed this project was more important to them.

The second project was to rewrite a fairy tale of the students' choice from the evil character's point of view. We read several examples, including *The True Story of the Three Little Pigs* by Jon Scieczka and *Interview,* a poem by Sara Henderson Hay that presents Cinderella's stepmother's point of view. Students had 2 weeks to write, revise, and type their stories. As a bonus, we sent each student's story in to Barry Lane's writing contest for recycled fairy tales.

With this project, I had very little problem with students being off task at any point, and all but maybe five students turned their stories in on time. I have not begun to assess them, but after reading through several of the stories during the past week, I am encouraged. I witnessed once again a positive attitude about the task, and students seemed very mindful of the scoring guide and task deadline.

With the results I have been getting, I have to pause to reflect upon why. Why are my students more focused? Why are they more likely to turn in their work? Why are they more interested and excited?

I think the shorter project time has a lot to do with the results I am getting. Middle school students seem to be in a time vacuum; without the immediacy of a task deadline to guide them, I think they are more apt to procrastinate. Students live in the here and now, not in the hazy, distant end of the quarter.

I have decided this realization does not mean I have to give up my longer projects; to the contrary, I think as long as I create intermediate deadlines with tangible products that will be assessed along the way to the larger assessments at the end of the unit, I can create the same sense of urgency and importance as with these smaller units. It is a matter of breaking down the task into manageable parts.

A second reason I think the past two projects have been so successful is that I have made a conscious effort to start first with what my students need to know in a backward design sort of approach. I have tried to do this with my larger units, but using Grant Wiggins's process on a smaller task helped me understand the process a little better, producing better results in task design.

The recycled fairy tale task was designed in response to my students' struggle with point of view, both in class and on a variety of district and state assessments. It felt good to be responsive to my kids, to remember I am teaching kids, not curriculum.

Just when I think I have task design mastered, I find I have much left to learn.

—*Ellen, middle school English/language arts teacher*

Please visit the Student Study site at **www.sagepub.com/mooreteachingk8** *for additional discussion questions and assignments.*

SOURCE: www.middleweb.com. Reprinted with permission.

Video Link 5.1:
Watch a video
about classroom
planning.

Unit planning functions as an educational GPS because it guides teachers in their efforts to link specific student academic and developmental needs, educational outcomes (goals and objectives), content knowledge and skills, sequential instructional activities, and evaluation. Teachers share the overall unit goals and objectives with students to explain the purpose and significance of the upcoming activities and to provide a "road map" of the academic journey they are about to begin. Students acquire content knowledge and skills through high-interest, authentic activities. Teachers use multiple evaluations to monitor students' progress toward mastering the unit objectives. Careful unit planning ensures that teachers avoid educational detours and that students arrive at their intended academic "destinations" on time.

Effective teachers carefully consider these nine components during the unit planning process: (1) topic, (2) context, (3) goals and objectives, (4) content outline, (5) learning activities, (6) resources and materials, (7) evaluation, (8) accommodations, and (9) reflection.

1. *Topic.* Review state/district standards, textbook chapter headings, or curriculum maps to identify unifying themes or clusters of related concepts.

2. *Context.* Consider students' academic, socioemotional, physical, and personal backgrounds. How will this unit extend and enrich what students have learned in other units, courses, or grade levels?

3. *Goals and Objectives.* Align cognitive, affective, and psychomotor unit goals and objectives with developmentally appropriate state and national standards.

4. *Content Outline.* Carefully consider the sequence and organization of the unit topics and subtopics. Include sufficient supportive detail.

5. *Learning Activities.* Create varied instructional activities that motivate students, address multiple learning styles, and align with unit goals and objectives.

6. *Resources and Materials.* Create a bulleted list of absolutely everything needed to teach the unit.

7. *Evaluation.* Systematically assess students' knowledge throughout the unit. Make sure the assessments align with state standards, unit goals and objectives, and unit activities.

8. *Accommodations.* Adjust instructional delivery, assignments, and assessments to address students' special needs.

9. *Reflection.* Improve instructional delivery and increase student achievement by reflecting upon the assessment results and lesson implementation.

Units vary greatly in scope and duration, depending on the grade level and subject. Kindergarten teachers might have a weeklong unit teaching about the five senses. Second grade teachers could teach a 2-week literature focus unit on folktales. Fourth grade teachers might create a month-long astronomy unit teaching about the phases of the moon and the earth's rotation around the sun. Seventh grade teachers could teach a month-long unit about the American election process.

Many teaching teams create thematic units, which integrate related instructional activities across multiple content areas (Roberts & Kellough, 2003). Thematic units may focus on one specific content area or they may be global in nature. For example, thematic units could focus upon saving the coral reefs or on westward expansion. Teachers can create thematic units independently, with grade level colleagues, or with interdisciplinary middle school teaching teams. Because team planning is often a complex process, teachers need sufficient planning time!

Many states and school districts have an explicit curriculum that mandates specific goals and topics. When this is the case, the prescribed goals and topics are usually presented in terms of minimum requirements, so there is still plenty of justification for the careful planning of additional learning units. Even when most of the instructional content has been predetermined, it is still necessary to plan the sequence, present the content, and test the outcomes. These demands for covering specific content do not preclude the need for planning, nor do they eliminate the opportunity to teach creatively! With careful planning and determination, teachers can still design instructional units that pique student interest while addressing mandated academic standards.

As a beginning teacher, keep in mind that although textbooks provide a foundation of information and some planning assistance, they do not constitute the entire curriculum. You will need to adjust the sequence of the topics and perhaps even include other topics or subtopics according to your school district's mandates, state standards, and your students' needs.

Once you have determined the sequence and timeline of standards-aligned topics, you are ready to develop unit goals and objectives related to that content. Write observable, measurable objectives that specify student outcomes at multiple levels of complexity across the three domains. Remember that well-written objectives are linked to lesson activities and authentic assessments.

With this framework in place, you are ready to identify teaching strategies and learning activities that support the unit's goals and objectives. The unit can be viewed as the whole, with the individual lessons as its parts. Analyze how you can achieve the desired outcomes by carefully grouping and sequencing the goals, objectives, and activities into a sequence of daily lessons for implementation. Remember that all lesson activities should align with state/district mandates, unit goals, lesson objectives, and evaluations.

Now you are ready to write the activity portion of your lesson plans. Some teachers like to script their lessons because it helps them to organize their thoughts, align activities with goals and standards, proactively plan good examples, and be more confident in front of students. Other teachers prefer to teach from a detailed outline of topics or bulleted key points. Find the system that works best for you! Regardless of the method, your description of learning activities should contain enough supportive details that a substitute teacher could teach from them in an emergency.

Systematically include activities addressing all students' learning styles and special needs. For example, if you design a unit on the court system, have students read about the court system in their textbooks, hold a mock trial, show a film about a court case, or take a trip to a nearby courtroom to observe a trial in session. You might even consider inviting an attorney or judge to be a guest speaker. Making these decisions in advance will allow time to arrange for these educational events.

High-quality instructional materials enhance and enrich the learning process. Work with your media specialist, curriculum specialist, and team teachers to discover available school, community, and technology resources. Technologically proficient teachers who have access to computers can conduct additional research on the lesson's content and use technology to produce course syllabi, lesson plans, record-keeping forms, and instructional materials. Take time to preview books, audiovisuals, Internet sites, and computer programs to ensure they are developmentally appropriate, support your instructional objectives, and use class time effectively. If you don't, you might end up in quite a predicament!

Finally, how will you know if the students have learned what you intended in your instructional unit? The answer lies in carefully planning for evaluation before, during, and after the unit. The evaluation process will be addressed in detail in Chapter 6.

BRAD, ANGELINA, AND JENNIFER: A REFLECTIVE CASE STUDY

Brad, Angelina, and Jennifer are all members of the Pittsburgh Middle School sixth grade team. They want to cooperatively create an interdisciplinary unit that encourages students to celebrate diversity. The unit needs to address their areas of specialization in social studies, literature, and English composition.

1. Write one objective for each of the three domains (cognitive, affective, and psychomotor).

2. Briefly summarize three possible activities that would support these unit objectives.

3. Which method would work best for presenting each activity (teacher-centered or student-centered)? Why?

Weekly Plans

Most school districts require teachers to submit a set of weekly lesson plans to ensure that learning is taking place even if the teacher is absent. A typical weekly plan, shown in Figure 5.2, outlines each day's lesson for one content area for 1 week.

Weekly lesson plan requirements vary greatly from school to school. Some districts require teachers to code each lesson according to prescribed academic standards to ensure that all activities relate to the mandates. Many principals require teachers to submit electronic or hard copies of the plans before they leave for the weekend while others ask teachers to leave the plans on their desks for "spot checks" during supervisory "walkthroughs." Although it might be tempting to rely totally upon an abbreviated lesson plan, especially after an especially tiring week, effective teachers still take time to write full-length lesson plans for their units so they can ensure quality educational experiences for their students.

Daily Lesson Plans

Making decisions about objectives, activities, experiences, and resources during the unit planning process sets the stage for more specific, detailed plans. The daily lesson plan

FIGURE 5.2	Weekly Lesson Plan Form

Teacher: _____ Subject: _____ Grade/Room: _____

Period(s)/Block(s) (Time): _____ Week of: _____

Accommodations for Students With Special Needs:
    1. Small Group 2. Extended Time 3. Test Read-Aloud 4. Modified Assignments 5. Preferential Seating
    6. Oral Testing 7. Other

Day: _____ Date: _____ Unit:_____	**Objective(s) and/or State Standard(s):**	
Materials: Transparency, manipulatives, dry erase board, informational resources, software, etc.	**Content:**	
Technology: YES NO **Assessment**: Formal Informal Alternative	**Teacher Procedure:**	*Reteaching/Enrichment:*
	Accommodations (circle): 7 Other _____	1 2 3 4 5 6
Day: _____ Date: _____ Unit:_____	**Objective(s) and/or State Standard(s):**	
Materials: Transparency, manipulatives, dry erase board, informational resources, software, etc.	**Content:**	
Technology: YES NO **Assessment**: Formal Informal Alternative	**Teacher Procedure:**	*Reteaching/Enrichment:*
	Accommodations (circle): 7 Other _____	1 2 3 4 5 6
Day: _____ Date: _____ Unit:_____	**Objective(s) and/or State Standard(s):**	
Materials: Transparency, manipulatives, dry erase board, informational resources, software, etc.	**Content:**	

(Continued)

(Continued)

Technology: YES NO **Assessment**: Formal Informal Alternative	**Teacher Procedure:**	*Reteaching/Enrichment:*
	Accommodations (circle): 7 Other _____	1 2 3 4 5 6
Day: _____ Date: _____ Unit: _____	**Objective(s) and/or State Standard(s):**	
Materials: Transparency, manipulatives, dry erase board, informational resources, software, etc.	**Content:**	
Technology: YES NO **Assessment**: Formal Informal Alternative	**Teacher Procedure:**	*Reteaching/Enrichment:*
	Accommodations (circle): 7 Other _____	1 2 3 4 5 6
Day: _____ Date: _____ Unit: _____	**Objective(s) and/or State Standard(s):**	
Materials: Transparency, manipulatives, dry erase board, informational resources, software, etc.	**Content:**	
Technology: YES NO **Assessment**: Formal Informal Alternative	**Teacher Procedure:**	*Reteaching/Enrichment:*
	Accommodations (circle): 7 Other _____	1 2 3 4 5 6

defines the objectives and class activities for a 1-day instructional period. The exact structure of the daily lesson plan depends on the lesson focus plus the individual needs, strengths, and interests of the teacher and the students. Lesson planning should never be dictated by rigid standards that prevent and stifle creativity. Indeed, effective

". . . and the reason we have summer vacation is so you can go
home to help with the crops."

teachers will rarely carry out a lesson entirely as planned. They must anticipate what is likely to happen as they teach the planned lessons and make modifications as needed. Good teachers expect to adjust their plans as they move along, and they have alternatives in mind in case they are needed. The fact that most plans must be modified as they are taught does not justify the avoidance of thorough initial planning. Few teachers can "wing it." Planning, however, does not ensure success. The instructional delivery is equally important.

Even daily lesson plans need to include an evaluation component. Because effective teachers are student-centered, they continuously evaluate students' learning by preassessing students' knowledge before instruction and formatively assessing their progress during the lesson. During post-lesson evaluation, or summative assessment, teachers reflect upon the degree to which learners have attained the lesson objectives to determine if reteaching is necessary.

Lesson Formats

Lesson Plan Format 1

Quality lesson plans provide structure yet allow for flexibility. Common components include the following:

1. *Objectives:* specific learning intent(s), selected from the unit plan

2. *Introduction (Set Induction):* starting activity used to pique students' interest

3. *Content:* brief outline of the lesson's content

4. *Methods and Procedure:* sequenced activities selected from the unit plan

5. *Closure:* wrap-up activity

6. *Resources and Materials:* list of needed materials

7. *Evaluation Procedure:* strategy for assessing students' progress towards meeting the objectives

8. *Assignment:* in-class or homework activity

Lesson Plan Format 2

This format, suggested by Madeline Hunter's instructional design, is a highly structured, detailed, and prescriptive eight-component plan that emphasizes student involvement and success. This format is appropriate for skill learning and many forms of teacher-centered instruction, such as telling and explaining, lecturing, and Socratic questioning. The eight components of this format follow:

1. *Anticipatory Set:* a teacher activity that "hooks" students' attention

2. *Objective and Purpose:* teacher statements that explicitly inform students what they will learn during the lesson and how they can use what they've learned

3. *Input:* direct instruction of new knowledge, processes, or skills

4. *Modeling:* teacher-provided examples that develop students' understanding of the content, processes, or skills

5. *Checking for Understanding:* method for assessing students' understanding and progress before or during the teacher-directed activity (modeling) or during student practice

6. *Guided Practice:* student practice of new knowledge, processes, or skills under teacher supervision

7. *Closure:* teacher action used to help students organize and make sense out of what has been taught

8. *Independent Practice:* unsupervised practice of new knowledge, process, or skill (assigned seatwork or homework)

Lesson Plan Format 3

This student-centered format works best for small-group work. Because small-group sessions require that students be prepared for their task and be debriefed once the assigned task has been addressed, this format includes the following components:

1. *Objectives:* statements specifying what students should be able to do upon completion of the lesson

2. *Initial Focus (Set Induction):* teacher-directed activity to focus students' attention on the upcoming task

Teachers must often plan for special students.

3. *Major Task:* teacher-directed presentation of assigned group task, directions for group work, and options available to students

4. *Group Activity:* students' efforts toward completing the task

5. *Debriefing:* students' presentation of the task's product; students' reflection upon the strategies they used and the overall group process

6. *Resources and Materials:* materials groups need to complete the assigned task

7. *Evaluation:* formal and informal techniques used to check whether students have achieved the objectives

Lesson Plan Format 4

This format is suggested for the backward design approach to instruction. It is based on the premise that students and teachers will have a firmer, clearer grasp of where learning is going when goals and assessments are clearly articulated right from the beginning.

1. *Enduring Understanding(s):* knowledge and skills students will be able to apply to their real-life experiences

2. *Essential Questions:* questions related to the enduring understanding(s) that guide and focus the lesson; overarching goals written in a question format

3. *Assessment/Acceptable Evidence:* demonstration of students' understandings, knowledge, and skills

4. *Strategies/Best Practices Used to Explicitly Teach Understandings:* sequence of motivational, authentic teaching/learning experiences that will equip students with the necessary knowledge and skills to demonstrate mastery of the learning intent

5. *Resources and Materials:* materials needed to accomplish tasks

These lesson plan formats are intended to be illustrative, not all-inclusive. Some alternate lesson plan formats are shown in Figures 5.3 through 5.7 (pages 122–126). Each alternate format has been logically structured for a specific type of lesson. Note the adaptation and extension planning section in the formats presented in Figures 5.5 through 5.7 (pages 124–126). You should vary your format according to the lesson content and teaching strategies. Remember that a lesson plan should lend direction to your lesson but not be a manuscript from which to read statements verbatim. Lesson plan templates are provided on the web-based student study site (**www.sagepub.com/mooreteachingk8**).

FIGURE 5.3 Outline of Key Questions/Discussion Lesson Plan Format

1. **Unit Topic:** _____

2. **Objectives:** _____
   _____

3. **Set Induction:** _____
   _____

4. **Procedures for Discussion:** _____
   _____

5. **Key Questions**

A. _____

Possible Answers: _____
   _____

Summary: _____
   _____

B. _____

Possible Answers: _____
   _____

Summary: _____
   _____

C. _____

Possible Answers: _____
   _____

Summary: _____
   _____

6. **Conclusions:** _____
   _____
   _____
   _____

7. **Closure:** _____
   _____
   _____
   _____
   _____

8. Assignment: _____

_____

_____

_____

_____

9. Evaluation: _____

_____

_____

_____

_____

_____

FIGURE 5.4   Outline of Inquiry and Problem-Solving Lesson Plan Format

1. Lesson Topic: _____

2. Objectives: _____

_____

3. Set Induction: _____

_____

4. Procedures or Steps

A. Problem Identification: _____

_____

B. Data Collection: _____

_____

C. Formulation of Hypotheses or Assumptions: _____

_____

D. Analysis of Data or Materials: _____

_____

E. Testing Hypotheses or Assumptions: _____

_____

F. Conclusion or Judgment: _____

_____

5. Closure: _____

_____

6. Assignment: _____

_____

7. Evaluation: _____

_____

FIGURE 5.5	Concept Attainment Lesson Plan

Your Name: _____ Grade Level: (circle one) K 1 2 3 4 5 6

Subject: (circle one) Language Arts Social Studies Mathematics Science

Lesson Title:

Materials Needed:

Prerequisite Skills:

Lesson Objective(s):

Concept Label (name):

Critical Attributes: [yes]	Non-Critical Attributes: [no]
A feature of a certain concept that distinguishes it from other concepts	Features found in some but not all members of a category

Definition of Concept

1. **Present objectives:** (What are students going to learn?) Time:

2. **Provide examples and nonexamples to the class:** (Input/modeling) Time:

3. **Test for attainment: (Do the students understand the concept?)** Time:

4. **Analyze student thinking processes and integration of learning:** (Are they able to provide additional examples and nonexamples?) Time:

5. **Assessment/closure:** (How do you evaluate student progress or provide closure for this lesson?) Time:

6. **Adaptation for students who need extra help, time, or attention:**

   AND

   Extension for students of high ability. Time:

TOTAL LESSON TIME: _____

References Consulted (Curriculum books, teacher resources, websites, etc.):

SOURCE: Developed by Dr. Sally Beisser, School of Education, Drake University. Copyright © 2000, Beisser. Used with permission.

FIGURE 5.6	Cooperative Learning Lesson Plan

Your Name: _____ Grade Level: (circle one) K 1 2 3 4 5 6

Subject: (circle one) Language Arts Social Studies Mathematics Science

Lesson Title:

Materials Needed:

Prerequisite Skills:

Lesson Objective(s):

   a. Cognitive

   b. Affective

   c. Psychomotor

   d. Social

Cooperative Learning Grouping Structure

   1. **Present objectives:** (What are students going to learn?) Time:

   2. **Present information for the academic goal:** Time:

   3. **Organize students into learning teams:** Time:

      (What is the social goal?)

      (How will you organize the groups?)

      (What group roles will you have?)

   4. **Assist team work and study:** Time:

      (How will you monitor progress of the academic and the social goals?)

   5. **Provide recognition:** Time:

      (How will students know they have met both academic and social goals?)

   6. **Assessment/closure:** Time:

      (How do you evaluate student progress or end this lesson?)

   7. **Adaptation for students who need extra help, time, or attention:**

      AND

      Extension for students of high ability. Time:

TOTAL LESSON TIME: _____

References Consulted (Curriculum books, teacher resources, websites, etc.):

SOURCE: Developed by Dr. Sally Beisser, School of Education, Drake University. Copyright © 2000, Beisser. Used with permission.

FIGURE 5.7	Direct Instruction Lesson Plan

Your Name: _____ Grade Level: (circle one) K 1 2 3 4 5 6

Subject: (circle one) Language Arts Social Studies Mathematics Science

Lesson Title:

Materials Needed:

Prerequisite Skills:

Lesson Objective:

1. **Provide objectives:** (What are students going to learn?) Time:

2. **Demonstrate knowledge or skill:** (Input/modeling by the teacher) Time:

3. **Provide guided practice:** (Guided practice with the teacher) Time:

4. **Check for understanding and provide student feedback:** (How will you know students understand the skill or concept? How will they know they "get it"?) Time:

5. **Provide extended practice and transfer:** (Independent practice of the skill) Time:

6. **Assessment/closure:** (How do you evaluate student progress or provide closure to this lesson?) Time:

7. **Adaptation for students who need extra help, time, or attention:**

   AND

   Extension for students of high ability. Time:

TOTAL LESSON TIME: _____

References Consulted (Curriculum books, teacher resources, websites, etc.):

SOURCE: Developed by Dr. Sally Beisser, School of Education, Drake University. Copyright © 2000, Beisser. Used with permission.

As the lesson formats presented in this section suggest, teachers vary widely in their approaches to daily planning. Some develop detailed daily plans, whereas others teach from a set of bulleted phrases or an outline. The sample lesson plans presented in Figures 5.8 through 5.12 (pages 127–133) illustrate how the various components can be constructed.

Block Scheduling

The length of lessons varies according to the subject area and whether or not the districts have adopted block-of-time schedules. **Block scheduling** is an instructional delivery pattern that divides schooltime into instructional blocks ranging from 20 to 110 minutes. There is no single, standard form of block schedule. All block schedules operate from the same premise:

FIGURE 5.8   Creativity Lesson Plan

Topic:

Creating a School

Objectives:

The students will be able to

1. give examples of the special features of different middle schools and
2. apply terms associated with middle schools to an original student project.

Materials:

School pictures, textbooks, glossary, large pieces of drawing paper or poster paper, felt pens or markers

Accommodations:

Depends on needs of special students in class

Introduction (Set Induction):

Spend 10 minutes using pictures to review various middle school terms. Students create a glossary of important middle school terms in the form of a three-column chart giving terms (e.g., curriculum, hidden curriculum, extracurricular activities, administration, scheduling, minicourses, flexible scheduling, modules, learning centers, staff, discipline, and school district), definitions, and examples (e.g., the principal is an administrator).

Content:

None

Procedure:

1. Divide the class into groups of four or five. Group members are to work cooperatively on planning and drawing an imaginary middle school.
2. Students give their school a name and decide on its main function (academic knowledge, prepare students for high school, develop character, etc.).
3. Each school should feature a curriculum, disciplinary process, class time scheduling, administration setup, and so forth.
4. Students are to decide on other special features of their school (music programs, sports, busing of students, clubs, etc.).

Closure:

Each group presents its proposed middle school. The class will discuss the drawbacks and advantages of each group's presented proposal.

Assignment:

Outline problems that must be overcome to implement the middle school that your group created. Be prepared to discuss the identified problems in class.

Evaluation:

Observe student participation as they work on assigned project. Check each group's imaginary middle school and its main function. Check each team's imaginary middle school to see whether it addresses the criteria specified in the procedural section.

FIGURE 5.9 A Sample Language Arts Lesson

Topic:
The Elements of Story Writing

Objectives:

Given a picture stimulus, students will be able to write a short fiction story that contains the needed elements for a short story.

Introduction (Set Induction):

Read aloud a short fiction story that will be of interest to the class. (Jumping Mouse, a short myth, demonstrates the elements in an interesting but condensed form.)

Content:

The Elements of a Short Story

    I. Short Story Beginnings
       A. Describe the setting
       B. Introduce the main character
       C. Introduce the plot (problem or goal the main character attempts to solve or achieve)

    II. Middle Story Elements
       A. First roadblock (character's attempt to reach goal)
       B. Second roadblock
       C. Climax of story (character reaches goal)

    III. Story Endings
       A. Make conclusions
       B. Wrap up any loose ends

Procedure:

1. After the oral reading, ask students to explain when and how the author introduced the main character.
2. Discuss the promptness that authors use to introduce the main character, setting, and plot in short stories. Record responses on the chalkboard using the bell-shaped curve to portray the elements of short stories. (Bell curve not shown here.)
3. At this point, ask students to summarize the elements needed in a short story's beginning. (They should be able to identify introduction of the main character, description of the story setting, and introduction of the story's plot.) It is important to convey to students that the order in which the elements are introduced is not important but rather that the inclusion of these elements is a crucial feature of the short story.
4. Next, ask students to recall the first roadblock (or difficulty the main character had in attempting to reach the intended goal). Record response on bell curve and stress that the middle of a story includes the majority of the story—including the story's climax.
5. As students recall the roadblocks presented in the short book, continue to record these on the bell-shaped curve to demonstrate the rising tension presented in the story.
6. Ask students to describe how the main character finally confronted and solved the problem presented in the introduction of the story. Explain that this element is called the climax of the story. The climax should be placed at the top of the bell-shaped curve to demonstrate it as the peak of the story.
7. Ask students to summarize the elements that constitute the middle parts of a short story. (The bell-shaped curve on the chalkboard should reveal that the middle story elements are composed of roadblocks in the main character's attempt to reach a goal and the climax or the reaching of that goal is at the peak of the bell curve.)
8. Finally, ask students to talk about the brevity the author uses to end the story once the main character has reached his or her goal. (Again, this is demonstrated by the falling line of the bell curve drawing on the board.)

Closure:

Ask students to make an outline of the elements of a short story using the information presented on the bell-shaped curve.

Assignment:

Let each student choose a picture from a magazine and instruct them to use the outline for short stories as a guide to write a short story about the picture selected.

Evaluation:

Answer questions during class discussions. Check students' outline of short story as work is being completed. Check to see if students' stories have clearly described settings, main characters, plots, roadblocks, climaxes, and conclusions.

Accommodations:

They will depend on needs of special students in class.

FIGURE 5.10   Sample Small-Group Lesson Plan

Topic:
Classifying Information

Objective:

Students will be able to classify information into categories on the basis of similar or common attributes.

Initial Focus:

Distribute a half sheet of colored paper to each student. Ask students to write the name of one of their favorite foods on the paper. Students stand up and arrange themselves into categories based upon their food preferences. Conduct a whole-class discussion of how they grouped themselves and what names they could give their categories. Then ask why they need to learn to group, or categorize, things.

Major Task:

Divide students into groups of three. Each group will be given a set of items to classify into categories.

Group Activity:

Give each group a small container of 15-bean mixture. Instruct teams to categorize the beans. As they near the end of this activity, give each group at least three jelly beans. Ask them to categorize those beans into one of the existing categories. Tell them they will need to choose one group member to report their classification schemes and rationales to the entire class.

Debriefing:

Each group presents their classification schemes and rationales to the whole class. Classmates react with questions, comments, and recommendations. How can students apply what they have learned to categorizing something in their personal lives? *(Accept all reasonable responses.)* After students carefully clean up all of the beans, they can eat their jelly beans.

(Continued)

(Continued)

Resources and Materials:

- half sheets of colored paper (one per student)
- one package of 15-bean mix
- one paper cup per team
- one bag of multicolored jelly beans

Evaluation:

Walk around and monitor group's efforts to classify beans. Ensure that all students participate. Ask questions about students' classification schemes.

Accommodations:

For students who have difficulty handling small objects, provide larger, multicolored foam shapes for classification. Have sugar-free jelly beans on hand as needed. Adjust the size of groups according to students' social needs.

FIGURE 5.11 Sample Key Question/Discussion Lesson Plan

Topic:
Traveling to School Safely

Objectives:

Students will identify at least three ways they can stay safe when traveling to and from school.

Set Induction:

Share the cover of *Make Way for Ducklings* by Robert McCloskey. Do a picture walk 'n' talk to familiarize students with the story line. Create a T-chart (two-column chart) on the whiteboard with these headings: Dangers/ Helpers. Set a purpose for reading: What dangers did the ducklings face as they walked to the Boston Public Garden? Who helped them on their walk? Read the story aloud. Stop at appropriate junctures to write phrases and draw sketches depicting the dangers and helpers. Tell students they are going to apply what they've learned in today's lesson about traveling to and from school safely.

Procedure for Discussion:

Conduct a grand conversation about ways to travel safely to and from school. Pose questions. Create a separate column or large box for each mode of transportation. Record students' responses using key words and sketches.

Key Question 1: How do you travel from your house to school?

Possible Answers: riding a school bus, carpooling, walking, riding a bicycle

Summary: We use many different ways to travel to and from school. Let's see how we can be sure we stay safe any time we travel.

Key Question 2: What are some dangers you might face? (repeat for each mode of transportation)

Possible Answers: Bus: getting hit by the bus or cars, crossing the street, getting on and off the bus safely, finding way to/from the bus. Car: entering/exiting car safely, having no seat belt or car seat, crossing the street. Walking: encountering strange people or animals, crossing the street, finding way to/from school, bad weather conditions. Biking: riding on sidewalk/street, falling and injuring self, crossing the street, finding way to/from school.

Summary: Just like the ducklings, we have to be very aware of traffic, busy streets, and strangers.

Key Question 3: How can I keep safe when I'm traveling to school? (repeat for each mode of transportation)

Possible Answers: Bus: wait till it comes to a complete stop, look both ways before crossing the street, don't walk in front of the bus, be sure you get on/off at the right stop. Car: enter/exit from the curbside, sit in a car seat and/or buckle up, stay quiet so you don't distract the driver, don't get into a stranger's car. Walking: steer clear of strange people or animals, know where safe houses are along your route, know how to get to school, walk with a friend, cross at crosswalks. Biking: ride facing traffic, know how to ride your book properly, wear safety equipment, ride with a friend, know your way to/from school, walk bike across at crosswalks

Summary: Basically, we need to be aware of cars and other people whenever we're near a street. We also need to take responsibility for keeping our bodies safe.

Conclusions: Today we've talked about many ways we can stay safe when we're traveling to and from school. Let's review what we've learned. Can we name FIVE ways to keep safe? *Accept reasonable responses.*

Closure: Tell your shoulder partner three ways you can keep safe when you're traveling to and from school each day.

Assignment: Students draw pictures depicting how they travel to and from school. The picture needs to show at least three ways they can be safe while traveling. When students share their pictures with the class, they say three ways they can be safe while traveling to and from school.

Evaluation: Monitor students' responses during the question/answer portion of the lesson to check for understanding. When students share their assignments, they should state one way they travel to and from school plus three ways they can keep safe while traveling.

Accommodations: Serve as a recorder/speaker for students with limited language proficiency so they, too, can share their pictures with the class.

Instead of using the traditional Carnegie approach of seven equal periods of time (or classes) each day, teachers vary the length of time devoted to selected subjects. Elementary teachers who use this approach plan independently or with a grade-level team; middle school teachers plan in interdisciplinary teams. At the upper elementary level, teachers create 90-minute periods, usually during reading and math, during which students rotate between classrooms. This allows teachers to group students by ability and to teach to their content area strengths. Middle school interdisciplinary teaching teams also rotate students for longer class periods; teachers teach in their preferred areas of content expertise.

Block scheduling offers many simple advantages. First, students have an opportunity to be taught by more than one teacher. Second, because teachers prepare for fewer classes and teach in their area of expertise, they tend to be more enthusiastic and creative in their instructional delivery. Third, students have the opportunity for in-depth study of subject matter. Fourth, minimal transitions between classes reduce chaos in the hall and lost teaching time. Finally, teachers tend to use more student-centered strategies to accommodate the longer class periods.

FIGURE 5.12 A Sample Block Pattern Lesson

Grade Level(s): 4–6

Subject: Conservation of Natural Resources

Duration: 90 minutes

Description: A first look at recycling

Goal: Students will understand the importance of conserving natural resources.

Objectives:

1. Students will be able to explain their feelings about conserving our natural resources.
2. Students will describe ways they can reduce, reuse, and recycle products.
3. Students will create personal conservation plans.

Materials Needed:

- whiteboard and markers
- *The Lorax* by Dr. Seuss
- assorted home products with three-arrow recycling symbol
- large chart paper
- markers
- tape
- yardsticks
- colored sticker dots (five per student)
- exit slips

Set Induction (Focus):

1. Quicklist: Students independently list five natural resources. Volunteers share with the class. Record students' answers on the whiteboard.
2. What would happen if people used up all of the existing resources (e.g., oil, water)?
3. Tell students they will be focusing upon ways to conserve natural resources during today's lesson.

Procedure:

1. Read *The Lorax* by Dr. Seuss. Conduct a grand conversation responding to this story. Possible questions/responses include the following: What natural resources were present in this story? (*truffula trees, water, clean air, grass*). What happened to these resources? (*In an effort to manufacture thneeds, all of the truffula trees were chopped down and the natural resources were polluted.*) What did the Once-ler mean by "Unless"? (*Unless they conserved the natural resources eventually the earth won't be able to sustain their lifestyles*). What do you think the Lorax will do next? (*Plant the truffula tree seeds and work to clean up the environment; ensure it never happens again*). How could this story relate to something happening in real life today? (*Accept all rational responses.*)

2. Point out the three-arrow emblem on multiple home products. Explain how this represents the three ways people can conserve natural resources. They can **reduce** the amount of natural resources they use, **reuse** items multiple times before discarding them**,** or **recycle** items.

3. Divide students into teams of up to four people. Give each team a display-size piece of chart paper, markers, tape, and a yardstick. Each team creates a three-column chart with these columnar headings: reduce, reuse, recycle. Team members brainstorm ways they can reduce, reuse, and recycle at school. Teams post their charts side-by-side on a classroom wall.

4. Give each student five colored sticker dots. Students do a walk 'n' gawk, reading one another's charts. They place one sticker dot by the five ideas they consider to be the most innovative or important.

5. Discuss how the most popular idea can be operationalized at the school level. Cooperatively create a classroom action plan to make at least one of the ideas a reality. Have student representatives present the plan to gain administrative approval. Put the plan into action!

Closure:

Students complete exit slips noting this information: three new ideas they have learned about conserving natural resources, two ways they can apply what they have learned at home, and one statement about how they feel about conserving natural resources.

Accommodations:

Create heterogeneous student groups of mixed abilities, demographics, and learning styles. Monitor students' efforts and assist as needed according to students' unique needs.

Lesson Analysis:

This is to be completed after the lesson has been taught. How well did students meet the stated objectives? How could the lesson plan be adjusted to increase student achievement? What remediation, extension, or enrichment activities could positively impact student learning?

When traditional schedules are restructured into larger blocks of time, teachers soon learn that they cannot take the simplistic approach of using the same methods they did before, only for a longer time, since nothing will disengage a group of students from the learning process more quickly than listening to the teacher talk for an entire class block. Numerous creative instructional approaches are possible within longer time frames; therefore, teachers should be cautious about relying too heavily on traditional, teacher-centered instructional routines. As a general strategy, teachers should consider planning three to four activities during the instructional block. For example, they could review previous learning, deliver direct instruction, engage students in performance activities, and provide guided practice or reteaching.

Team Planning

Lesson planning can be a collaborative process. Many middle school and upper elementary teachers work in interdisciplinary teams representing mathematics, social studies, language arts, and science. These teams plan for a common group of students who rotate classes taught by members of the teaching team. Elementary teachers who do not rotate students also work in grade-level teams to plan quality units. In schools that embrace full inclusion of students with special needs, a reading teacher, gifted education teacher, special education teacher, or other specialists may also be part of the team.

Let's now look at the structure of a lesson. However, first review Table 5.1 and complete Reflect and Apply Exercise 5.2, which addresses the importance of teacher planning.

TABLE 5.1	Planning Concepts
Type	**Description**
Team planning	Group or team of teachers organizing instruction so that each supplements the other
Teacher–student planning	Involvement of students in planning process. Learning activities are based on students' interests and their involvement promotes ownership.
Course planning	Broad planning of instruction for year or term
Unit planning	Discrete segment of a year's work organized around a specific theme or cluster of related concepts
Weekly planning	Short-form outline of instruction for 1 week on a single sheet of paper
Daily lesson planning	Detailed description of objectives and activities for one instructional period. Daily plans should flow naturally out of the unit plan.

REFLECT AND APPLY EXERCISE 5.2: Unit and Daily Planning

Reflect

- Why do unit, weekly, and daily plans need to be planned and developed? Wouldn't one level of planning be adequate? Why or why not?

- Should teacher planning be part of the teacher evaluation process? Why or why not?

Apply

- In your own experiences, did you ever have a teacher who did not plan well? What was the effect on learning? What was it like for students?

- Consider a college-level lesson you've recently experienced. What lesson plan format did the professor use? How do you know?

Video Link 5.1:
Watch a video about anticipatory set.

LESSON PLAN STRUCTURE

As a teacher, you will probably imitate a favorite teacher in your initial planning. Later, you will modify the initial structure to fit your individual teaching style and educational philosophy. Regardless of which format you use, it is imperative you include these common elements: the set induction (cognitive set), the lesson itself (instructional strategies), and the lesson closure.

Set Induction (Focus)

Use a set induction at the outset of a lesson to get students' undivided attention, to arouse their interest, and to establish a conceptual framework for the information that follows.

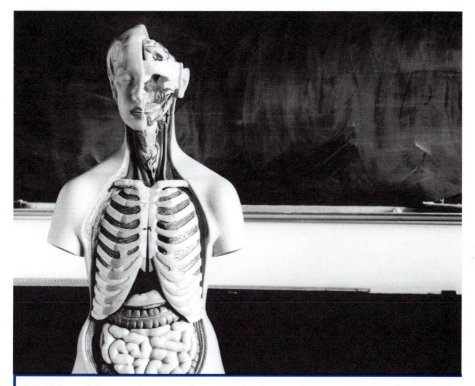

Colorful models can often get a lesson started.

This opening activity is frequently related to the homework assignment, a recent lesson, or students' personal experiences. Without establishing this cognitive set, students aren't ready to listen or learn, so valuable instructional time could be wasted. Thus, you must plan strategies for getting students' undivided attention.

One way to gain students' attention is to do nothing. Stand quietly. Students will soon focus their attention on you. Another technique is to begin talking in a very low tone, gradually increasing volume. Most people want to hear what they cannot hear. Some teachers turn the lights on and off. This, however, might damage the ballasts of the fluorescent light fixtures. Many teachers use a pretaught attention-getting signal such as a raised hand, rhythm clapping, a little bell, or a special phrase (May I have your attention, please. Give me five). If you use one of these techniques on a regular basis to cue the students to attend, chances are they will begin to look for your cue even before you start. The lesson is guaranteed to be more successful if everyone is focused and ready to learn.

Once students are listening, you need to spark their interest and motivate them to learn. Use inspirational or intriguing quotes, questions, or scenarios that connect with students' previous academic or personal experiences. The quotations and Before You Begin prompts at the beginning of each chapter of this book are examples of motivational devices.

To maximize learning, share your lesson objectives and an overview of the lesson events in student-friendly talk. Use "you" instead of "the students will" since you are talking to (not about) the students. Provide a cognitive framework, or an **advance organizer**, for learning. For multifaceted information, provide students with a partially completed outline or other graphic organizer (Ausubel, 1963). You can also use generalizations, definitions, analogies, or planned remarks to give students a "what to look for" frame of reference. For example, you might start a lesson about light by asking students to describe how rainbows are formed or begin a lesson on the importance of exercise by asking students what they like to do during their free time. No matter what form it takes, an advance organizer acts as a conceptual bridge between students' prior knowledge and the new information.

You must set the stage for the learning process. If you fail to gain students' attention, arouse their interest, and establish a conceptual framework for your lesson, the remainder of the lesson may be wasted.

Instructional Strategy

A well-planned lesson consists of the content to be taught as well as the **instructional strategy,** or global plan, for teaching a particular lesson. It can be viewed as analogous to the overall plan for winning a tennis match or basketball game. The instructional strategy consists of two components: the **methodology** and the **lesson procedure**.

Methodology

The methodology is the planned patterned behaviors by which the teacher influences learning. The methodology should be designed and organized so that it sets a positive tone for learning, captures and holds students' attention, and involves them as much as possible in the learning process.

Instructional methods can influence students directly through focused, teacher-centered instruction or influence them indirectly by actively involving them in their own learning (student-centered instruction). Comparisons of these two methods of instruction are given in Table 5.2. The teacher-centered instructional approaches are more "traditional" or didactic. In the teacher-centered instructional approach, students are passive recipients of information who listen to the teacher and/or read a textbook. In contrast, the student-centered instructional approach actively engages students in their learning experiences. Both instructional approaches are equally effective in bringing about learning. The distributive property of mathematics, for example, can be taught through a presentation (teacher-centered approach) or through hands-on manipulation of objects or discovery learning (student-centered approach). To help you decide which method to use, consider the lesson's purpose, your personal teaching style and educational philosophy, the students' characteristics, and the learning environment.

Your lesson must have a purpose. Are you mostly focusing on the cognitive, affective, or psychomotor domain? Select a methodology and related experiences that relate to that teaching domain plus the lesson's content, goals, and objectives.

Like all teachers, you have a unique set of personal experiences, background knowledge, teaching skills, and personality traits that make you more comfortable and more effective with certain methodologies than with others. Because teachers are inclined to select the methodology that makes them feel most comfortable, it is easy to get into a teaching rut. Therefore, you should be prepared to experiment with different methods. You cannot become comfortable or

TABLE 5.2   Comparison of Teacher-Centered and Student-Centered Methodologies

Method	Amount of Teacher Control	Intent and Unique Features
Teacher-Centered Instructional Approaches		
Lecture	High	Telling technique: Teacher presents information without student interaction
Lecture–Recitation	High to Moderate	Telling technique: Teacher presents information and follows up with question-and-answer sessions
Socratic	Moderate	Interaction technique: Teacher uses question-driven dialogues to draw out information from students
Demonstration	High to Moderate	Showing technique: Individual stands before class, shows something, and talks about it
Modeling	High	Showing technique: Teacher or individual behaves/acts in way desired of students. Students learn by copying actions of model
Student-Centered Instructional Approaches		
Discussion	Low to Moderate	Interaction technique: Whole class or small group interact on topic
Panel	Low	Telling technique: Group of students present and/or discuss information
Debate	Low	Telling technique: Competitive discussion of topic between teams of students
Role Playing	Low	Doing technique: Acting out of roles or situations
Cooperative Learning	Low	Doing technique: Students work together in mixed-ability group on task(s)
Discovery	Low to Moderate	Doing technique: Students follow established procedure in an attempt to solve problems through direct experiences
Inquiry	Low	Doing technique: Students establish own procedure to solve problem through direct experiences
Simulations/Games	Low	Doing technique: Involvement in an artificial but representative situation or event
Individualized Instruction	Low to Moderate	Telling/doing technique: Students engage in learning designed to fit their needs and abilities
Independent Study	Low	Telling/doing technique: Learning carried out with little guidance

SOURCE: Moore, K. D. (2007). *Classroom Teaching Skills* (6th ed.). New York: McGraw-Hill. Used with permission.

even familiar with methods you have not used. Indeed, you might even discover a new method that you want to make part of your permanent teaching repertoire!

The methodology must also match the maturity level and experiences of your students. Just as teachers often prefer one teaching style, students feel comfortable and learn better when the method fits their abilities, needs, and interests. Keep in mind that when your method is mismatched with students' preferred styles, learning does not take place at the maximum level. Thus, you should select the best method for the class as a whole. To address the abilities, needs, and interests of every student, you must use a variety of teaching methods and be willing to use a mixture of individualized instruction and teacher-centered instruction so that all students gain a common foundation of knowledge and skills.

Finally, the environment and related environmental factors also must be taken into account when you select your methodology. Factors such as the space available, time of day, and weather can influence a lesson greatly.

Procedures

The lesson procedure is the sequence of steps designed to lead students to the acquisition of the learning objectives. For example, you may decide on the following sequence for a lesson on creating a voice in personal writing:

1. Ask students to identify their favorite singers. Students independently reflect and then share with a partner. A few volunteers share with the whole class. The teacher shares a personal choice also (accompanied by a *YouTube* video clip if available).

2. Provide a "bridge" to the day's lesson. Explain how musicians excel if they have developed personalized styles and have unique voices. Writers need to find their own voices also.

3. Conduct a brief lesson about creating a personalized voice by writing from personal experiences, selecting words carefully, maintaining an insider's perspective, and sharing sensory details.

4. Students select one exceptionally memorable event in their lives. Capture the moment by completing a sensory table (see, hear, taste, smell, touch, emotional feelings).

5. As a guided practice activity, students use the sensory chart to assist them as they talk about the special moment with a classmate.

Students progress through the rest of the writing process (drafting, revising, editing, publishing) to create personal narratives about that special moment. They share their final pieces with peers. As you see, the procedure consists of the sequenced teacher and student activities used for achieving the lesson objectives.

Practice

When you plan, don't overlook student practice. Students must have the opportunity to test themselves on the content. Providing these opportunities must be a regular part of the daily lesson plan. Two types of practice are important and should take place during the course of each lesson: (1) *guided practice*, or individual/small-group practice with the help and encouragement of the teacher, and (2) *independent practice*, or individual practice without the help and encouragement of the teacher.

Closure

Lessons must have some type of closure. Ringing a bell or telling students to put their reading books away and take out their math books does not represent closure. A closure activity should provide a logical conclusion by consolidating the lesson's main concepts and ideas and assessing whether students have learned what was intended.

Video Link 5.3: Watch a video about lesson closure.

Closure should be more than a quick review of the ideas covered in the lesson; it should show the relationship among the major ideas and tie together the parts of the lesson. Instead of doing all the talking, have students verbalize their understanding of the interrelatedness of the lesson's key points and how this information connects with prior learning and real-life applications. Closure is an important, and often overlooked, component in the teaching–learning process. Indeed, it is as vital as the set induction and the lesson itself.

Closure isn't something that takes place only at the conclusion of a lesson; sometimes you may want to achieve closure partway through a lesson. Closure can be appropriate after a video clip, a guest speaker's presentation, a class field trip, a science experiment, and at the end of a unit as a capstone activity.

Effective teachers employ multiple ways to provide closure to lessons. They can do a "quickwrite" or "quickwhip" during which students take turns stating the most important things they learned during that day's lesson. Through question-and-answer sessions, cueing, and summary questions students can relate what they've learned back to the general theme. Have students fill in an outline that includes the main points of the lesson or have them create a product to show what they have learned. If they cannot demonstrate or apply the new concept or skill, then learning is questionable.

Every student in your class must achieve closure on a lesson. Just because one student is able to answer closure questions correctly does not mean that all can. Therefore, you must take care to ensure that all students achieve closure.

Evaluation

You have set the stage, identified the objectives, developed the strategies, and planned for practice. Now you need to plan how you will evaluate student learning. We will discuss multiple methods of assessment of student learning in detail in Chapter 6. Always keep in mind that well-written lesson objectives lead to observable, measurable assessments. Evaluations need to align with the unit goals, lesson objectives, and lesson activities! Complete Application Activity 5.1 to gain additional skill at planning lessons.

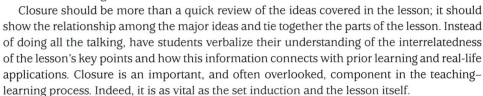

APPLICATION ACTIVITY 5.1 Planning Format

1. Compare and contrast the lesson plan formats presented in this chapter.

2. Develop a *unique* lesson plan format that will best fit your teaching philosophy and style. Share your format with classmates.

Lesson Planning for Everyday Use

The formats described in this chapter are probably more detailed than the formats you will use in the schools. However, some master teachers still create fully detailed lesson plans for new thematic units to ensure that all of the necessary components are in place. They reference these plans in their weekly plan book. Other experienced teachers may use an abridged format commonly found in lesson plan books. They still need to identify unit goals, objectives, activities, and assessments that are aligned with state and district

---

REFLECTIONS ON TEACHER PRACTICE 5.2: A Year Plan

1. What are the benefits of having teachers plan for the year at the beginning of school?

2. How will technology make teachers better planners? Better teachers?

I spend many hours at the beginning of the year making a Year Plan, with the objectives and concepts, topics, or stories that I plan to teach each week, trying to make sure all objectives will be covered and introduced in some sort of logical or sequential manner. I've written my plans on the computer for the past several years, just setting up a table and copying the master to a new document each week, saving by date and main topic. Like the other savers, I find this to be a great resource in later years—especially now that I have them on computer, I can just search and find my topics so easily. Since my schedule and special things change throughout the year, my table/template will also change as needed. Since Texas has made such a push to cover all of the objectives and to retain children who can't pass state tests, I have started writing the state objective numbers after each entry in my plans. At first this was a real pain, but I found that it actually turned out to be an excellent training for learning exactly what my objectives are. I believe that I am much better at including things that I might have left out in the course of teaching because I do know my objectives better. I usually look at my plans at the first and last of the day, and occasionally to check for a page number or other specific detail. I don't feel bound by the plans, and give myself the freedom to go with the flow if the lesson leads . . . but with plans I know I won't stray too far for too long. Unless you are following a textbook or other pre-planned series or routing, I would question whether or not a person could keep in mind where they were going, what they had covered, and what hadn't been addressed without some sort of reference. I probably go to the extreme in detailing my plans, but I have had a few weeks when they just didn't get made. Those have never been weeks that I would count as my most effective. I think you can be an excellent teacher without lesson plans, but don't see how having them could do anything but make you even better. (The clearer the target, the more precise the hit.)

—SJ, elementary teacher

Please visit the Student Study site at **www.sagepub.com/mooreteachingk8** *for additional discussion questions and assignments.*

SOURCE: Reprinted with permission from ProTeacher, a professional community for elementary teachers (www.proteacher.net).

mandates and provide sufficient information for a possible substitute teacher, however. Because preservice students, student teachers, and beginning teachers have yet to internalize this effective lesson plan design, they need to take the time to create fully detailed plans.

Reflective Teaching

After you've designed and taught a lesson, you need to analyze the results of student learning and reflect upon your instructional effectiveness. These reflections will help you decide how to improve your instruction to maximize student achievement. In short, you need to be a teacher who is a reflective decision maker. Donald Cruickshank (1987), the primary architect of **reflective teaching**, suggests that reflective teachers consider their teaching carefully and, as a result, are more thoughtful and alert students of teaching. These careful reflections on past experiences result in teacher growth and lead to more effective planning and teaching. Reflective teachers ask themselves such questions as "What am I doing and why?" "How can I better meet my students' needs?" "What are some alternative learning activities to achieve my objectives?" "How could I have encouraged more involvement or learning on the part of the students?"

Self-knowledge and self-assessment are hallmarks of reflective practice. Good teachers are constantly evaluating their efforts and finding better instructional approaches. Even when lessons go well, reflective teachers analyze the lesson to determine what went well and why and how else things might have been done. Teaching practices tend to become routine with time and are repeated with very little or no forethought. Through reflective teaching, however, a teacher might examine student satisfaction with a lesson, the level of student engagement, or the degree of student academic success. Teachers who carefully examine and reflect on their practices become better decision makers and, consequently, better planners and more successful teachers. Think about your teaching, test new ideas, and evaluate the results; you will improve your teaching practice and increase your students' learning.

This concludes the discussion of lesson plan structure. Table 5.3 gives a summary of section concepts. Review Table 5.3, and then complete Reflect and Apply Exercise 5.3, which will check your understanding of the concepts presented in this section.

TABLE 5.3	Lesson Plan Structure Concepts
Component	**Description**
Set induction	Activity at outset of a lesson to get students' undivided attention, to arouse their interest, and to establish a conceptual framework
Instructional strategy	The methodology and procedure. It is the global plan of a lesson.
Methodology	Planned patterned behaviors that are definite steps by which the teacher influences learning
Procedure	Sequence of steps designed to lead students to the acquisition of the desired learning
Closure	An activity designed to pull a lesson together and bring it to a logical conclusion

---

REFLECT AND APPLY EXERCISE 5.3: Lesson Plan Structure

Reflect

- Are a set induction and closure really necessary in lessons at all grade levels? Why or why not? What do teachers need to consider when designing set induction and closure activities?

- How is an advanced organizer related to a set induction?

Apply

- What kinds of lesson plans would be most appropriate for the grade level you expect to teach? Why?

- Think of a topic you might teach one day. Develop a set induction and a closure activity related to that topic. Be ready to share.

SUMMARY

This chapter covered teacher planning. The main points were as follows:

- Effective teaching requires planning. Novices, as well as experienced teachers, must plan and plan well.

Planning Instruction

- Teachers engage in four levels of planning: curriculum mapping, unit, weekly, and daily.

- Curriculum mapping is the broadest and most general type of planning.

- Comprehensive unit plans that include a title, a contextual student narrative, goals and instructional objectives, an outline of content, learning activities, resources and materials, and evaluation strategies are necessary for coherent instruction. Accommodations for exceptional students and reflections should also be important components of unit plans.

- Planning daily lessons is one of the most important components of effective teaching.

Lesson Plan Structure

- A strong set induction (focus) is crucial for a lesson. It sets the tone and establishes a conceptual framework for the coming activities.

- The methodology and procedure form the lesson instructional strategy. The selected method forms the heart of a lesson because it determines whether you use a teacher-centered or a student-centered mode of delivery.

- When selecting a lesson method, students should actively respond in some manner or should at least be mentally alert.

- Lessons should have a well-planned ending, or lesson closure.

- Effective teachers are reflective decision makers who learn from their past experiences to improve their teaching and to increase student learning.

DISCUSSION QUESTIONS AND ACTIVITIES

1. **Instructional Planning.** Obtain the teacher's edition of a textbook for a subject that you expect to teach. Consider the learning outcomes that you accessed in Reflect and Apply Exercise 5.1. Determine which units you would choose to teach. Provide rationales for your decisions. Create a timeline for presenting the units. How did you determine the sequence of units? How much time would you allot to each unit? Be ready to share.

2. **Research.** Using the library or Internet, collect three examples of lesson plans addressing a topic related to your field of interest. Analyze the plans. Are they teacher-centered or student-centered? How do you know? Which lesson format do they most closely resemble? What changes, if any, would you make to improve the lessons?

3. **Planning a Lesson.** Plan a lesson presentation for the topic of your choice for the grade level or content you expect to teach. Include the three key components that constitute a well-written lesson plan.

TECH CONNECTION

The Internet offers numerous resource sites that will assist teachers in developing unit and daily lesson plans. Complete the following two application activities, which will help you identify resources that will make you a better planner.

- An excellent Internet resource for teachers is the ERIC Resource Information Center (www .eric.ed.gov/), which provides a wide range of free information about educational topics. What information on the site would be useful to you at the grade level you expect to teach? Summarize the information, and share it with your classmates.

- Access the lesson plan at these URL websites: www.lessonplanspage.com, www.eduref.org/ Virtual/Lessons, and www.teachnology.com/teachers/lesson_plans. Locate five lesson plans relative to the grade level and subjects you expect to teach. Analyze and modify the sets and closures to make them more effective for your future students. Do all the lessons include a set and closure? If the selected lesson does not have a set and/or closure, design one. Summarize your findings and modifications with classmates.

CONNECTION WITH THE FIELD

1. **Classroom Interviews.** Visit with teachers at local schools. Find out how the standards, assessment, and accountability movement has affected these schools and how the teachers are affected in their classrooms.

2. **Classroom Observation.** Observe in several classrooms. Note the structure of the lessons being presented. Can you identify the elements that constitute the lesson plan? How is set induction achieved? How is closure achieved? Can you draw any conclusions as a result of your observations?

3. **Teacher Interviews.** Interview several teachers. Are they required to write and submit lesson plans? Describe the content and procedures. Do they include the three major components in their daily lesson plans?

STUDENT STUDY SITE

Visit the Student Study Site at **www.sagepub.com/mooreteachingk8** for these additional learning tools:

- Video clips
- Web resources
- Self quizzes
- E-Flashcards
- Full-text SAGE journal articles
- Portfolio Connection
- Licensing Preparation/Praxis Connection

CHAPTER 6

Evaluating and Measuring Student Learning

Too often we give children answers to remember rather than problems to solve.

—Roger Lewin

Before We Begin

All teachers test! Is high-stakes testing beneficial to students, families, and society? Does high-stakes testing result in better teaching? Improved learning? Be ready to compare your view with classmates.

OVERVIEW

Today's teachers and students are entangled in a dragnet of standardized assessment. This recent, heavy emphasis on assessment is the result of accountability and reform movements that have impacted this nation's schools. The American public is demanding that children know the facts and only the facts. However, will knowing just the facts equip them with the problem-solving skills and strategies they'll need to become productive global citizens?

Like every other aspect of the teaching–learning process, assessing educational outcomes is a complex and sometimes confusing endeavor. First, teachers need to realize that the terms *assessment*, *evaluation*, and **measurement** are related but not synonymous. Next they need to become proficient in using multiple forms of assessment, evaluation, and measurement, including standardized tests and teacher-made tests. Then they need to interpret assessment results to determine students' progress, to improve instruction, and to assign grades. Furthermore, they need to share information about students' progress with parents and patrons who are interested in the quality of their schools' programs and instruction.

Today, more than ever, it is critical that beginning teachers build a repertoire of effective evaluation strategies for assessing students' knowledge, behaviors, skills, and abilities in the cognitive, affective, and psychomotor domains. Because assessment and evaluation is such a vast topic, this chapter will provide an overview of basic evaluative topics and procedures. This information should equip beginning teachers with an initial understanding of how to use assessment, measurement, and evaluation to make teaching more productive, learning more engaging, and explaining outcomes more tenable.

OBJECTIVES

After completing your study of Chapter 6, you should be able to

- define and explain the purposes of assessment, measurement, and evaluation;
- compare and contrast **preassessment**, **formative assessment**, and **summative assessment**;
- differentiate among competitive, noncompetitive, and **performance assessment** systems;
- compare and contrast norm-referenced and criterion-referenced evaluations;
- describe the various sources of evaluative information and identify the advantages and limitations associated with the use of each; and
- explain the purposes and strategies for assigning grades.

In an effort to raise academic standards, 49 states have adopted state-mandated testing, thus increasing school district and teacher accountability. Students can no longer be promoted to the next grade based solely upon their report cards—even though some teachers continue to do so. An increasing number of states require testing at certain grades to determine if students should continue to the next grade. One practice that has received considerable attention is the increased use of **minimum competency tests** to award graduation diplomas. At issue is whether such tests are accurate measures of the scope of knowledge and skills learned in school. Students who fail the tests usually receive a certificate of attendance. Many believe this practice will have a chilling effect on minority students and students with special needs. Elementary and middle school teachers can ensure that *all* K–8 students are learning by using a mixture of standardized and teacher-made assessments (Wright, 2010).

THE ASSESSMENT AND EVALUATION PROCESS

Assessment, measurement, and evaluation are vital parts of the instructional process. Assessment is the process of documenting students' knowledge, skills, attitudes, and beliefs. Measurement provides specific data about the quality or degree of students' efforts. Evaluation is the process of making judgments or placing value on the students' efforts based upon the data.

Assessment and Measurement

Assessment is the process of gathering information about students, the curriculum, and the school environment through informal observations, discussions, performance tasks, formal assignments, portfolios, or tests. Although many assessments are created at the district, state, or national levels, teachers can also construct quality assessments. Students demonstrate their learning through presentations, products (artwork, models, etc.), performances, or traditional tests. Teachers might also gather information to assess the quality of instruction or the classroom environment to improve their teaching efforts.

Usually, teachers are interested in measuring the degree to which students attain mastery based upon predetermined criteria. For example, teachers might want to gather specific information about students' group skills, reading fluency, or ability to adjust a microscope during an experiment. Measurement generates specific data. Each day, teachers take hundreds of different types of measurements that vary in degrees of precision. The accuracy of the data varies depending upon what is being measured and how it is being measured.

The Evaluation Process

Once teachers have gathered pertinent data regarding the desired outcomes and measured the degree to which students have acquired the outcomes, they are ready to evaluate, or judge, the quality of students' performances or products. TenBrink (2003) suggested that the evaluation process consists of four steps:

1. *Preparation.* Determine what information is needed, as well as how and when to collect it.

2. *Information Collecting.* Gather a variety of information as accurately as possible.

3. *Making Judgments.* Compare information against selected criteria to make judgments.

4. *Decision Making.* Reach conclusions based on formed judgments.

These four steps require teachers to be reflective decision makers who make judgments based upon information generated by multiple assessments.

The motivational, social, and attitudinal effects related to the "desired outcome" should also be considered in making judgments. Teachers make all kinds of evaluations based upon assessment information and data. Can my kindergartners identify letters of the alphabet? Are my fourth graders ready to learn long division? Is this book appropriate for my eighth grade English class? Is John's behavior improving? Should students make team or individual presentations? Has Mary earned a B or C on her science project? In effect, teachers assess any time they collect information and evaluate any time they determine a course of action based on that information.

Because evaluation is an integral part of the teaching process, effective teachers use evaluation to monitor students' progress, to gauge the appropriateness of the curriculum, to identify what must be retaught, to ensure proper placement of individual students within a program of instruction, and to make sure that prescribed academic guidelines for achievement have been met. Viewed in this context, evaluation performs a dual function in the educational process by providing student achievement results plus valuable information for future curriculum planning.

Technology Support

Effective teachers use a wide array of technological resources such as recordings, databases, electronic grade books, online test banks, test generators, scantrons, CPS clicker systems, online exams, rubrics, games, and digital portfolios to track students' progress. Available software can also be used to align instructional objectives, content, and assessment. These resources reduce assessment development and grading time. Some of these assessment tools can be found here: www.internet4classrooms.com/teachertools4htm#assess.

EVALUATION TYPES

Evaluation occurs throughout the instructional design and implementation process to provide continuous feedback so teachers can adjust their instruction accordingly. This feedback may be obtained through any one of three main types of evaluation: (1) preassessment, (2) formative assessment, and (3) summative assessment (see Table 6.1).

Before beginning a unit of instruction, chapter, or course, teachers assess students' prior knowledge of a topic through informal and formal activities. These preassessments might include class discussions, students' responses to provided prompts, quick games of topical questions, or pretests. Teachers use this information to differentiate instruction by varying content, grouping, and instructional strategies according to students' knowledge and skill level. Formative assessments occur during instruction while students are *forming* their knowledge. Examples include daily student work, student responses during discussions, journaling, and writing conferences. Teachers use this continuous feedback to monitor students' progress and to adapt further instruction. Summative assessments occur at the end of a unit of instruction, chapter, grading period, semester, or course. Teachers evaluate students' achievement and their teaching success through posttests, presentations, conferences, performances, and products. Summative evaluation usually yields grades. Grades provide the school with a rationale for passing or failing students and are usually based on a comprehensive range of accumulated behaviors, skills, and knowledge.

TABLE 6.1 Characteristics of Preassessments, Formative Assessments, and Summative Assessments

	Preassessments	Formative Assessments	Summative Assessments
Purpose	To identify difficulties and place students	To promote learning through feedback	To assess overall achievement
Nature	Many questions related to general knowledge	Few questions related to specifics of instruction	Many questions related to specific and general knowledge
Frequency of administration	Varied—usually before instruction	Frequently—usually during instruction	Once—usually in the final phase of instruction

Evaluation is a continuous process fostered by daily teacher–student interaction.

SYSTEMS OF EVALUATION

Evaluation systems can be grouped into two categories: (1) competitive and (2) noncompetitive. **Competitive evaluation** systems compare students' progress with other students' efforts (norm-referenced); in effect, students are competing with their peers for academic standing. Traditionally, many middle schools have required competition among students because of the belief that it stimulates motivation. All schools use some form of norm-referenced testing to compare their students' achievement with students from other school systems, states, or countries. **Noncompetitive evaluation** systems evaluate each student's progress toward meeting established sets of standards of mastery (criterion-referenced). Many teachers use criterion-referenced evaluations to determine if individual students have mastered the intended outcomes.

Competitive Evaluation

When evaluators are concerned with students' standing within a large, diversified group, they use the **normal curve** (see Figure 6.1). This curve, commonly called the *natural curve* or *normal distribution curve*, reflects the natural distribution of all sorts of things in nature. Standardized test results are interpreted using a normal curve and "**norm group**." Teachers use the curve to compare how well an individual student has performed in comparison with a peer group representing a cross section of students at the same age and grade, or norm group. They can further analyze specific results using standard statistical measurements such as z scores, T scores, stanines, or percentiles. To augment your understanding of the normal curve and standard scores go to the web-based student study site (**www.sagepub.com/mooreteachingk8**).

FIGURE 6.1 Normal Probability Curve

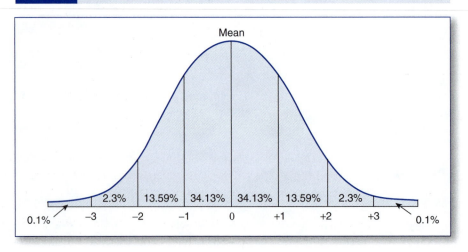

Noncompetitive Evaluation

Fantini (1986) suggested that criterion-referenced evaluation is more indicative of students' progress than is norm-referenced evaluation because competition with a norm group might intimidate or discourage struggling students. Competition can even be harmful to more capable students because it often teaches that winning is all-important. Criterion-referenced evaluation protects all students' academic dignity because it focuses on assessing their mastery of specific skills, regardless of how other students performed.

Today, many educators believe grades should reflect students' efforts as well as learning mastery. No one should receive an A without really trying, nor should students who are exerting themselves to their fullest potential receive an F. There is now a national call for changing assessment practices. Performance assessments and the use of portfolios show promise as more viable assessment techniques because they reflect students' progress. We will discuss performance assessments and portfolios later in this chapter.

This concludes the discussion of the assessment process. Before you continue, complete Reflect and Apply Exercise 6.1.

REFLECT AND APPLY EXERCISE 6.1: Evaluation Information

Reflect

- What forms of preassessment, formative assessment, and summative assessment have you experienced?

- What are the advantages and disadvantages of using competitive evaluation? Noncompetitive evaluation?

Apply

- Is it best to use competitive or noncompetitive evaluation at the grade level you expect to teach? Why?

INFORMATION SOURCES

Effective evaluators make decisions based upon assessment information and data. The quality of their decisions is impacted by the quality and amount of information available to them. Where can they acquire this information?

Cumulative Record

Cumulative records are paper or electronic files containing information about students' academic careers, such as grades, standardized test data, health records, family data, vital statistics, and extracurricular activities. Some districts require teachers to include short summaries of parent–teacher conferences; others allow teachers and principals to insert notes about students' behaviors. Educators need to be very careful of what they include, however, because the Family Educational Rights and Privacy Act (FERPA) allows parents access to the files. To further protect students' confidentiality, many districts require people to sign a form indicating their name, position, and reason for accessing the file. Teachers need to treat the information found in these records with great care because it might cause them to alter their perceptions of students' abilities, lead to inaccurate judgments, and predispose them to hold unrealistic expectations.

School personnel—such as counselors, assistant principals, nurses, secretaries, and other teachers—can also be excellent sources of information. For example, counselors can help interpret test results, as well as identify personality factors that might affect student performance. Assistant principals, nurses, and secretaries maintain records of students' office visits, health data, and attendance. Former teachers can provide additional insight into students' academic and behavioral needs as well.

Personal Contact

Effective evaluators are "kid-watchers" who gather formative information during daily teacher–student interactions and classroom activities. They listen in on students' interactions during group work, examine students' papers, visit with students during writing conferences, monitor students' progress in the computer and science labs, and attend to students' answers and questions during classroom discussions. Kid-watching provides plentiful, pertinent assessment information to guide teachers' instructional efforts. Formal and informal conversations with students may be among the best techniques for gaining diagnostic and formative evaluative information.

ALBERT: A REFLECTIVE CASE STUDY

Paulina paused to ponder as she packed the proofs into her briefcase. Her algebra class had gone well today. Most of the students had seemed to grasp the concept of logarithms. Her thoughts were interrupted when Beatrix stopped by with her usual benign beatitudes, hoping to schmooze her way to an A. In the background, Paulina overheard Albert mutter, "I hate this class!" She glanced up, but he had already left the classroom. Paulina was perplexed. She'd noticed that Albert had started sitting in the back of the room. He spent most of the class muttering to Alexi. His posture had changed until he was almost sitting horizontally. Homework had become extinct. Queries were met with indifferent shrugs and silent stares. Something didn't add up! What variable was she missing?

1. How can Paulina discover what's causing Albert's attitude?

2. What can Paulina do once she identifies the cause? Please give a specific example.

Many teachers record, organize, and reflect upon their observations to gain insights into students' learning and development. For example, elementary teachers maintain reading conference folders containing anecdotal records on students' reading fluency and acquisition of reading skills and strategies. Some teachers use note cards to track students' behavioral growth by recording the frequency of misbehaviors, identifying possible causes and describing students' reactions to consequences. Other teachers create folders to house general comments such as "Mary has difficulty remembering to bring her book to class," "John must be continuously reinforced to study," and "Ron has trouble with fine motor adjustments in science." Without written records, teachers only have general impressions of students' efforts and behaviors; the information isn't specific enough to make informed decisions. Anecdotal record forms can facilitate teachers' efforts (see Figures 6.2 and 6.3). More refined forms such as checklists, **rating scales**, and **questionnaires** evaluate students' mastery of intended outcomes. For more information about how to develop these instruments, visit the web-based student study site (**www.sagepub.com/mooreteachingk8**).

Analysis

Effective evaluators constantly analyze students' work for possible errors or misperceptions. **Analysis** is a powerful formative assessment tool that takes place during or immediately after instruction. It is more formal than personal contact because it provides specific feedback to students and their parents.

FIGURE 6.2   Anecdotal Record Form

Student: _____ Date: _____

Description of environment/class: _____

_____

_____

Description of incident: _____

_____

_____

_____

_____

Reported by: _____

FIGURE 6.3   Seating Chart Record of Classroom Behaviors

1 – 1 – 1 1 – 1 – 4 Sherry	1 – 1 – 2 2 – 1 – 2 Julie	2 – 1 – 2 1 – 2 – 1 Sue	2 – 1 –2 3 – 3 – 3 Chad	1 – 3 – 1 3 – 3 – 3 Paul	1 – 3 – 1 5 – 1 – 2 Mary
1 – 1 – 1 1 – 1 – 2 Joe	2 – 2 – 2 2 – 2 – 1 Mike	1 – 2 – 1 1 – 4 – 1 Sally	3 – 3 – 2 2 – 3 – 1 Conrad	3 – 3 – 1 1 – 1 – 1 Aaron	1 – 2 – 2 2 – 2 – 2 Scott
Empty Seat	2 – 2 – 2 2 – 3 – 3 Jan	1 – 1 – 1 2 – 2 – 2 Billie	5 – 5 – 1 1 – 2 – 1 Susan	1 – 1 – 1 3 – 3 – 3 Pat	1 – 1 – 1 3 – 3 – 3 Jean
2 – 1 – 1 1 – 1 – 1 Lisa	2 – 1 – 1 1 – 3 – 3 Lila	2 – 1 – 1 1 – 1 – 4 Dawn	3 – 1 – 1 1 – 1 – 4 Skip	3 – 1 – 1 2 – 2 – 5 Ben	Empty Seat

Legend: 1. Quiet and on task
2. Quiet, not working
3. Talked to other student
4. Finished work early
5. Talked with teacher

"I can accept and process data, but I have trouble generating it on my own."

SOURCE: Created by Martha Campbell.

Teachers actively monitor and provide immediate feedback by analyzing students' work as it is produced. This enables them to address misperceptions or faulty practice, reteach skills, probe for understanding, and suggest alternative strategies. When combined with observation and inquiry, analysis provides insight into students' thinking processes and skills acquisition. Effective teachers adjust their instruction according to students' perceived needs.

Students learn that making mistakes is part of the learning process and develop confidence in self-correcting their work. They have an opportunity to reflect upon and critique their own work and the work of their peers based upon prespecified performance criteria. After a peer review session, students revise their work before submitting it for grading. Teachers keep and share student work samples with students and their parents during teacher–student and parent–teacher conferences.

Journals

One technique that can be used for gaining valuable information about students is journaling. Elementary teachers train students how to record events and feelings by collaboratively writing a summary of each day's events in a class journal. Older students use a variety of journals. In *learning logs*, students record key concepts and draw sketches demonstrating what they've learned. *Buddy journals* encourage dialogue between journaling partners on topics of shared interest. Students write from another person's perspective in *simulated journals*. In *double-entry journals*, students record intriguing quotations or facts in the left column and their personal reactions in the right column. Students expound upon content topics, peer relations, or personal circumstances in *personal journals*. They fold over the pages of personal entries they do not want to have read by the teacher. Teachers peruse journal entries to evaluate students' progress. Sometimes they grade journal entries according to preestablished criteria. Other times, teachers react to students' responses with comments or questions to precipitate more conversation.

Journaling is an excellent way to gain insight into students' feelings and understandings of school and life experiences. Some of their viewpoints might not be accurate, but their perceptions of reality are revealed through their writing.

Parental Conferences

Parental conferences are an excellent way to gain insight into students' social and academic problems. Because these conversations usually only last up to 20 minutes, they need to be scheduled in advance. Teachers can ensure positive results if they plan well (see Table 6.2). Before the conference, create a folder of students' work representing the major topics that have been taught since the last conference. Carefully arrange furniture so parents who are comfortably waiting do not overhear the current parent–teacher conversation. Sit on the same side of the table as the parents to build a sense of teamwork and collegiality. Include educational specialists and a translator as needed. Begin with a positive statement. Ask parents if they have something they want to share before continuing. This usually takes care of major issues everyone's been concerned about. Do not use conference time to chastise parenting skills or demonize the student. Maintain a positive, professional tone. Focus on the students' personal and academic growth. Have suggestions for parent assistance (if asked). Consider using student-led conferences to ensure the student's voice is heard. Be sure to prepare carefully, however, so the student knows how to contribute to the conversation. End the conference on a planned positive note and follow up on future successes.

TABLE 6.2	**Framework for a Successful Conference**
Step 1	*Plan ahead*. Establish your purpose. Plan what you intend to say, what information you want to obtain, and what your concerns are. Plan what your next step will be in the classroom as a result of the conference.
Step 2	*Starting the conference*. Be positive. Begin the conference with a positive statement.
Step 3	*Holding the conference*. Establish a positive sharing relationship. Be an active listener. Be accepting with regard to input and advice. Establish a partnership, so all concerned can work toward a common goal.
Step 4	*Ending the conference*. End the conference on a positive note. Communicate the fact that in working together, the common goals will be reached.
Step 5	*Conduct follow-up contact*. Keep all parties informed. Send notes and make phone calls to share successes and/or further concerns.

Testing

A **test** may be defined as task(s) used to obtain specific information presumed to be representative of preestablished attributes, or performance criteria. Effective evaluators design tests according to established guidelines, describe the criteria being measured, and establish scoring procedures. Tests are classified according to how they are created (teacher-made or standardized), administered (individuals or groups), scored (objectively/subjectively, norm- or criterion-referenced), focused (speed or accuracy), and responded to (performances or traditional paper–pencil).

Effective evaluators use multiple types of tests, including pretests, diagnostic tests, posttests, chapter exams, unit exams, midterms, final exams, standardized tests, and quizzes. The type of testing depends on their purpose for collecting data. The two main types of tests, selected-response and constructed-response, will be discussed later in this chapter.

Assessment information should be shared with students.

Because of problems associated with reliability, validity, and usability, extra care must be taken in selecting tests that measure attitudes, feelings, and motor skills. Even under the best of conditions, pencil-and-paper tests—which are used more often than other kinds of assessment techniques—tend to place more value on knowing than on thinking and verbalizing than on doing. It also places more value on teacher expectations than on student beliefs and values. With careful thought, however, teachers can construct tests that assess thinking ability. The problem is that most teachers lack either the skill or time to construct proper tests.

This concludes the formal discussion of information sources and evaluative instruments. Complete Application Activity 6.1, which will let you further explore the measurement of student learning.

APPLICATION ACTIVITY 6.1 Effective Evaluation

1. What forms of personal contact, journaling, and conferencing did your elementary and middle school teachers use?

2. What types of tests have you experienced? What is your preferred type of test? Why?

3. Think about the following statement: A teacher should never use a single measure to assess learning. Do you agree or disagree with the statement? Why?

TYPES OF TESTS

In response to recent reform efforts accentuating standardized testing results and academic accountability, most schools primarily emphasize learning in the cognitive domain. The most common way to measure knowledge in the cognitive domain is through the use of standardized and teacher-made tests. This section will explore the basic characteristics and purposes of these tests. Detailed guidelines for constructing these tests are beyond the scope of this book. For more information on tests, please consult a basic textbook that details the creation, validation, and administration of tests.

Standardized Tests

Ebel and Frisbie (1991) define a standardized test as one that has been constructed by experts with explicit instructions for administration, standard scoring procedures, and tables of norms for interpretation. Standardized tests measure individual performance on a group-administered and group-normed test. Standardization means that the examinees respond to the same questions within the same amount of time under the same conditions with the same directions. Furthermore the same procedures are used to score the tests.

Standardized tests are generally used to determine student placement in differentiated instructional tracks, provide information for individualizing instruction, diagnose students' academic strengths and weaknesses, gauge program effectiveness, evaluate student progress, and determine teaching emphasis and effectiveness. Because they address a broad range of material, standardized tests play an important role in educational decision making and public reporting on student achievement.

REFLECTIONS ON TEACHER PRACTICE 6.1: Keeping Up With Students

1. How important is homework in the teaching process? Should you grade all homework?

2. Are the benefits derived from the use of rubrics worth the time and effort it takes to develop them? How else might student learning be assessed and evaluated?

Keeping up with all those student papers can be a chore. I find that having a system definitely does help.

Homework Policy: I always make sure that I collect all assignments and let students know that "everything counts." I do want them to take their assignments seriously, so I review all assignments after I collect them, and then assign a letter grade of E, S, or N. If they really appear to get the idea, let's say on a math sheet, they receive an E. If they appear to be doing reasonably well with the assignment, I assign an S. If they miss the point altogether, I assign an N. Most of my students strive for an E. I let them know that homework is part of their grade. Each week, I assign a grade of 1 to 5 for homework completion. If they miss one assignment in the week, they get a 4. If they miss two, they get a 3, and so on. At the end of the marking period, I use homework completion as a means of deciding whether or not a borderline student can be raised up to the higher grade, or should be dropped down a grade. Quality of homework also enters into the picture when it comes to grading. Shoddy work receives a shoddy grade.

Student Writing: This is the most challenging and time consuming thing to keep up with. You need to obtain or create a rubric for your students' writing exercises. Creating a rubric takes time, but once you have it, you can use it from year to year, and it provides a quick and objective means of grading writing. I created a rubric for each type of writing piece the kids do. I have rubrics for persuasive, expressive, descriptive, narrative, and informative writing. Books like those published by "Teacher's Mailbox" have writing ideas and rubrics to go along with them. These published rubrics can help. I tend to use my own, so that I am meeting state standards. Our students are graded on voice, conventions, organization, and content, so I take these into consideration when I am creating rubrics for my students. In one writing piece, I may not look for *everything*. I may tell the students that they will be graded on organization in a particular writing piece. In another, I may be grading for voice. Toward the end of the school year, I will grade on everything—all domains, and expect them to have the work as "picture perfect" as they can possibly make it.

Tests: I use the tests that come with the text series as often as possible to save myself time, but I do have some of my own quizzes made up. Of course, you probably realize that multiple-choice tests take a great deal less time to grade than essay. But I do believe that students should write in all areas, so I typically assign at least two to three essays with each test I give.

—*Carolyn, elementary school teacher*

Please visit the Student Study site at **www.sagepub.com/mooreteachingk8** *for additional discussion questions and assignments.*

SOURCE: Reprinted with permission from ProTeacher, a professional community for elementary school teachers (www.proteacher.net).

Standardized tests are particularly useful in comparing the performance of one individual with another, of an individual against a group, or of one group with another group. Such comparisons are possible because of the availability of the norming-group data and the uniformity of the procedures for administration and scoring the test. Thus, people can compare the testing results of a single school with other schools in a district, compare districts, compare states, or compare students in one state with all students in the nation. Standardized test results generally include a percentile norm, an age norm, a grade-level norm, or a combination of these norms. Your school district should train you to interpret these norms.

Standardized tests also have certain limitations. For example, they might test content and skills that are inconsistent with the teachers' or school districts' goals and objectives. Moreover, standardized tests are likely to have some social and cultural bias, which means that the test may discriminate against certain social and cultural groups that lack prerequisite language, background experience, or testing experiences.

Teacher-Made Tests

Teacher-made tests are designed to measure student learning for an instructional unit. There are four main reasons why these are the most common school evaluative instruments. First, test items align with classroom goals, objectives, and instructional activities. Second, because teacher-made tests present the same questions to all students under nearly identical conditions, teachers can make comparative judgments about students' achievement. Third, teacher-made tests are readily accessible for review by students and parents when explaining how grades were determined. Fourth, teacher-made tests are much less expensive to construct and administer.

Standardized tests provide valuable information for making curriculum decisions.

Teacher-made tests contain selected-response and/or constructed-response items. Students can *select* one of the provided responses when answering true–false, multiple-choice, and matching test items (selected-response). They have to *construct* their own responses when answering completion, short answer, essay, on-demand, and open response items (constructed-response). Teachers carefully choose the question types that align with their objectives and the nature of the behaviors being measured. The advantages and disadvantages of major types of test items are detailed in Table 6.3. Test items should align with the taxonomical level of the objectives. Contrary to common belief, this can be accomplished with almost any type of test item. Generally speaking, true–false and matching test items usually test at the knowledge and comprehension levels. Multiple-choice, completion, and short answer items can test at the knowledge, comprehension, analysis, and application levels. Essays, open-response, and on-demand items may test at the application, synthesis, and evaluation levels. Although it is more difficult to write selected-response items at the higher levels, it is also difficult to write high-level constructed-response items.

Instructional objectives usually suggest the best type of test item. For example, an objective that involves solving math problems would probably be best evaluated through a short answer or brief essay, whereas definitions of terms would probably be best evaluated through the use of matching or multiple-choice items. In general, however, when objectives lend themselves to more than one type of test item, most teachers prefer selected-response items over constructed-response items because of their scoring ease and reliability.

Classroom tests generally should not contain more than two types of test items. Students may have trouble when they must shift to different types of responses. Therefore, limit your test item types to the one or two formats that best fit your objectives. Keep these two principles for writing

TABLE 6.3 Advantages and Disadvantages Associated With the Different Types of Test Items

Type	Advantages	Disadvantages
Alternate choice	Large sampling of content Easy to score	Guessing Writing clear items difficult Tends to test memorization
Multiple choice	Large sampling of content Scoring simple and fast Measures wide range of cognitive levels Reduces guessing	Question construction time-consuming Often used to test trivial content
Matching	Large sampling of content Can test associations Easy to construct and score	Tests for recognition Guessing
Completion	Large sampling of content Easy to construct Limited guessing	Tests for memorization Writing good items difficult Difficult to score
Essay	Measures higher cognitive levels Less time needed to construct	Difficult to score Questions sometimes ambiguous

SOURCE: Created by Martha Campbell.

"I studied for this test, and the ploy paid off."

test items in mind: (1) Every test item should directly relate to an intended outcome. (2) Every item should separate the students who have mastered the objectives from those who have not. To augment your understanding of the standardized tests, teacher test construction, and test reliability and validity, go to the web-based student study site (www.sagepub.com/mooreteachingk8).

Choosing the "right" type of assessment can be quite confusing. As a rule, there are no absolute guidelines relative to the superiority of one type of assessment over another in every situation. Effective teachers use a variety of assessments, depending upon the grade level, content area, intended outcomes, and students' needs and learning styles. In general, the best procedure is to use the best assessment instrument that will measure the type of objectives the teacher has for a particular lesson or unit and the type of knowledge expected of students.

To further explore various information sources, complete Reflect and Apply Exercise 6.2.

REFLECT AND APPLY EXERCISE 6.2: Different Types of Evaluation

Reflect

- What kinds of information can teachers obtain from cumulative records, personal contacts, analysis, journals, parental conferences, and testing?

- Compare and contrast the purposes, advantages, and disadvantages of standardized tests and teacher-made tests.

Apply

- In addition to the sources mentioned in this chapter, what other sources of evaluative information would you use at the grade level you expect to teach?

- Identify a topic you might teach one day. What type of test would work best to assess students' knowledge of that topic? Why?

AUTHENTIC ASSESSMENT

Video Link 6.1:
Watch a video about authentic assessment.

Although traditional tests are an effective way to assess students' achievement, they only comprise part of the overall portrait of a student's capabilities. Some learning goals and objectives, particularly those in the psychomotor, affective, and higher levels of the cognitive domains, simply do not lend themselves to paper–pencil assessments. To meet this challenge many teachers now use **authentic assessment** techniques. Authentic assessment requires students to demonstrate skills and competencies that realistically represent real-world problems and situations. Students are required to integrate knowledge and to complete tasks that have real-life applications. Authentic assessments can include exhibitions, oral presentations, and other projects. Students might be asked to count a small set of objects, demonstrate a cooking technique, create infomercials for new scientific inventions, perform role-plays, or share original poems in a Poets Theatre. Authentic assessment usually includes a carefully-written performance task and a rubric by which the task performance will be evaluated.

Some educators use the term *performance assessment* in place of, or in conjunction with, *authentic assessment*. They call upon students to apply the skills and knowledge they have mastered but don't necessarily provide a real-life connection to make the task authentic. In performance assessment, students demonstrate the behaviors that the assessor wants to measure (Airasian, 2001; Meyer, 1992). For example, if the desired behavior is writing, students write; or if the desired behavior is identification of geometric figures, they point to or create geometric figures.

When creating authentic assessments, teachers need to consider these guidelines:

1. Design meaningful, motivational projects or tasks that align with the content and instructional outcomes.

2. Make sure tasks have real-life applicability.

3. Emphasize product and process, and convey that both development and achievement matter.

4. Provide opportunities for learner self-evaluation.

5. Develop rubrics to ensure consistent, fair evaluation.

Through the Eyes of an Expert

Designing Authentic Assessments

As a new teacher, my mind was brimming with creative lessons and activities that I couldn't wait to share with my students. My approach to curriculum design in those first couple of years was to teach a lesson, assign a core content standard that seemed relevant to the lesson and save assessment as an afterthought. It didn't take long for me to come to the understanding that this was not an effective way to teach! Putting in the time and effort to construct curriculum based on standards with an emphasis on assessment has definitely made me a more successful teacher.

The first step in curriculum development is to understand the standards and benchmarks that you are expected to teach. Work within your professional learning community to identify the essential content and skills that students need to learn. Use assessments from prior years (formal and non-formal) to target areas of weakness. Group the content standards that are compatible together and use a calendar to decide how much time you will devote to each unit of standards.

Designing authentic assessments should be your next priority. Create tests, quizzes, exit-slips, writing assignments, open response questions, etc. that are based on the content standards that you have grouped together. Use the expertise of your peers within your content area to develop objective, standards-based assessments that you can all use. Compare the results of your assessments within your professional learning community and see this as an opportunity to learn and grow as an educator.

The more I teach, the more I come to understand the importance of constant assessment! Good teachers are always aware of their students' progress and understanding of the material being taught.

Lesson planning is much like putting a puzzle together. The standards and benchmarks are the corner pieces. The assessments are the edges and the lessons and activities are the pieces in the middle. They take on many different forms and functions, and it's our job to make sure they all fit together perfectly. Begin with standards, assemble your assessments and fill in with lessons and your curriculum-development will be picture perfect!

SOURCE: Jennifer Dunnaway, Calloway County Middle School, Murray, Kentucky. Used with permission.

Portfolios

Portfolios are a very popular form of authentic assessment. Teachers use portfolios to document and evaluate students' efforts, progress, or achievement over a period of time. Students, their teachers, or both carefully select samples of students' work (artifacts) to place in portfolios. Portfolios come in many forms. Struggling students document their academic or personal progress through *growth portfolios*, which include artifacts clearly demonstrating the knowledge and skills they have slowly acquired. *Process portfolios* document every step of a long-term project, from the initial brainstorming ideas to the drafts, revisions, and final product or prepared accomplishment. As a capstone experience for long-term efforts, students might create *showcase portfolios*, highlighting their best efforts. Student artifacts may include research papers, book reports, journals, logs, photographs, drawings, videotapes and audiotapes, abstracts of readings, group projects, software, slides, and test results. Portfolio artifacts should document the students' history of learning and accomplishments in an organized way. Moreover, they can serve as a catalyst for reflection on students' growth as learners. Some teachers also require students to include written reflections about their skills and accomplishments as part of their portfolios. These develop students' reflective decision-making skills by requiring them to explain why they selected particular artifacts.

Video Link 6.2: Watch a video about portfolios.

Rubrics

Most teachers develop scoring rubrics to evaluate performance tasks and portfolios as objectively as possible. A rubric is a summarization of the performance criteria at different levels of performance. There are two main types of rubrics—holistic and analytical. To create holistic rubrics, teachers create multiple columns labeled with levels of performance such as novice, apprentice, proficient, or distinguished. In each column, they describe criteria associated with each level of performance. Analytical rubrics also have performance terms across the top and up to seven performance criteria listed in the left-hand column. Teachers write brief descriptions of representative performances in each cell of the resulting grid. Rubrics communicate standards and scoring criteria to students before the performance so they can produce their best work. When possible, teachers invite student input on determining these performance criteria. A sample scoring rubric that can be used to assess a Readers' Theatre presentation is shown in Table 6.4. Additional samples and rubric templates can be accessed at http://rubistar.4teachers.org and other sites.

TABLE 6.4 Analytical Rubric for a Readers' Theatre Presentation

Criteria	Excellent (4)	Very Good (3)	Satisfactory (2)	Unsatisfactory (1)
Expression	Student used expressive voice tone, extensive eye contact, and appropriate gestures when delivering lines.	Student used some expression, periodic eye contact, and some gestures when delivering lines.	Student used a neutral voice tone, minimal eye contact, and few gestures when delivering lines.	Student used an inappropriate voice tone, no eye contact, and no gestures when delivering lines.
Preparation	Student spoke at the correct times and read fluently with no mistakes.	Student missed some cues and misread a few words.	Student missed several cues and misread several words.	Student did not participate in most of the presentation.
Group work	Student actively participated in the group planning process.	Student somewhat participated in the group planning process.	Student minimally participated in the group planning process.	Student did not participate in the group process.
Etiquette	Student listened actively during peers' presentations.	Student fidgeted and looked away during peers' presentations.	Student visited with neighbors during peers' presentations.	Student turned around and didn't watch peers' presentations.

Constructing a rubric is not an easy task. A clearly defined purpose is essential as each component is developed. With this in mind, follow these steps:

Step 1. Examine the standards or objectives that the product or performance is meant to address.

Step 2. Write or identify no more than seven criteria that will be used to judge the students' product or performance. Make sure they match the standards or objectives. Invite student input if appropriate.

Step 3. Design a frame by deciding on the major categories or attributes the rubric will address. Will a holistic or analytical rubric work best?

Step 4. Describe the different levels of performance (exceptional, very good, adequate, etc.) that match each criterion. Write the highest level first and then the lowest level. Be sure to choose words or phrases that show the actual differences among the levels. Make sure they are observable.

Step 5. Test the rubric with students to make sure it is understandable.

Step 6. Revise the rubric as necessary.

A well-designed rubric enables students to understand what is expected of them. Furthermore, once students gain experience with rubrics, they can help construct their own rubrics.

REFLECTIONS ON TEACHER PRACTICE 6.2: Using Portfolios

1. How does the use of portfolios improve teaching and student assessment?

2. How can students be involved in the use of portfolios?

I have seen different teachers implement portfolios in many different ways. Some teachers use subject based portfolios, some use an all purpose portfolio, and some even use electronic portfolios (those were the coolest)! As for how often, I saw one teacher do it this way: On the last part of the day on Friday's while students were finishing work or reading, she would have portfolio conferences. After saving ALL work that the child had completed the entire week (either in a work folder or in those cardboard shelving systems with labels for each child), the student and teacher would have a short conference at the desk to decide which pieces of work should be included in the portfolio. The student was allowed to choose one, and the teacher was allowed to choose one. Both the student and teacher have to explain why they are choosing this piece. Of course, sometimes more than one piece of work was chosen. They actually filled out paperwork on each piece that had title, reason picked, and some other things.

Good luck with portfolios. This is a wonderful authentic assessment, and I think all teachers should implement it in some form.

—*Beth, elementary teacher*

Please visit the Student Study site at **www.sagepub.com/mooreteachingk8** *for additional discussion questions and assignments.*

SOURCE: Reprinted with permission from ProTeacher, a professional community for elementary school teachers (www.proteacher.net).

Work Samples

Student work samples portray the students' efforts over a sufficiently long period of time for appreciable progress in learning to occur. Work samples might include written documents such as a report, science experiment results, test, or story; artwork; recordings; special projects; and other types of finished products depending on the subject area. Teachers use work samples to assess and reflect upon the impact their instruction has had on students' academic progress and make revisions accordingly. Work samples also encourage teachers to think reflectively about teaching—planning, instruction, assessment, classroom management, and professionalism. They give teachers the opportunity to demonstrate with hard evidence that they are in fact able to foster learning gains in students.

This completes our study of authentic assessment. Complete Reflect and Apply Exercise 6.3 to check your understanding of the authentic assessment concepts presented in this section.

Video Link 6.3:
Watch a video about portfolio conference.

Reflect and Apply Exercise 6.3: Authentic Assessment

Reflect

- What forms of authentic assessment have you experienced? Were they positive experiences? Why or why not?

- Does your teacher preparation program require a portfolio? How does it compare with the portfolios discussed in this chapter?

- How can portfolios be used in assessment? Work samples?

Apply

- How could you use portfolios for the grade level you plan to teach one day?

- What types of student work samples could you collect in your future classroom?

Gathering student data does not complete the evaluative process. Teachers must interpret these data to assign grades. Grades help students and their parents know how well they are mastering the required material. A review of students' past grades can help teachers identify areas of strength or weakness and possibly even precipitate additional diagnostic testing to identify a learning disability or giftedness.

GRADING SYSTEMS

Effective teachers are confident in their ability to grade students' work because they know how to use multiple assessments to evaluate students' work. Most school districts assign grades of A, B, C, D, and F. Some elementary schools use S (satisfactory performance), MP (making progress), and N (not making progress). This section will explore three ways of assigning grades: (1) mastery learning system, (2) absolute grading system, or (3) relative grading system.

In a mastery learning system, teachers reteach material and allow students to revise their work until they achieve mastery of the intended outcomes. They use growth portfolios to document students' progress toward eventually achieving mastery. Students earn As or SPs. This approach works well in elementary classrooms because students must acquire the knowledge and skills to set a firm foundation for future learning.

In an absolute grading system, teachers use established criteria to grade students' performances (see Table 6.5). In this criterion-referenced grading system, grades are assigned based on the number of items answered correctly. Grading is simple: A student either does get an established percentage of the responses correct or does not. Student scores depend on the difficulty of the test. Most teachers use the absolute standard of grading. The major advantage of such a system is that it makes students responsible for the quality of their assignments and test results.

TABLE 6.5	Examples of Absolute System of Grading		
Percentage Grade	**Correct**		**Percentage Correct**
A	90 to 100		85 to 100
B	80 to 89		75 to 84
C	70 to 79	OR	65 to 74
D	60 to 69		55 to 64
F	Less than 60		Less than 55

Teachers frequently use a relative grading system in which they compare one students' performance with their peers' efforts. Some use a normal (bell) curve, which distributes students' grades in this pattern: 3.5% As, 23.8% Bs, 45% Cs, 23.8% Ds, and 3.5% Fs. Because of the normal curve's lack of flexibility, many teachers implement a simple ranking system instead. In a ranking system, the teacher establishes a fixed percentage for each assigned grade. For example, they might create the following curve:

A = Top 10%

B = Next 20%

C = Next 40%

D = Next 20%

F = Next 10%

Another common method of grading with curves is the inspection method. Teachers create a frequency distribution of raw scores on a vertical or horizontal line, as shown in Figure 6.4. They then assign grades according to natural breaks in the distribution. It is possible that this type of system will not yield A or F grades. There is no correct or incorrect division. Figure 6.5 shows three possible inspection grading patterns for grade distribution.

FIGURE 6.4   The Inspection Method

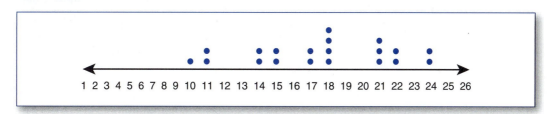

FIGURE 6.5 Examples of Inspection Grade Distributions

100			100			100		A
95			95			95		
94	(1)	A	94	(1)	A	94	(1)	B
91	(1)		91	(1)		91	(1)	
90	(1)		90	(1)		90	(1)	
85		B	85			85		
81	(2)		81	(2)	B	81	(2)	
75			75			75		
74	(4)	C	74	(4)		74	(4)	C
70	(3)		70	(3)		70	(4)	
65			65		C	65		
64	(2)	D	64	(2)		64	(2)	
60	(1)		60	(1)		60	(1)	
55			55			55		
50			50			50		
45			45		D	45		D
44	(1)	F	44	(1)		44	(1)	
43			43			43		
42			42		F	42		F

ASSIGNING FINAL GRADES

Teachers usually arrive at final grades by combining the results of students' work for a grading period. There are three major ways of accomplishing this end: (1) a point grading system, (2) a weighted grading system, and (3) a percentage grading system.

A point grading system is fairly simple and easy to use. The importance of each assignment, quiz, or test is reflected in the points allocated. For example, teachers may decide that assignments will be worth 10 points, quizzes will be worth 25 points, and tests will be worth 100 points. At the end of the grading period, the teacher adds up the points and assigns grades according to the established grade range (see Figure 6.6). A weighted grading system is more complex than the point grading system. Every assignment is given a letter grade, and all grades are then weighted to arrive at a final grade (see Figure 6.7). The percentage grading system is probably the simplest of all grading systems and the most widely used. Teachers calculate the percentage of correct responses for each assignment. For example, a student who gets 20 of 25 correct on a homework assignment has a score of 80 written in the grade book, 6 of 8 correct on a quiz has a 75 recorded in the grade book, and 40 of 60 correct on an examination has a 67 written in the grade book. In this approach, each assessment event carries equal weight.

A more detailed description of the three grading systems and assigning grades is provided on the web-based student study site (www.sagepub.com/mooreteachingk8). Before we finish this section on grading systems, complete Application Activity 6.2, which will help you develop your philosophy on grading.

FIGURE 6.6   Example of a Point Grading System

Student Work	Points
Assignments	250 (25 × 10 pts.)
Quizzes	150 (6 × 25 pts.)
Tests	300 (3 × 100 pts.)

Total points possible = 700

Grade Range
A 650 to 700
B 600 to 649
C 550 to 599
D 500 to 549
F 499 or less

IGURE 6.7   Example of a Weighted Grading System

Student Work	Weight
Homework assignments	25%
Quizzes (6)	25%
Tests (3)	50%
Total	**100%**

APPLICATION ACTIVITY 6.2 Grading

How do you plan to assign grades in your future classroom? What criteria will you use? Be ready to share.

SUMMARY

This chapter focused on student assessment and evaluation. The main points were as follows:

The Assessment and Evaluation Process

- Evaluating student learning is a complex endeavor that requires careful planning.

- Evaluation helps teachers key in on students' abilities, interests, attitudes, and needs in order to better teach and motivate them.

Evaluation Types

- The three types of evaluation are (1) preassessment, (2) formative assessment, and (3) summative assessment.

- Teachers use preassessment before instruction to assess students' prior knowledge and skills. Formative evaluation is used during instruction to monitor students' learning and adjust teaching. Summative assessment judges students' overall mastery of the intended outcomes.

Systems of Evaluation

- Evaluation can be competitive, noncompetitive, or performance based. Competitive evaluation compares students' efforts. Noncompetitive evaluation assesses individual's attainment of goals and objectives. Performance assessment requires students to demonstrate teacher-specified behaviors.

Information Sources

- Evaluation requires information obtained from cumulative records, personal contacts, analysis, journals, conferences, and testing.

Types of Tests

- Testing and grading represent two challenges for teachers.

- Standardized test results indicate how individual students and classrooms compare with local, regional, or national norm groups.

- Teacher-made test results provide information about students' attainment of classroom goals and objectives.

Authentic Assessment

- Authentic assessment requires students to demonstrate skills and competencies in real-world situations.

- The most widely used authentic assessment technique is the portfolio.

- Portfolios are a collection of learners' work over time.

- Student work samples can be used to offer credible evidence of student learning.

Grading Systems

- The mastery learning system, absolute grading system, and relative grading system are the principal grading systems commonly used in schools. A mastery standard uses growth portfolios to document students' progress towards eventually achieving mastery. An absolute standard compares student performance against an established set of criteria. The relative standard compares students with one another.

Assigning Final Grades

- Three systems are available to teachers for assigning grades: (1) the point system, (2) the weighted system, and (3) the percentage system.

DISCUSSION QUESTIONS AND ACTIVITIES

1. **Test-Bank Critique.** Examine and critique the test materials included in a published program of study for the subject area and grade level you would like to teach. What changes would you make before using the materials?

2. **Evaluation Purposes.** List five purposes of evaluation. Why should there be a match between the method of evaluation and the purpose of evaluation?

3. **Conferences.** Plan a general conference with a parent for the first time. Discuss what topics might be important to include in a conference.

4. **Evaluating Students.** Create a list of evaluation dos and don'ts. What evaluation practices are beneficial? Harmful? Explain.

TECH CONNECTION

Today's teachers use a wide array of technology and related software programs designed to support classroom assessment. Complete the following two application activities to help you identify ways technology can be used to support classroom assessment.

- Use one or more available search engines, and conduct a search for software programs relative to the following teacher tools:

  1. Electronic grade books

  2. Test generators

  3. Rubric generators

  4. Digital portfolios

  Select and describe the two or three teacher tools you think are the best. Be ready to share with your classmates.

- Access and analyze the rubrics on the following websites: www.rubrician.com and www.rubrics4teachers.com. Using the information gleaned from your analysis of the Internet rubrics, develop a rubric for a student project or activity of your choice. Share your rubric with the class.

CONNECTION WITH THE FIELD

1. **Teacher Interview.** Interview an elementary and middle school teacher.
   a. How important do they feel assessment is for promoting learning?
   b. How do they assess students' learning?

    c. Do they use standardized assessments? Teacher-made assessments? Authentic assessments?

    d. How do they assign grades?

STUDENT STUDY SITE

Visit the Student Study Site at **www.sagepub.com/mooreteachingk8** for these additional learning tools:

- Video clips
- Web resources
- Self quizzes
- E-Flashcards
- Full-text SAGE journal articles
- Portfolio Connection
- Licensing Preparation/Praxis Connection
- Part II View from the Classroom
- Part II Public View of Education

part III

Designing Instruction to Maximize Student Learning

In his play. *As You Like It*, Shakespeare penned, "All the world's a stage, and all the men and women merely players. . . . and one man in his time plays many parts. . . ." As we have discussed in Parts I and II, effective teachers play many roles in meeting students' academic needs: They create a climate conducive to learning; form a common vision of educational goals, objectives, and curriculum; and design standards-based lessons, instructional units, and assessments. The stage is set. Now the teachers bring the lesson "script" to life by drawing upon a repertoire of varied teaching strategies to teach students what they need to know in the way they learn best, or "as they like it." The four chapters in Part III focus on helping you develop the art of teaching so that you won't "break a leg" once you're center stage in your future classroom.

Just as amazing actors employ multiple strategies to evoke emotions, effective teachers use multiple methods to promote student learning through active involvement, thought-provoking discussions, and high-interest activities. Chapters 7, 8, and 9 explore the direct, authentic, and integrated teaching approaches to instructional delivery. Chapter 10 focuses upon developing students' critical thinking skills.

CHAPTER 7

Using Direct Teaching Methods

Not only is there an art in knowing a thing, but also a certain art in teaching it.

—Cicero

Before We Begin

One common teaching strategy is teacher presentation (telling and explaining). We've all experienced this "sage on the stage" approach. Sometimes the presentation is memorable; other times it's regrettable and forgettable. What makes a teacher presentation a Tony award-winning event? Be ready to compare your view with classmates.

OVERVIEW

Like any complex skill, it takes awhile for teachers to learn the craft of developing a set of actions and skills to produce learning. In this chapter, you will study direct instruction and exposition approaches to teaching integrated bodies of knowledge. Because direct instruction involves teacher–student interaction, you will learn the art of questioning as well. This chapter will teach you how to vary the levels and kinds of questions while using proven questioning techniques. These procedures will prevent prolonged pontifications.

OBJECTIVES

After completing your study of Chapter 7, you should be able to

- identify factors that should be considered in selecting teaching techniques and strategies;
- define and discuss the strengths and weaknesses of the **direct teaching** and **exposition teaching** approaches;
- describe ways to improve teacher presentations through effective questioning;
- identify and differentiate between the different categories of questions, as well as the levels within these categories;
- compare and contrast focusing, prompting, and probing questions; and
- define and explain the benefits derived from the use of the **redirecting** technique, **wait time**, and **halting time**.

Children often need help in learning how to learn. Basically, you will have three types of students in your classes: (1) students who can learn on their own, (2) students who need some help in learning, and (3) students who need a lot of help in learning. Your job will be to provide challenging activities for the independent learners while assisting students who need help in building new concepts. You can accomplish this by making information meaningful, helping students develop learning and study skills, and teaching students how to apply or **transfer** knowledge to other areas. You need to carefully select the methods and procedures that will deliver the content in such a way that all students can master the instructional objectives. If you just arbitrarily choose these strategies, then effective teaching won't take place, and students won't learn.

How do you decide which teaching strategy is best for a particular lesson? Experience can often be the best basis for selection. You should also consider the students' needs, age, intellectual abilities, physical/mental characteristics, and attention spans to select strategies that best serve students' needs as well as the lesson's purpose and content.

Some strategies emphasize focused, teacher-directed instruction, whereas others involve students actively in their own learning. Thus, there are two major ways of delivering instruction: (1) directly or (2) indirectly. The direct delivery of instruction ("telling and explaining") is the "traditional" or didactic mode, in which knowledge is passed on through the teacher, the textbook, or both. The indirect avenue of instruction ("showing and doing") provides students with access to information and experiences whereby they develop knowledge and skills.

Direct instruction is an effective way to help students master fundamental facts, rules, formulas, or sequences. Although it is an efficient way to provide information quickly, it does not develop students' higher level thinking skills. In contrast, indirect instructional strategies involve students in authentic activities that require them to develop ideas, test hypotheses, make generalizations, and discuss results. This allows students to discover patterns and relationships in their learning and knowledge and to develop their critical thinking skills.

Although instructional strategies can be categorized as direct or indirect, the distinctions are not always clear-cut. For example, a teacher may provide information through a **teacher presentation** (a direct instructional strategy) and then use small-group discussions to help students process the information (an indirect instructional strategy).

How much time should be devoted to each of the two modes of instruction? The amount of instructional time varies, depending on the subject, grade level, students, time, and material available, as well as the teacher's and school's philosophies. Experience suggests, however, a compelling relationship between method of instruction and student retention, depicted in Table 7.1, in which a blend of "telling" and "showing" techniques results in

TABLE 7.1 Relationship Between Method of Instruction and Retention (in Percentages)

Methods of Instruction	Recall 3 Hours Later	Recall 3 Days Later
Telling when used alone	70	10
Showing when used alone	72	20
Blend of telling and showing	85	65

greater retention. Furthermore, varying the strategy can positively affect students' motivation to learn. It is a fortunate situation when you have a choice of equally effective strategies for achieving your instructional intent. In such instances, it is possible to choose a method and procedure (strategy) that will foster motivation, improve classroom control, or cost less to implement. Indeed, you should become skilled in combining various strategies into a total lesson package.

The ultimate goal of teaching and learning is to develop students' ability to apply knowledge and skills acquired in one situation (such as the classroom) to new situations. For example, students should be able to apply their knowledge of measurement to cook new recipes at home. This ability is referred to as transfer. Teachers can enhance the likelihood of transfer by making the original learning experience as similar as possible to the situation to which information or skills will be applied. For example, primary teachers use learning stations replicating real-life situations such as a doctor's office or grocery store. Older students can apply map-reading skills by creating maps of their communities or homes. Of course, another means for accomplishing transfer is through learning: Students cannot use information they do not thoroughly understand. Effective teachers motivate students by providing authentic reasons for them to learn the information so they can apply it in their everyday lives.

The remainder of this chapter will elaborate on the direct modes of instruction: direct teaching, exposition teaching, and exposition with interaction teaching. We will review the more indirect, authentic modes and procedures in Chapters 8 and 10 and some integrated teaching methods in Chapter 9.

DIRECT TEACHING

Direct teaching is a teacher-centered, skill-building instructional model with the teacher as the primary information provider. Teachers disseminate facts, rules, information, or action sequences through presentations, explanations, examples, and opportunities for student practice and feedback. The direct teaching format calls for teacher–student interactions involving questions and answers, review and practice, and the correction of student errors. This strategy works best for establishing a common foundation of knowledge in skill-based subjects such as reading, writing, mathematics, grammar, computer literacy, and the factual parts of science and history. The direct teaching approach is especially effective when teaching very young children, struggling students, or students who are learning new or difficult concepts.

Video Link 7.1:
Watch a video about instructional strategies.

Direct teaching lessons usually follow a standard sequence of events. First, teachers tell students what they are going to learn, review prerequisite knowledge and skills, and connect the new topic with students' prior knowledge or experiences. Then they teach the content, provide opportunities for students to practice the skills and process the information, and assess students' learning. This is very similar to Madeline Hunter's "Mastery Teaching" approach (see Chapter 5). The general lesson structure varies according to the subject area and grade level. Primary teachers may complete the entire process in one instructional period, using informal assessments to assess students' learning. Intermediate and middle school teachers may take several days to complete the instructional sequence, ending with a formal test or quiz.

REFLECTIONS ON TEACHER PRACTICE 7.1: Motivating Students to Read

1. Why should reading be an important part of the curriculum in all subject areas?

2. How can students be motivated to read?

I go to the public library every three weeks and check out high interest picture books that center around whatever I am currently teaching, picture books that are nonfiction, for the most part, and appropriate for middle school students. Lots of DK books, Science Encyclopedias, all-in-one volumes, and Seymour books. They sit in a laundry basket at the front of my room as resources to read.

Here's my one tip that I have used and found wildly successful. Every once in a while, we do a science "read around day." On that day, I take those books from the basket and put them in the middle of the lab tables. When I say, "go"! They have to select a book and read until I say stop. Usually it's about 3–4 minutes. Then they send their book to the next person. This continues until all four people have read the books at that table.

They don't have to start at the beginning; they can just look at pictures, or use the index to find something that interests them. From here each table interviews each person on what they learned, or what they liked. From here we switch that pile of books with another table and continue with the process.

They love it, and they hate it. They want to read more of at least one book and they can't because it has rotated around. Well, let me tell you, books fly out of the basket in extra time before class, or if they finish early. The afterglow only last a couple of days, but it works. And sometimes, oh how I love those sometimes, someone will ask to have a library pass so they can go see if that book is in our library or if the media specialist can help them interlibrary loan it.

That's what I've tried in science. Now math, well, that's another story. I'm still working on it—mostly working to find read-alouds beyond the standards.

—*Marsha, middle-level teacher*

Please visit the Student Study site at **www.sagepub.com/mooreteachingk8** *for additional discussion questions and assignments.*

Here is a brief description of the components of a direct teaching instructional sequence:

1. *State Learning Objectives and Orient Students to the Lesson.* Tell students the lesson goals, objectives, and teacher expectations in student-friendly terms. Help students establish a mental set or attitude of readiness to learn. This is the set induction.

2. *Review Prerequisites.* Go over any skills or concepts students will need to understand the lesson. Provide advance organizers to give students a framework for understanding the new material.

3. *Present New Material.* Give concrete, varied examples and nonexamples, demonstrate concepts, and present material in small steps. Provide an outline when material is complex.

4. *Provide Guided Practice and Conduct Learning Probes.* Pose questions and give students practice problems to assess their level of understanding and to correct misconceptions. Have students summarize new information in their own words. Reteach as necessary.

5. *Provide Independent Practice.* Give students an opportunity to practice new skills or use new information through independent activities or cooperative group work.

6. *Assess Performance and Provide Feedback.* Review students' independent practice or give a quiz. Give feedback on correct answers, and reteach skills as needed.

7. *Provide Distributed Practice and Review.* Give students assignments to complete in class or at home to provide distributed practice on the new material.

Keep in mind that not all elements of the direct teaching strategy belong in every lesson, although they will occur in a typical instructional unit composed of several lessons. Complete Application Activity 7.1 to explore your thoughts on the implementation of the direct instruction strategy.

APPLICATION ACTIVITY 7.1 Direct Instruction

List the sequence of steps that you feel should characterize a direct instruction lesson at the grade level you expect to teach. How does your sequence of activities compare with the seven steps presented in the text? What is your rationale behind any differences? Share your steps with several classmates. Do they agree?

Let's now look at the various components of direct instruction in more detail. Expository teaching (telling and explaining) and questioning hold key roles in the success of direct instruction.

EXPOSITION TEACHING

Exposition teaching is considered to be the best way to communicate large amounts of information in a short period of time. In this approach, an authority—teacher, textbook, film, or computer—presents information with limited, overt interaction between the authority and the students.

Presentation: Teaching as Telling and Explaining

Teacher presentation (telling and explaining) is probably the most widely used exposition teaching method at the elementary and middle school levels. Teachers tell, explain, and share knowledge. Usually the instructional content comes directly from the textbook. The "teacher talk" is peppered with question-and-answer sessions to help students consolidate and organize the new information. Virtually every teacher employs teacher presentation to some degree, and some use it almost exclusively. Teacher presentation is similar to lecturing. However, lecturing is more like giving a speech on some subject, whereas a presentation is an informative talk made by a teacher.

Teacher presentations vary in length and formality. They can last for an entire class period or for just a few minutes, depending upon the content, students' age, and teacher's teaching style. Formal presentations allow no interruptions or questions; less formal presentations invite periodic student participation. Though often criticized by some educators, the teacher presentation does possess some unique strengths.

Strengths of the Teacher Presentation

The teacher presentation is an excellent way to set up an atmosphere for learning about a new topic, to create a frame of reference, to introduce a unit, or to provide a focus for student activities. Moreover, a short presentation can effectively wrap up an activity, unit, or lesson. Finally, a teacher presentation is time-efficient because teachers use their planning time organizing content information instead of devising instructional procedures. Thus, they have ample opportunity to collect related materials, assemble them into a meaningful framework, and present the information to students in a relatively short period of time. The teacher simply plans a presentation for the desired length of time.

Weaknesses of the Teacher Presentation

Presentations have several serious flaws, however. First, because they are teacher-centered they promote passive learning with very low student involvement. Students are expected, and even encouraged, to sit quietly, listen, and perhaps take notes. Thus, presentations are not a good way to teach younger students or to help students develop skills in thinking, problem solving, and creativity. Indeed, because presentations tend to focus on the lowest level of cognition, understanding and transfer are often limited.

Second, presentations are often so boring that students are inattentive and undermotivated, especially if aural learning is not their preferred learning style. For this reason—except in unusual cases—very little of a presentation information is retained by students. The lack

"It's difficult to reprimand some children for inattention in class."

SOURCE: Created by Martha Campbell.

of student involvement can also cause students to find other ways to occupy their minds, which can lead to student misbehaviors. Therefore, wise teachers vary instructional strategies several times an hour. Teacher presentation is just one teaching tool in their repertoire.

Planning the Presentation

Teachers need to carefully plan presentations to pique and maintain students' interest while accomplishing lesson objectives. Although teacher presentations are ever-present in today's classrooms, they should be used judiciously, especially with younger students, and mixed with other appropriate methods. The most successful presentations are relatively short. Even older, brighter students probably won't listen to a presentation for more than about 10 minutes. Therefore, alternate short presentations with other engaging activities. For example, a teacher presentation about the water cycle (with time allotted for each activity) might be as follows:

1. Have a quick talk about the craziest precipitation students have experienced (5 minutes)

2. Share lesson objectives; present the water cycle (10 minutes)*

3. Show a film or Internet clip of the water cycle (10 minutes)

4. Discuss the film (10 minutes)*

5. Present a physical demonstration of the water cycle (10 minutes)*

6. Have student teams create a visual representation of the water cycle (30 minutes)

7. Have the students do a "gallery walk" to view everyone's efforts (5 minutes)

8. Wrap up and review (5 minutes)*

---

*Denotes activities where the teacher is presenting

Notice that this plan intersperses short teacher presentations with other engaging activities (discussion, media, demonstration, group work). Only part of the time is devoted to presenting; most of the time encourages student involvement.

As you learned in Chapter 5, you should begin your presentation with a quality set induction that arouses students' interest, hooks into previous learning, creates a mind-set for learning, and establishes a framework for the information you will present. Share your academic and behavioral expectations in student-friendly language. Use visual aids—a whiteboard, overhead projection, SMART Board, handout, or PowerPoint. Keep students involved taking notes or completing advanced organizers. Finally, create a quality closure to review the major points of your presentation.

In summary, a good presentation must be well planned if it is to be clear and persuasive. To help you remember the importance of including a set induction and closure in your presentation, try following this presentation planning formula:

- Tell students what you are going to tell them.

- Tell them.

- Tell them what you have told them.

The use of instructional materials and media enhances most presentations and stimulates student interest.

The proper application of this formula will result in a logical, well-organized presentation with a firm introduction and a well-planned wrap-up.

Presentation Delivery

Effective presentations maintain student interest and attention from beginning to end. Factors such as the tempo, audiovisual aids, **stimulus variation**, and language can impact students' interest and attention.

Pace your presentation to maintain student interest without causing information overload. Periodically check student comprehension; adjust your pace accordingly. Speak in an expressive, enthusiastic voice tone that all students can hear. Use stimulus variation techniques, such as gestures, pauses, enthusiasm, and teacher movement, to maintain students' attention.

Finally, make regular eye contact with every student in your classroom. This maintains students' attention, promotes positive teacher–student relationships, and decreases misbehaviors. Eye contact gives students the feeling that you are addressing each of them personally. Indeed, watching students' body language provides you with valuable feedback on how well a presentation is being received and lets you know if it's time to switch strategies to keep students interested.

Enhancing Direct Instruction With Technology

The effectiveness and quality of direct instruction can be greatly improved through the use of technology. By integrating technology into instruction, teacher presentations come alive and teachers are better able to capture and keep the attention of students while presenting current information in novel ways. Indeed, make your presentations as multisensory and multimedia as is feasible through the use of interactive videos, print media, photographs, films, computer graphics, and hypermedia.

PowerPoint and SMART Boards are probably the best-known teacher presentation tools available. PowerPoint is an ideal tool for creating memorable classroom presentations. For example, you can use PowerPoint to create study shows of vocabulary words that students need to learn, run study shows with words appearing along with pictures and definitions (and sound, if appropriate) to help students remember meanings, animate words and graphics, show QuickTime movies, give instructions on adding two

---

GABRIELLA: A REFLECTIVE CASE STUDY

Gabriella sighed inwardly and looked at the clock again. It was 8:23 a.m. Mr. Tockalott was firmly entrenched in his monologue about the three branches of government. His drone was punctuated by the sound of a frustrated fly trying to exit through a closed window. Gabriella wished she could escape, too. She busied herself by doodling in her spiral notebook, hoping he would think she was taking notes. She already knew the material, though, because she'd finished her homework assignment. Good grief! Now Mr. Tockalott was reading from the book! Ticktock, ticktock! Mr. Tockalott sure does talk a LOT! Hermione raised her hand (like she always did) to ask a question, but Mr. Tockalott didn't notice. Ticktalk, ticktalk. Gabriella watched the fly circle then land on Mr. Tockalott's toupee. She watched, entranced, as it made its way toward his right sideburn. Mr. Tockalott caught her eye and smiled, thinking she was focusing on his monologue. At 8:50, the bell rang. Free at last!

1. Why was Gabriella having difficulty focusing in class?

2. How could Mr. Tockalott improve his teacher presentation?

one-digit numbers without regrouping, teach the concepts of speed and motion, and even give tests.

SMART Boards are an excellent way to display PowerPoints and various other technology applications. Teachers or students can write on the SMART Board screen and save the notations as typed or handwritten text for future reference. Students can also use interactive software that requires them to group objects, select objects, and activate links. They can take quizzes using response systems and questions displayed on the SMART Board screen. The uses of PowerPoint and SMART Board technology in presenting information and teaching are unlimited.

Table 7.2 summarizes the different direct teaching and the exposition teaching methods. Review the summary and complete Reflect and Apply Exercise 7.1.

TABLE 7.2 Exposition Teaching

Method	Descriptions
Direct teaching	Teacher controls instruction by presenting information and giving directions to the class; associated with teacher-centered, teacher-controlled classrooms; an instructional procedure for teaching content in the most efficient, straightforward way
Presentation	Teacher presents information, with limited overt interaction with students
Illustrated talk	Teacher gives a presentation that relies heavily on visual aids to convey ideas to students
Teaching lecture	Teacher gives an oral presentation that allows some participation by the students
Textbook teaching	Teacher talks about and explains material presented in the textbook

REFLECT AND APPLY EXERCISE 7.1: Teacher Presentations

Reflect

- Reflect on the teaching methods used by your past teachers. Did they use teacher presentations? Were they effective? Why or why not?

Apply

- What are some things you want to keep in mind when making teacher presentations in your future classroom? How will you ensure you're meeting the needs of your students?

- How much time should be devoted to direct teaching and to indirect teaching at the grade level you expect to teach? Which mode of delivery do you favor? Why?

EXPOSITION WITH INTERACTION TEACHING

Exposition with interaction teaching is a two-phase instructional strategy. First, information is disseminated by teacher presentations or assigned readings. Second, the teacher uses questions to assess students' understanding of the material. Because this strategy requires teachers to be knowledgeable, effective questioners, let's analyze this important teaching skill in greater detail.

The Art of Questioning

Presentations need not be passive learning. They can be made stimulating.

Proper questioning is a sophisticated art at which many of us are less than proficient even though we have asked thousands of questions in our lives. Research indicates that questioning is second only to telling and explaining in popularity as a teaching method. Teachers spend anywhere from 35% to 50% of their instructional time conducting questioning sessions. Effective questioning can

- pique students' interest and curiosity,
- motivate students,
- emphasize key points,
- clarify and connect concepts,
- develop critical thinking skills and problem-solving abilities,
- assess students' knowledge and preparation, and
- review and summarize previous lessons.

Questioning is an important way to capitalize on students' cognitive potential by developing their reflective, metacognitive, and critical thinking skills. Effective questioning activities promote problem-solving and reasoning skills, provide a structure for examining ideas, and assess students' mastery of the intended learning outcomes.

Emphasizing the art of quality questioning to develop students' higher order thinking skills is not a new concept, but it is a very important one! Most students don't score well on tests that require them to recognize assumptions, draw inferences, or evaluate arguments. They can develop these skills, however, if they are taught *how* to think through careful questioning. Answering challenging questions enhances students' self-esteem and motivates them to participate. Therefore, careful questioners select a variety of carefully worded questions representing the full spectrum of cognitive thinking levels and follow-up on students' responses. Let's explore the different levels of questions these careful questioners use.

Levels of Questions

Researchers have verified that teachers ask hundreds of questions a day. Most of the questions are teacher-generated and fact-oriented. Choosing the right types of questions to ask students is necessary to spark thought-provoking answers and engage students in productive discussions. By asking challenging questions, teachers call upon students to explore ideas and apply what they have learned to novel situations. Furthermore, using different types of questions encourages students to think in different and unique ways.

There are two main kinds of questions: **narrow questions** and **broad questions**. Narrow questions solicit factual recall or one right answer. They limit the discussion because once the answer is given the teacher moves on to another question. Broad questions require students to reach beyond simple memory to defend or explain their positions. There can be diverse or limitless answers. Broad questions develop students' critical thinking skills, elicit a range of responses by multiple students, increase classroom communication, and stir discussion and debate in the classroom. Both narrow and broad questions contribute to the learning process. Unfortunately, many teachers rely too heavily on narrow questions; they don't realize the importance of using broad questions as well.

Artful questioners adapt the level of their questions to assess the depth and breadth of students' learning. Therefore, they ask questions that reveal whether students have gained specific knowledge, as well as questions that stimulate the thinking process. Because thinking can take place at several levels of sophistication, it is important that teachers learn to classify—and ask—questions at these different levels.

Although many effective question classification systems have been developed, this text focuses upon the two systems that benefit teachers most in the classroom. The first widely used system classifies questions as either *convergent* or *divergent*; the second categorizes questions according to the mental operation that students use in answering them.

Convergent and Divergent Questions

One of the simplest ways of classifying questions is to determine whether they are convergent or divergent. **Convergent questions** allow for only a few right responses, whereas **divergent questions** allow for many correct responses.

Questions regarding concrete facts that have been learned and committed to memory are convergent. Most who, what, and where questions are also classified as convergent:

"What is the square root of 225?"

"Who was the 43rd president of the United States?"

"What is the chief export of Brazil?"

"Mirror, mirror, on the wall, who's the most sensitive, open,
student-centered, and innovative teacher of all?"

SOURCE: Created by Ford Button.

"How many legs does an insect have?"

"What should you do before crossing the street?"

Convergent questions may also require students to recall or analyze information to arrive at *one expected* correct answer. Thus, the following questions would also be classified as convergent:

"Based on our discussion, what could be causing global warming?"

"Explain the process of photosynthesis."

"Based on our definition of a preposition, can you name three prepositions?"

"Name one animal whose name begins with the letter C."

Most alternate-response questions, such as yes/no and true/false questions, would also be classified as convergent because the responses available to students are limited.

Conversely, questions calling for opinions, hypotheses, or evaluation are divergent because many possible correct responses may be given:

"Why do you suppose we need houses?"

"What would be a good name for this painting?"

"Can you give me a sentence in which this word is used correctly?"

"What did Shel Silverstein's *The Giving Tree* teach you about life?"

Divergent questions should be used frequently because they encourage students to think, personalize their responses, and participate in the learning process. Convergent questions, however, are equally important because they establish that students have the background knowledge and skills necessary to deal with higher-level divergent questions. Therefore, it is generally desirable to use convergent questions initially and then move toward divergent questions.

Mental Operation Questions

Based on the work of J. P. Guilford and Benjamin Bloom, Moore (2007) developed the **Mental Operation system** for classifying questions. Table 7.3 shows the relationship between the Mental Operation system, Guilford's Structure of the Intellect model, and Bloom's (1956) *Taxonomy of Educational Objectives*. The Mental Operation system is basically a four-category system that combines the cognitive and memory categories of the Guilford model into a single factual category. In addition, it combines four of Bloom's categories of higher order thinking into two categories (see Chapter 4). The categories of questions that make up the Mental Operation system are factual, empirical, productive, and evaluative.

TABLE 7.3 Categories of Questions

Mental Operation Questions	Guilford's Structure of the Intellect	Bloom's Taxonomy
1. Factual	Cognitive/memory	Knowledge/comprehension
2. Empirical	Convergent thinking	Application/analysis
3. Productive	Divergent thinking	Synthesis
4. Evaluative	Evaluative thinking	Evaluation

Factual questions test the student's recall or recognition of information that has been committed to memory through some form of repetition or rehearsal. Some examples of factual questions are listed here:

"Ginger, what should you do in case you catch on fire?"

"Joe, tell us the syllable count formula for a haiku."

"Which of these is the chemical formula for water?"

"Who was the first president of the United States?"

Empirical questions require that students integrate or analyze remembered or given information and supply a single, correct *predictable* answer. Empirical questions are also narrow questions because although they may involve more thinking, students are expected to arrive at a correct, predictable answer. Some examples of empirical questions include the following:

"Based on our study of California, what conditions led to its becoming a state?"

"Given that this circle has a radius of 5 centimeters, what is its area?"

"According to the information provided in the text, what is the most economical source of energy presently being used in the United States?"

"Who are the main characters in *The Cat in the Hat*?"

Productive questions require students to use their imaginations, develop unique ideas, and think creatively. They have no single, correct answer. Indeed, it may be impossible to predict what the answer will be. Students still need to know basic information to answer productive questions, but they are prompted to go beyond the simple recall of facts. Following are some examples of productive questions:

"Describe ways you can make a new student feel welcome."

"What changes would we see in our school if we were to eliminate rules?"

"What are some possible solutions to the problem of world hunger?"

"What do you suppose Norman Rockwell was trying to communicate through this painting?"

Finally, **evaluative questions** require that students put a value on something or make some kind of judgment. These open-ended questions require students to use related information while applying internal or external criteria to make a judgment. The responses to evaluative questions can often be predicted or limited by the number of choices. For example, the question of "Which of these two short stories is the best?" limits the responses to two, whereas the question "What is the best automobile made today?" allows a variety of responses. Other examples of evaluative questions are these:

"Who was our greatest scientist?"

"How would you rate our success in controlling drugs in our city?"

"Which community helper's job is the most important?"

"Are Native Americans portrayed accurately in the movies?"

Because these questions call on students to make judgments based on internal criteria, all answers are acceptable. When student responses are formally evaluated, however, teachers must establish external criteria that they can evaluate, confirm, or refute. They should couple evaluative questions with empirical or productive questions that require students to provide a rationale for their judgment. Follow up the evaluative questions.

Refer to the Mental Operation system of classifying questions (Table 7.4) to ensure you help students develop their critical thinking skills by asking a full spectrum of questions instead of just factual-level questions, as many teachers do.

| TABLE 7.4 | Levels of Classroom Questions | |

Category	Type of Thinking	Examples
Factual	Student simply recalls information "Who was . . ." "What did the text say . . ."	"Define . . ."
Empirical	Student integrates and analyzes given or recalled information "Explain in your own words . . ." "Calculate the . . ."	"Compare . . ."
Productive	Student thinks creatively and imaginatively and produces unique idea or response "What's a good name for . . ." "How could we . . ."	"What will life be like . . ."
Evaluative	Student makes judgments or expresses values "Why do you favor this . . ." "Who is the best . . ."	"Which painting is best?"

Questions can often give a lesson life and arouse student interest.

Types of Questions

Effective teachers match the type of question to the specific instructional purpose. For example, they may want to ask questions to determine students' preparedness, to increase student involvement and interaction, to clarify conceptual development, or to stimulate student awareness. These purposes call for different types of questions.

Rhetorical Questions

Teachers ask rhetorical questions to emphasize a point or to capture students' interest. They do not necessarily expect an answer, however! The question can be effective as an attention getter at the beginning of a lesson or to maintain interest throughout the lesson. Some possible examples of rhetorical questions might include the following:

"What has science done for us?"
"Can fish drown?"

"Is it possible to exist in this world without leaving a carbon footprint?"

"Is establishing a colony on Mars really possible during our lifetimes?"

A rhetorical question normally does not require an answer from students, but the teacher may answer it if desired.

Focusing Questions

Focusing questions, which may be factual, empirical, productive, or evaluative, are used to direct student attention. Teachers use focusing questions to motivate and arouse students' interest at the start of a lesson or during the lesson, to stimulate student involvement, and to check students' understanding of lesson material throughout a lesson.

Was the assigned chapter read by students? There's no use in discussing the material if it wasn't read! Did the students learn and understand the material? Can students apply the information? Focusing questions can provide valuable information regarding these concerns. Ask factual questions to check on basic knowledge at the beginning of or during a lesson. Use empirical questions to have students figure out correct solutions for problems related to assignments or issues being discussed. Pose productive and evaluative questions for motivating and stimulating thinking and interest in the topic.

When opening a lesson or discussion with a question, it is good practice to use a productive or evaluative question that focuses on the upcoming topic. The question should arouse students' interest and thinking:

"What do you suppose would happen if I were to drop these two objects at the same time?"

"How could we test the hypothesis suggested by the results?"

"Should we do away with taxes in the United States?"

These questions should then be followed with questions at all levels to develop understanding and to maintain interest.

Prompting Questions

Prompting questions use clues that help students answer questions or correct initially inaccurate responses. Thus, teachers reword the original question and add clues. Consider this example of a prompting questioning sequence:

Teacher: Can you give me an example of a noun, Pat?

Pat: No.

Teacher: Well, let's see if we can figure it out. What words are nouns?

Pat: Names of persons?

Teacher:	What else?
Pat:	Places and things!
Teacher:	Right! So, can you give me an example of a noun?
Pat:	[*Pause*] Run.
Teacher:	Is run the name of a person, place, or thing?
Pat:	[*Pause*] No.
Teacher:	So, can you give me an example of a person, place, or thing?
Pat:	[*Pause*] Chicago. It is a place!
Teacher:	Very good, Pat.

Using prompting questions sets students up for success, resulting in even greater participation.

Probing Questions

Sometimes students' responses are incorrect; other times they are correct but lack sufficient depth. In such cases, teachers use **probing questions** to correct an initial response, elicit clarification, develop critical awareness, or refocus a response. Students are required to rethink, revise, or provide additional supportive details. Here are some examples of probing questions:

"What do you mean by the terms . . . ?"

"Would you say that in another way?"

"Could you elaborate on those two points?"

"Please explain that point more fully."

Asking students to justify their answers fosters their critical awareness. This also can be accomplished with probing questions. Probing questions that could be used to develop critical awareness include these:

"What is your factual basis for these beliefs?"

"Why do you believe that?"

"What are you assuming when you make that statement?"

"What are your reasons for those assumptions?"

Finally, teachers may want to probe to refocus a correct, satisfactory student response to a related issue. Examples of questions that could serve this function follow:

"Let's look at your answer with respect to this new information."

"Can you relate your answer to yesterday's discussion?"

"What implications does this conclusion have for . . . ?"

"Can you relate Mary's earlier answer to this issue?"

These different types of questions are invaluable teaching tools. When used effectively, they can increase student participation and involve students in their own learning.

Questioning Techniques

Teachers enhance the quality of students' responses by using redirection, wait time, halting time, and **reinforcement**. Let's now learn more about these questioning techniques.

Redirecting

Redirecting increases student participation by asking students to react to another student's response. Because this technique requires several correct responses to a single question, the question must be divergent, productive, or evaluative. The following is an example of how a teacher can redirect a question:

Teacher: We have now studied many of the U.S. presidents. Which president do you think made the greatest contributions to the nation?

[*Pause. Several hands go up.*] Cindi?

Cindi: Lincoln.

Teacher: Jeff, do you agree?

Jeff: I think it's Washington.

Teacher: Mary, what is your opinion?

Mary: John Kennedy.

Please note that teachers who use redirecting correctly do not react to the student responses; they simply redirect the question to another student. Thus, this technique leads to greater student participation and involvement and, consequently, to greater learning and increased interest.

The redirecting technique can also be used effectively with students who are nonvolunteers. It is important to remember, however, that nonvolunteers should never be forced to answer; rather, they should be given the opportunity to contribute to the discussion. In addition, teachers should give nonvolunteers ample time to consider a response. This is called wait time. Let's now look at the appropriate use of wait time in questioning.

Video Link 7.2:
Watch a video
about wait time.

Wait Time

Students need time to ponder possible responses to posed questions. Higher level questions require even more time to process. However, the typical pattern of questioning in the average classroom is nothing more than a question-and-answer period. The teacher asks a question, the student answers, the teacher moves to the next student and asks a question, the student answers, the teacher moves to the next student, and so on. The average teacher waits only about 1 second for a student response. Increasing the wait time to 3 to 5 seconds increases the number of successful, thoughtful responses; builds student confidence; and prompts students to ask more questions and respond.

Basically, there are two types of wait time. *Wait time 1* is the time provided for the first student response to a question. *Wait time 2* is the total time a teacher waits for all students to respond to the same question or for students to respond to other students' responses. Wait time 2 may involve several minutes. To more actively engage students, teachers must learn to increase their wait time tolerance, so students have more opportunities to organize their thoughts.

Halting Time

When presenting complex material, teachers need to stop periodically to give students time to process the information. No questions are asked, and no student comments are elicited. In using the halting time technique, teachers present some complex material or complicated directions and then stop momentarily, so students have time to consider the information or carry out the directions. During this pause, they silently scan the class to monitor students' reactions. If students seem confused, teachers rephrase the explanation or repeat the directions.

Reinforcement

Once teachers have received an acceptable response to a question, they must react to that response. Some accept the response without comment while others offer praise for a job well done. The teachers' reinforcement, or pattern of positive reaction, powerfully impacts the direction of the classroom interaction.

General praise often encourages students to participate. Teachers reward students' correct answers with nonverbal behaviors such as smiles or nods as well as phrases such as "Fine answer," "Great," "What an outstanding idea," and "Super." Specific praise is even better—"It was interesting how you built upon Greg's answer by saying . . . " or "I had never considered it in that light before, Sylvester. That is a creative perspective." Teachers need to vary their reinforcements so that students perceive it to be genuine.

Reinforcement is often a good idea, but using it too frequently or at the wrong time can negate the benefits of using wait time. If reinforcement is given too early in an answering sequence, other students may decide not to respond because they fear their answer could not match an earlier response. After all, didn't the teacher say the earlier response was "great"? Rather than give reinforcement early in the questioning–answering sequence, teachers should allow as many students as possible to respond to the question, then reinforce all of them for their contributions. They can always return to the best answer for further comment.

Through the Eyes of an Expert

Direct Instruction Involving Student Response Systems

Student response systems are handheld student devices that promote engagement between students and the teacher. One of the purposes of this technology is to help teachers appropriately pace their instruction to maximize student achievement and not be surprised by the level of understanding of their students. They allow students to submit answers to questions posed by the teacher during a lecture or discussion, and the instantaneous posting of results allows the teacher to gauge student understanding or misconceptions.

Through direct instruction, the teacher is often providing content in a more traditional approach such as lecturing. Student response systems allow teachers to use traditional methods such as lecturing while increasing student engagement and therefore student achievement. In many classrooms where the teacher is using direct instruction, attempts of asking questions that will trigger feedback from the students often fail. The students are usually embarrassed about stating an incorrect answer in front of their peers or they are disengaged from the lesson altogether. Student response systems allow all students to respond anonymously with only class totals being displayed. The teacher is then able to analyze the level of understanding on a particular concept within a matter of seconds.

This technology can transform traditional direct instruction methods! It adds the engagement component which is often missing. Students are more likely to pay attention knowing that they will be asked to input an answer or opinion on a particular topic at any moment. However, they are not paying attention to the lesson due to the fear of being called on. Rather, they are paying attention because they have an active role in the learning process.

SOURCE: Meagan Musselman, PhD, assistant professor of Middle School Education, Murray State University, former middle school math and science teacher, National Board Certified Teacher. Used with permission.

Tips on Questioning

With sufficient practice, teachers can learn the art of questioning. The improper use of questioning can negatively affect learning. Teachers who strive for higher level questions, for example, may lose interest in asking the just as important bread-and-butter memory questions. They may even tend to cater to the capacities of superior students. Let's now look at some questioning tips that may help you avoid questioning pitfalls in your future classroom.

Create a climate conducive to communication. Use eye contact, proximity, and facial expressions demonstrating you are truly listening to students' responses. Model the importance of respecting different perspectives. Encourage all students to participate in the discussion, even if they aren't adept at answering difficult questions.

Ask clearly stated questions, give sufficient wait time, then designate who should answer. As usual, there are exceptions to this rule. When you call on an inattentive student, it is often wise to designate the individual first, so that the student is sure to hear the question. Similarly, you should call the name first of slow or shy students so that they can prepare themselves.

Distribute your questions fairly. Avoid directing all questions to a few bright students. Also avoid going by alphabetical order or row by row because students will only pay attention when it is their turn. Use a random process instead, such as drawing name cards out of a container. Return students' cards to the container before asking the next question so they see they might have to respond again in the near future.

Do not ask more than one question at a time. Asking too many questions at once often confuses students. Simultaneous questions permit no time to think, and when several questions are asked, students are not sure which question to answer first.

Finally, ask questions representing all levels of difficulty from basic knowledge level to evaluation and synthesis. Also, use prompting and probing questions to help students think more thoroughly about and modify their inaccurate responses. Artful questioning will increase student involvement, develop student's critical thinking skills, and reinforce student success.

The key to the effective use of exposition with interaction is good questioning. Therefore, you must refine your ability to think, plan, and ask questions throughout your lessons.

REFLECTIONS ON TEACHER PRACTICE 7.2: Answering Questions

1. How can you encourage students to find their own answers to all questions?

2. Why is it important that teachers work on improving students' listening skills? How are listening and questioning related?

I teach sixth grade and was going home each and every day mentally wiped out because I think I answered 9,000 questions. Questions like "Should I put my name on my paper?" (Of course.) "Can I write in red pen?" (Never.) I started calling these "self explanatory questions" because they pertained to policy that they should have had under control by now—and I think some of them just liked to hear themselves talk. Anyway, I started with discussing strategies of how they could find answers to their questions before asking me—basically just wanting to work on their listening skills (Hey, isn't that a standard?!) I even went so far as to give them each three tickets for the day—if they had a question to ask me (not content related) that they could have found the answer for themselves, I took a ticket away in exchange for an answer. Some kids didn't even make it through first period.

As a result, I had a parent COMPLETELY flip out and call our assistant principal. She totally supported me to this parent, but I had to write a "letter of explanation" about why I had to use the ticket system in my classroom. I made sure that I filled it with things like "listening is a skill that will benefit all students" and "by answering fewer self-explanatory questions I have more time for one-on-one instruction with students" and so forth and so on. It just made me angry that they would even waste time questioning it. At any rate, the ticket system has worked. If students make it to the end of the day with a ticket, they get a piece of candy. Now, we have stretched it to three tickets for the week—make it to Friday and you get candy. My days go much smoother!

—*Michelle, elementary teacher*

 Please visit the Student Study site at **www.sagepub.com/mooreteachingk8** *for additional discussion questions and assignments.*

SOURCE: Reprinted with permission from ProTeacher, a professional community for elementary school teachers (www.proteacher.net).

This concludes our discussion of various direct teaching methods. Apply the concepts developed in this chapter in Application Activity 7.2 and complete Reflect and Apply Exercise 7.2.

APPLICATION ACTIVITY 7.2 Direct Instruction

Teachers devote a lot of time and effort developing plans, activities, and instructional resources to maximize learning. Create a two-column chart of the direct instructional strategies covered in Chapter 7, and indicate your feelings as to the value of each strategy at the grade level you expect to teach. Use these three categories to evaluate each strategy for your chart: (1) appropriate and useful, (2) limited usefulness, and (3) not appropriate and not useful.

REFLECT AND APPLY EXERCISE 7.2: Questioning in the Classroom

Reflect

- Why is questioning an art?
- Are you a good questioner? How can you improve your skills?
- What are the strengths and weaknesses of the exposition with interaction instructional approach?
- Should teachers use a question classification system? Why?

Apply

- What question classification system do you plan to use at the grade level you expect to teach? Why?
- Describe the different types of questions that will be most useful for you at the grade level you expect to teach.

SUMMARY

This chapter focused on direct teaching methods. The main points were as follows:

- There are two basic approaches to teaching: direct and indirect.

Direct Teaching

- Direct teaching is a teacher-centered skill-building model.

Exposition Teaching

- Exposition teaching offers an effective way to convey a great deal of information in a short period of time.
- The effectiveness of direct instruction can be improved through the use of technology.

Exposition With Interaction Teaching

- Exposition with interaction teaching is often more effective than exposition teaching.
- The key to exposition with interaction teaching is questioning. Asking good questions is an art that is essential to the recitation and textbook recitation methods.

- The recall of information requires the use of narrow questions (convergent) while the desire to stimulate thinking and reasoning calls for the use of broad questions (divergent).

- The Mental Operation system categorized questions as factual, empirical, productive, or evaluative.

- Focusing, prompting, and probing questions can be used to arouse interest and increase involvement.

- Redirecting questions, using wait time and halting time, and using reinforcement can enhance questioning skills.

DISCUSSION QUESTIONS AND ACTIVITIES

1. **Strategy Selection.** Your new class consists largely of slow learners who are restless, undermotivated, and hard to manage. What teaching strategies and methods would be best to use with these students? Would your strategies change if they were a different age level? Provide rationales.

2. **The Preparation Method.** When would it be appropriate to use the presentation method? Consider objectives and purpose. How would you plan an effective presentation? Consider motivation, length, aids, clarity, and interest. How could you tell whether a presentation has been successful?

3. **Preparing Questions.** Choose a topic you might teach one day. Prepare examples for each level within the following question categories.
   a. Convergent and divergent
   b. Mental Operation system

4. **Textbook Questions.** Obtain the teacher's edition of a textbook for a subject you expect to teach. Analyze the questions contained in the text. What levels and types of questions are most frequently suggested?

TECH CONNECTION

Teachers should always be looking for ways to make teaching strategies more motivating and student-centered. Complete the following two application activities to help you identify ways technology can be used to enhance direct instructional methods.

- Find a lesson plan that incorporates one or more of the direct instruction models found in this chapter. Identify the model. How could a teacher use technology to enhance the lesson? You might want to access the following Internet URL websites for ideas: www.teachnology.com, www.nvo.com/ecnewletter/teacherstoolresources, www.readwritethink.org/, or www.eduref.org/Virtual/Lessons/index.shtml.

Form groups of four or five to share ideas. Use PowerPoint and SMART Board technology to share your group's findings with the class.

- Access www.adprima.com and www.adprima.com/direct.htm. The first address has general information for teachers; the second address has information and links about direct instruction. Identify ideas and resources that will improve direct instruction at the grade level you expect to teach. Form groups of four or five to share ideas. Use PowerPoint and SMART Board technology to share your group's findings with the class.

CONNECTION WITH THE FIELD

1. **Questioning in the Classroom.** Attend a class in a public school or college classroom. Keep a tally of the levels of questions, as well as types of questions, used by the instructor. Did you see any patterns? What other questioning techniques did you observe? Were they successful? Why or why not?

2. **Teaching.** Prepare and teach a mini lesson using a direct methods approach. Use the mini teaching guidelines and forms in Appendix A to plan and analyze your mini lesson.

3. **Teaching Analysis.** Make a videotape of your mini teaching lesson; then critically analyze it with your peers.

STUDENT STUDY SITE

Visit the Student Study Site at **www.sagepub.com/mooreteachingk8** for these additional learning tools:

- Video clips
- Web resources
- Self quizzes
- E-Flashcards
- Full-text SAGE journal articles
- Portfolio Connection
- Licensing Preparation/Praxis Connection

CHAPTER 8

Using Authentic Teaching Methods

Discovery consists of seeing what everybody has seen and thinking what nobody has thought.

—Albert Szent-Gyorgyi

Before We Begin

What is something you discovered for yourself? How did you feel? How can teachers set the stage for student discovery and problem solving? Be ready to compare your view with classmates.

OVERVIEW

For centuries, humankind has embraced the challenge of discovering new worlds. That's why it's so appropriate that NASA named one of its space shuttles Discovery. To inspire our "star tech" generation to seek and conquer new intellectual horizons, teachers need to use authentic teaching methods such as discovery learning, discussions, and inquiry experiences.

Many educational theorists argue that students learn best by constructing their own knowledge while being engaged in meaningful, high-interest activities that teach them content knowledge and problem-solving skills they can apply to their current and future lives. Teachers set the stage for authentic learning by providing participatory experiences and facilitating, or guiding the academic "missions." This chapter will examine how teachers can create authentic educational experiences that will launch students into becoming enthusiastic, lifelong learners with the confidence to go intellectually where no one has ever gone before.

OBJECTIVES

After completing your study of Chapter 8, you should be able to

- describe the primary roles associated with various discussion techniques and explain the four areas that must be addressed in effective discussion planning;
- compare and contrast the purpose, function, strengths, and limitations of **brainstorming**, buzz groups, and task groups;
- describe the major tenets, characteristics, strengths, limitations, and teacher's role associated with each of the heuristic methods;
- define *problem solving*, and distinguish between the three levels of problem solving;
- differentiate between discovery and inquiry learning and describe the major purpose, characteristics, teacher role, and desired environment associated with each approach; and
- outline and explain the five-step discovery model, the three-step inquiry approach, and the basic features of Richard Suchman's inquiry learning.

Authentic instructional methods promote the development of students' critical thinking and problem-solving skills and give students a voice in the learning process. Furthermore, when students are actively engaged in the learning process, they are motivated to take responsibility for their own learning (Cornelius-White & Harbaugh, 2010). Such involvement is often difficult to achieve through direct teaching strategies. Although **authentic methods** are typically student-centered, providing a wide range of participatory activities requires a considerable amount of careful planning and classroom time. As we explore these various strategies, think of ways you can use them in your future classroom.

Through the Eyes of an Expert

Reaching All Students

Knowing WHAT to teach is only part of being an effective teacher. Equally important is knowing HOW to teach in a way that motivates students and increases their retention. My strategy is to know what I need to teach and find creative means to connect it to students' lives. For example, 4th grade students LOVE to blog. Therefore, I added a blogsite to our class website. Students logged in and described what they received for Christmas and connected to science using vocabulary. One girl wrote, "I receive gerbils for Christmas. I know that they are mammals which are covered with fur/hair, warm blooded and have live young. Gerbils are also herbivores (plant eating animals) which eat nuts, berries and grains." Then, other students would post comments. Again, this is a great opportunity to build classroom community while connecting science to their individual lives. This gives me an inside look at their thoughts and understandings while the students believe they are just "chatting" back and forth to each other.

(Continued)

(Continued)

Another example would be the way that I teach about how heat travels, conduction/convection and insulators/conductors. Students roast hot dogs and marshmallows over a campfire while I teach them the concepts of conduction and convection (coming off the fire). In addition, we begin to explore various conductors with which to roast the hot dogs. This experience was published in our local paper with one student commenting, "I learned that heat travels from hot to cold objects. The heat traveled from the hot dog to the bun to my mouth! Yum!" Experiences such as this connect with student lives while teaching them in depth science concepts.

I ensure academic rigor by creatively teaching to ALL the various learning styles through EVERY unit. Numerous opportunities exist to help ALL students excel beyond their individual potential and goal. Community volunteers, collaboration with faculty, compacting curriculum, projects/team challenges are all ways to reach ALL learners. For example, some of my students are gifted in fine arts. During my space unit, I had a community volunteer work with these students to create a quilt square (for our local quilt museum challenge) demonstrating their knowledge of the space content.

The bottom line is ALL students can learn the goals set before them, and I do what it takes EVERY DAY to guarantee that success!

SOURCE: Keri Dowdy, 4th grade teacher, Sedalia Elementary School, Mayfield, Kentucky, Nationally Board Certified Teacher, Presidential Award Winner for Excellence in Math/Science Teaching. Used with permission.

THE DISCUSSION METHOD

An important but infrequently used authentic teaching method is the classroom **discussion**. What all too frequently passes for a classroom discussion is really nothing more than a teacher presentation with periodic questioning–answering sequences. In a true discussion, students should talk more than the teacher. A discussion is not an informal conversation; it is a carefully structured exchange of ideas directed toward a specific cognitive or affective goal.

Quality classroom discussions promote the development of students' critical thinking skills. Many subjects pose questions that are open to interpretation. For example, how can policemen help us? Is there a cure for obesity? What can be done about oil spills? How are Patricia Polacco's books influenced by her life experiences? Discussion is an excellent instructional vehicle for exploring varying perspectives related to current world events and "hot topics."

Listening to others' perspectives and expressing opinions about issues helps students clarify their personal beliefs, attitudes, and values. A discussion about the effects of drug use, for example, would likely tap into students' personal experiences and attitudes more than a presentation would. Similarly, discussions on issues such as poverty, democracy, bullying, pollution, treatment of animals, and favorite musical groups can lead to the establishment of such attitudes as civic duty, patriotism, behavior, responsibility, and a commitment to the arts.

To provide an open forum in which students feel free to express their opinions, teachers need to create a supportive learning community that encourages open teacher–student and student–student communication. Part of that process is establishing certain teacher–student roles and procedures.

Because discussions are student-centered, students need to learn how to lead, record, and participate in discussions. Leaders ensure that everyone understands the discussion's purpose and topic. They pose questions designed to involve disruptive or reluctant group members, prevent anyone from dominating the discussions, and address alternative viewpoints. Leaders ensure that all participants' perspectives are heard and periodically summarize major discussion points.

Student or teacher recorders record key points and the group's conclusions. They might display these records on the whiteboard, chart, SMART Board, or an overhead projector so that all participants can reference the information during and after the discussion.

Students are more likely to participate in a discussion if they feel they have knowledge of the topic. Therefore, they prepare in advance by reading and reflecting upon teacher-provided and student-discovered materials about the topic. During the discussion, students listen actively, respect other's opinions, take turns talking, express their perspectives, ask relevant questions, and keep on task.

Throughout the discussion, teachers act as guides on the side. They empower students to lead the discussion as much as possible but remain ready to assume the roles of model, leader, recorder, or consultant as needed. Whatever role they assume, teachers must carefully plan in advance and allow enough class time for a meaningful discussion to take place.

Planning the Discussion

For discussions to be effective, they must be well organized. If not, most discussions will disintegrate into chaos. Basically, teachers must address four areas when planning a discussion activity.

First, teachers must carefully consider their cognitive and affective goals and the amount of student preparation needed to achieve these goals. Because students need to be conversant about the discussion topic in order for the discussion to be educational and worthwhile, teachers must provide a common foundation of student knowledge through pre-discussion activities such as assigned readings, student research, or, in the case of value-related discussions, prior reflection upon a personal position.

Second, teachers must decide whether lesson goals would be met best by a whole-class or small-group discussion activity. If the goals are to develop students' comprehension, analysis, synthesis, and evaluation skills, a whole-class discussion would be most appropriate. The development of leadership skills, social skills, listening skills, or other related skills, however, would probably call for a small-group discussion. Some advantages of whole-class discussions are the teacher's ability to keep students on task and on topic. However, whole-class discussions do not give students as much opportunity to practice active listening, edit or build upon ideas, communicate, and turn taking. Small group discussions might take the form of buzz groups, brainstorming sessions, or task groups. All students have more opportunity to participate and to share their perspectives. Effective teachers select the approach that best matches their intended learning outcomes. We will take a closer look at group size later in this chapter.

Because a productive discussion requires interaction, teachers should arrange the seating so students can look directly at each other when they interact. Students should all be sitting at the same eye plane level as well. Figure 8.1 shows two possible whole-class arrangements.

Note that every student can make direct eye contact with every other student. Similarly, Figure 8.2 shows three possible small-group arrangements that maximize interaction.

| FIGURE 8.1 | Large-Class Discussion Seating Arrangements (To maximize interaction, students should be seated in a circular or hollow square arrangement. Arrows pointing through the center indicate that the individual is speaking to the total group. Leader and recorder positions are marked with an X.) |

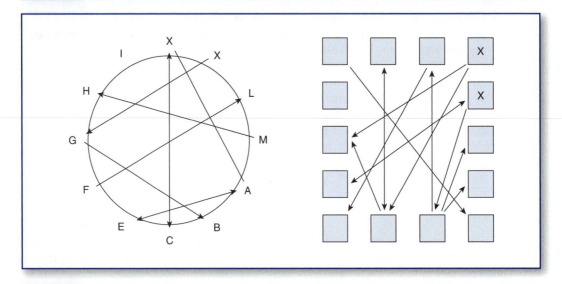

| FIGURE 8.2 | Small-Group Discussion Seating Arrangements (Leader and recorder positions are marked with an X.) |

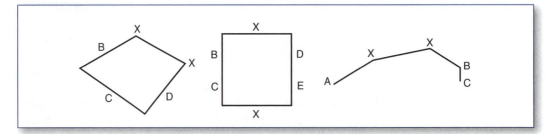

Finally, teachers need to schedule enough time for meaningful discussions to take place. The amount of time varies depending upon the size and function of the group. Most small-group discussions tend to be relatively short—about 20 minutes for older students and shorter periods with younger students. To ensure productive use of group time, effective teachers give explicit directions about what the group needs to accomplish during the discussion period and remind groups when their time is drawing to a close.

Careful planning results in quality classroom discussions. To make good decisions about discussion activities in your future classroom, you need to have a thorough understanding of the characteristics and functions of whole class and small group discussions.

Whole-Class Discussion

In some respects, whole-class discussions are similar to the class recitation method. You or a designated discussion leader pose questions, listen to student answers, react, and probe for more information. In the true whole-class discussion, however, you assume the role of passive moderator and create a pleasant atmosphere conducive to free interaction. Neither you nor any class member should dominate the discussion. Your major task is to make the total class session more interactive.

Conducting a whole-class discussion takes careful advanced planning. First, select a suitable topic. Then, provide an adequate knowledge base so the students will have something to discuss. Next, determine the procedure (discussion agenda), time limits, and discussion ground rules. Then you are ready to conduct the whole-class discussion.

For example, a teacher presentation about the benefits of a healthful diet could be followed by a 20-minute discussion, then a closing activity. To promote equitable participation opportunities, you might set a 2-minute time limit for each student to speak. You also could establish ground rules such as these: (a) summarize the last speaker's comments before making your own, (b) respect others' perspectives, (c) be a positive participant, (d) disagree in an agreeable way, and (e) stay on topic.

Spark off discussions with a *YouTube* clip, **role-playing**, an open-ended question, or a high-interest scenario. Once the discussion has begun, the leader keeps it on track, summarizes as needed, and involves all class members through the use of questioning, redirecting, and reinforcing before bringing all the discussion points to a logical conclusion.

Textbooks can be used to establish a common foundation of knowledge for whole-class discussions. One strategy, called the *listen-read-and-discuss* method, begins when the teacher makes a short presentation on the textbook material to create a cognitive framework. After reading assigned textbook pages, students compare and contrast their understanding of the material with the teacher's presentation. The teacher continuously monitors the discussion to assess students' comprehension of the material.

Another option for a whole-class discussion is an informal debate. Near the end of a unit of study, students conduct additional research exploring contrasting viewpoints on a controversial issue. For example, eighth grade students might explore the perspectives of Northerners and Southerners during the Civil War. Third grade students might debate whether or not the city should build a water park. On the day of the debate, divide the class into two teams and randomly assign which viewpoint each team will support. Teams have time to share their notes, strategize, and select a spokesperson. The teacher or a capable student serves as the moderator. Teams take turns presenting their viewpoints and counterpoints before delivering closing statements.

Small-Group Discussion

Successful small-group discussions also require careful planning. As with any discussion, you need to provide a common foundation of information through presentations, assignments, books, or films. Set clear guidelines regarding the small groups' task and responsibilities. Once students are adequately prepared, they start their discussions, usually in different areas of the room. Because it is impossible for you to be with multiple groups simultaneously, responsible student leaders must be selected to keep their groups on task

Instruction should provide students with real-life experiences.

and ensure all group members participate. Group recorders write down the group's ideas and conclusions using chart paper, transparencies, or laptops. Each group reports their ideas to the rest of the class using a visual aid such as large display charts, overhead transparencies, PowerPoints, graphs, brochures, videos, or electronic timelines.

What is the optimal size for small-group learning? The general rule is the younger the student, the smaller the group. In larger groups, it is too easy for students to remain silent and not participate in the interaction. In smaller groups, one person might dominate the conversation and there are not enough people to present a diversity of opinions. Generally speaking, groups of five to seven work best.

Students who participate in small-group activities develop their communication skills, leadership abilities, open-mindedness, persuasive arguing, and other interpersonal skills. In addition, group work often leads to a stronger sense of personal commitment to group decisions compared to those made by the whole class or individuals. Finally, students involved in small-group work are usually given more opportunity for active verbal participation and, in some cases, for physical movement.

Small-group discussions have limitations as well. One of the primary problems is the tendency for students to quickly drift off task, which wastes valuable classroom time. Another danger of small groups concerns the group composition. Teachers need to carefully consider the students' abilities, interests, and personalities when forming heterogeneous (mixed ability) or homogeneous (similar ability) groups. Furthermore, because some elementary and middle school students don't have their social skills in place, it is possible—and quite likely—that some groups cannot work together cooperatively or that they cannot reach consensus because they have very different perspectives. Careful teacher planning and supervision, however, can proactively prevent difficulties of small group work.

The kinds and purposes of the small groups you can form are limited only by your creativity. Let's look at three common small group types.

Brainstorming

Brainstorming is a small-group activity used to generate ideas. The leader introduces a complex topic such as ways students could help the community go green. After each person independently generates ideas, solutions, or comments, they meet in small groups to share their ideas and to "piggyback," or add to group members' ideas. Then groups share their ideas with the whole class.

Because the quantity of suggestions is paramount during each brainstorming session, teachers should emphasize decency and decorum. During each brainstorming session, all answers, no matter how wrong, are accepted as possible solutions. No comments about or reactions to contributions are allowed until all groups have reported their ideas. Positive, productive brainstorming sometimes results in a mood of delightful quest.

Brainstorming is an excellent springboard for other activities such as discussions, research, problem solving, or small-group work. For example, after brainstorming a list of famous women throughout history, each student can select one person to study further.

Buzz Group

A **buzz group** is a small group of four to seven students who meet for a few minutes to quickly share opinions, viewpoints, or reactions to certain ideas or course content. The group can be formed easily by counting off or by having those in close proximity form a group.

One variation of a buzz group is the interview approach. After teams are formed, students partner up to take turns interviewing one another by asking clarifying questions about the topic or issue. Then they share their responses with their team. Another variation is the three by three by three strategy. After a short presentation, three students meet for three minutes to generate three questions or comments related to the topic. These buzz group sessions should be followed up with a whole-class discussion.

Task Group

A **task group** sets out to solve a problem or complete a project. Unlike other types of small-group discussions, however, students have assigned roles, and the group has a task to complete. Group size usually ranges from four to seven members, depending on the problem or project.

Teachers' and students' roles vary in task group activities. The teacher selects the tasks, assigns team member roles, provides resources, establishes a work schedule, and monitors the groups' activities. Students need to be self-directed and able to work in an uninhibited, but productive, environment in which discussion can be free and open.

This concludes the examination of the various discussion techniques. Complete Reflect and Apply Exercise 8.1 to explore the use of the discussion method at the grade level you expect to teach.

REFLECT AND APPLY EXERCISE 8.1: **Discussion Techniques**

Reflect

- Describe the characteristics of the true discussion. What are some pros and cons of this teaching method?

- Describe the teacher–student roles and basic characteristics of the various discussion formats.

Apply

- Can the discussion approach to learning be adapted to any grade level? What format would work best at the elementary level? Middle level?

- Did you ever have teachers who used the discussion method extensively? How successful were they? How would you change the teachers' roles and procedures?

- Name some topics or tasks that would be appropriate for small-group discussions. What type of small-group structure would be best for each topic or task?

HEURISTIC METHODS

Teachers who use *heuristic* teaching methods provide opportunities for students to learn through problem solving, discovery, inquiry, reflection, and experimentation. In this section, we will address these heuristic approaches: problem solving, discovery learning, and inquiry learning.

People often confuse the discovery and inquiry methods. Some educators use the terms interchangeably, whereas others feel they represent subcategories of each other. For the purposes of this textbook, the discovery and inquiry methods are considered as unique, yet somewhat related, techniques. Because the **heuristic approach** actively involves students in problem solving, let's begin our study of the heuristic modes by looking at the problem-solving process.

Problem Solving

Video Link 8.1:
Watch a video about problem solving.

Progressive educators such as John Dewey have long advocated a curriculum centered around problem solving. Some contemporary curricula and textbooks rely upon Dewey's problem-solving approach coupled with direct experiences provided by the teacher. Therefore, for the purposes of this text, problem solving is the intentional elimination of uncertainty through direct experiences and under supervision.

Because preparing students to solve everyday problems is an important function of schools, curricular specialists who advocate a problem-solving instructional approach suggest that schools should develop traits (or behaviors) that enable students to be effective problem solvers. Furthermore, these school experiences should articulate the content and processes needed to produce successful problem solvers.

Problem solving actively involves students in their own learning. The amount of student decision making can be classified according to three levels of involvement. As depicted in Table 8.1, Level I is the traditional teacher-directed or guided problem-solving approach. The teacher provides the problem as well as the processes and procedures leading to an intended conclusion. Because Level I problem-solving activities are highly manageable and predictable, they work well to teach basic concepts to students who are not yet equipped with the critical thinking skills to solve problems independently.

TABLE 8.1	Levels of Problem Solving		
	Levels		
	I	**II**	**III**
Problem identification	Generated by teacher or textbook	Generated by teacher or textbook	Generated by students
Processes for solving problem	Decided by teacher or textbook	Decided by students	Decided by students
Establishment of tentative solution to problem	Determined by students	Determined by students	Determined by students

In Level II, problems are usually defined by the teacher or the textbook, but students get to devise their own means of solving the problems. Level II problem solving gives the learners the opportunity, often for the first time, to explore something independently.

Level III represents almost total self-direction. Students generate the problems and then design ways to solve these problems. This level is often referred to as open problem solving.

Ideally, once students have critical thinking skills and self-direction in place, teachers can have them independently identify and solve problems. For example, second graders can investigate ways to befriend lonely senior citizens. Sixth graders can design and implement a school recycling program. To ensure a successful learning experience, teachers need to monitor students' activities carefully and be ready to step in as needed if students aren't as independent and self-directed as they perceived.

Discovery Learning

Discovery learning is a means by which students engage in problem solving to develop their knowledge or skills. A good working definition of discovery learning is intentional learning through supervised problem solving following the scientific method of investigation. Thus, with discovery, the learning must be planned, it must be supervised, and it must follow the scientific method of investigation (see Figure 8.3).

Although people confuse discovery learning and inquiry, they are actually specific kinds of problem solving. Whereas discovery follows the general scientific method of investigation (see Figure 8.3), inquiry learning doesn't have an established pattern.

FIGURE 8.3	General Scientific Model of Investigation

Identify problem
1. Be aware problem exists
2. Write problem statement(s)

Develop possible solutions
1. Propose testable hypotheses

Collect data
1. Gather evidence
2. Conduct experiment(s)
3. Survey a sample

Analyze and interpret data
1. Develop data-supported meaningful statements
2. Test hypotheses
3. Establish relationships or patterns
4. Make generalizations

Test conclusions
1. Obtain new data
2. Revise original conclusions

"Earth science, close up."

SOURCE: Created by Martha Campbell.

The collection of data is a significant component of discovery learning.

Discovery learning can take place at each of the three levels of problem solving (review Table 8.1). At Level I, discovery learning is carefully structured (*guided discovery*); at Level II, a moderate amount of guidance is administered (*modified discovery*); and at Level III, students' problem-solving activities are very casually supervised (*open discovery*).

Discovery Learning Strategies

To ensure successful discovery learning experiences in your future classroom, you need to plan carefully and execute the problem-solving process effectively. Your role is to provide a situation that lets students identify a contradiction or uncertainty and then to assist them in finding a relationship between what they already know and the newly discovered knowledge. Essentially, you direct the planning, organization, and execution of the general scientific method of investigation (review Figure 8.3). Let's explore the steps involved in the discovery learning approach.

Video Link 8.2: Watch a video about discovery learning.

Selecting the Problem. Students often lack the sophistication to identify their own problems (open discovery); they aren't prepared to operate at the Level III problem-solving level (review Table 8.1). Therefore, you must be prepared to suggest appropriate problems or areas for which students may seek problems.

Science, geometry, social studies, art, and mathematics all provide many opportunities for discovery learning. For example, students might examine the pollution in the local river, identify geometric shapes in local architecture, build shelters using available natural resources, mix paint to learn about secondary colors, or investigate ways mathematics skills are used in everyday life.

Other subjects such as the language arts, which are not as discovery oriented, can still be presented with the discovery method. For example, students could complete diagramless crosswords or cryptoquizzes, interpret quality literature, present impromptu unscripted plays, and create puppets. Figure 8.4 offers some additional discovery learning activities.

FIGURE 8.4   Discovery Learning Activities

Flashlight Fixing

Materials:

- Shoe boxes
- Working flashlights with bulbs and batteries
- Paper and pencil

Take the flashlights apart. For younger children, simply remove the batteries. For older children, also remove the lightbulb. Put the flashlights and the various parts into the shoe boxes. Instruct the children to put the flashlights together so they will work. Children should record their discoveries.

Car Design

Materials:

- Books about automobiles, transportation, and/or simple machines such as the wheel
- Several small boxes such as shoeboxes, tissue boxes, or gift boxes
- Items to create wheels and axles such as paper towel tubes, cardboard, dowel rods, plastic coffee can lids, rubber balls, spools, etc.
- Scissors
- Glue
- Tape
- Crayons, watercolor markers, or paints—optional

Read to the children, or have the children read one or more of the selected books. Instruct children to use the craft items or others they find to create cars with wheels that roll.

Baking Bread

Materials:

- A gingerbread or cornbread recipe, or for younger children a mix
- The ingredients for making the bread and all the bowls and utensils
- Adult supervision for the baking

Provide children with all the ingredients and tools needed to make the mix and ready it for the oven. Supervise the baking, placing into and removing the bread from the oven if need be. Once it has baked and is sufficiently cool, have the children serve and taste the results.

Suitable problems should not be left to chance. Left alone, students often flounder or select problems that are not suitable, ones that are too broad in scope, or problems whose solutions require unavailable materials and equipment.

Once students have a general grasp of the problem, help them restate the problem in clear and precise terms to determine exactly what they need to find out. If this critical step is neglected, students often have difficulty in knowing exactly where to start in attempting to find a solution.

Proposing Possible Solutions. Once students clearly define the problem, they are ready to develop hypotheses, collect and analyze data, and seek solutions. At this stage, you should provide resources and make suggestions where data can be located.

When students are proposing possible solutions, or hypotheses, you should promote guessing and intuitive thought. Also, encourage healthy skepticism and practice in suspending judgment. Ideally, you want to give students the opportunity to express all their ideas in a nonthreatening environment.

Collecting Data. Next, students need to check their proposed solutions for validity. Thus, they amass additional, usable data through experiments, surveys, Internet searches, and other measures. Students may need your assistance in designing and implementing valid data collection tools and techniques. Be sure to monitor their experiments to promote physical safety. Supervise Internet searches to ensure they don't access undesirable sites.

Data Analysis and Interpretation. Next, students establish criteria and judge the validity of their hypotheses by analyzing and interpreting the data against these criteria. You might need to guide students as they carefully examine and evaluate data to arrive at conclusions. Although you cannot establish conclusions for the students, you can use probing and open-ended questions to help them discover patterns and relationships. With this assistance, students will develop skill in reaching plausible conclusions to their identified problems.

Testing Conclusions. Once established, students test and revise their conclusions. Consequently, the final step in the problem-solving component of discovery is the generation of data that will lend support to the identified conclusions or that will lead to revisions of the conclusions.

Benefits of Discovery Learning

Discovery learning is active rather than passive learning. **Active learning** tends to result in a higher degree of intrinsic motivation. With other teaching methods, students are motivated from teachers' feedback during class discussions and through grades received on assignments. During discovery learning activities, students are motivated by the activity itself, direct involvement, and group dynamics. Furthermore, students tend to learn more and retain information longer when they are actively involved in constructing their own knowledge. Explore further benefits of discovery learning by completing Application Activity 8.1.

Discovery learning also fosters the development of positive social skills because students work cooperatively throughout the process. They must develop skill in planning, follow established procedures, and work together toward the successful completion of common tasks.

APPLICATION ACTIVITY 8.1 Discovery Learning

Is discovery learning related to the constructivist theory? Form a small team. Investigate the constructivist theory using this text and Internet sites. Cooperatively create a faux discovery learning activity. Does it evidence the characteristics of constructivism? Support your findings. Be ready to share.

Limitations of Discovery Learning

The greatest limitation associated with discovery learning might be the demands it places on the teacher and students. Because discovery learning is a cooperative process rather than a competitive one, it calls for an adjustment—by students and teacher alike—to the very nature of discovery. The lack of competition and traditional grading practices often leads to uncertainty for the teacher and the students.

Because discovery learning takes more time, it can be an inefficient system for addressing large amounts of material. This limitation is a major concern to teachers who feel they are expected to cover all the material in the textbook.

REFLECTIONS ON TEACHER PRACTICE 8.1: Learning by Doing

1. If students learn best by doing, can we teach all subjects, attitudes, and skills "by doing"? Why or why not?

2. Is "learning by doing" more applicable to the elementary, middle school, or high school classroom? Why?

It is unfortunate that Columbine High School has changed the reputation of our young people. All the stereotypes of "sex, drugs, and violence" are, after all, true, and we must change our schools to prevent such a disaster from ever taking place again! Fortunately, Columbine is merely an aberration—tragic, but in no way typical of today's young people.

At Shawnee Mission Northwest High School just the opposite has been true since the day it opened in 1969. The students have collected food, clothing, and even presents for all the men at the state prison. In 1991, it was decided to make this an autonomous class. It was eventually called "Cougars Community Commitment." It is a social science offering for a half-credit per semester. It is open to juniors and seniors, and, with approval of the sponsor, students may enroll for as many as four semesters.

Seventeen students were enrolled the first year, and those 17 set a standard few classes have met. Few in the community took the class seriously: Rake the lawn, mow my grass at no charge?! The class motto was simply "THE DOER OF GOOD BECOMES GOOD!" It was and is our opinion that what we used to take for granted now has to be taught. Goodness needs to be nurtured but never taken for granted.

—Ronald W. Poplau, high school social studies teacher,
Shawnee Mission Northwest High School, Shawnee, Kansas

Please visit the Student Study site at **www.sagepub.com/mooreteachingk8** *for additional discussion questions and assignments.*

SOURCE: Randi Stone's *Best Practices for High School Teachers: What Award-Winning Secondary Teachers Do.* Thousand Oaks: Corwin. Reprinted by permission.

Inquiry Learning

Like discovery, inquiry is a problem-solving technique. Unlike discovery, however, the emphasis is placed on the process of investigating the problem, rather than on using the scientific method to reach a correct solution. Indeed, different students may use different strategies in obtaining information related to a problem. Students may even take intuitive approaches to problems.

As with discovery learning, there are three levels to inquiry learning: (1) guided inquiry, (2) modified inquiry, and (3) open inquiry. Thus, you may want to identify the problem and then decide how to investigate it (guided inquiry), you may want to identify the problem and then have students decide how to go about finding out about it (modified inquiry), or you may want the students to identify the problem and then design ways for obtaining information (open inquiry).

Inquiry Learning Strategies

The inquiry approach is flexible yet systematic. Students follow a basic, three-step problem-solving procedure. The approach is flexible, however, because the activities used in addressing the problem may vary. Let's now look at this three-step procedure.

Identifying the Problem. Inquiry learning is closely related to discovery learning. Thus, the problem selection processes are essentially identical. Either the teacher selects the problem (guided or modified inquiry) or more sophisticated students select a problem (open inquiry). Be prepared to monitor the problem selection process and to provide guidance or suitable alternatives for consideration.

Working Toward Solutions. Next, students work on a solution to the problem. Inquiry learning activities emphasize *finding* a problem's solution, not on the solution itself. Instead of using the scientific method (as in discovery learning activities), students devise their own strategies. Decisions regarding strategies can be teacher orchestrated (guided inquiry) or student orchestrated (modified or open inquiry). Some students may want to attack a problem through the literature and reference materials, others may want to interview experts in the field, and still others may want to design and carry out experiments. Teachers should support students' creative problem-solving efforts. These opportunities show students how inquiry works in the real world.

Establishing Solutions. The success of inquiry learning is not necessarily dependent on reaching a predetermined conclusion. Even when directed by the teacher, inquiry learning should be a highly personal experience for each individual involved. Students should be given the opportunities for applying themselves totally—so they may put their fullest talents, ideas, skills, and judgments to work in reaching their own conclusions.

During an inquiry-based lesson, the teacher or students identify a problem, investigate ways to solve the problem, and cooperatively arrive at solutions by discussing, reflecting upon, and interpreting results. Another version of the inquiry-based learning sequence is the five-E model: Engage, Explore, Explain, Elaborate, and Evaluate.

Step 1. Engage. The teacher provides high-interest activities that stimulate students' thinking. Students ask questions and make connections between past and present learning experiences to define a problem.

Step 2. Explore. Students actively explore their environment or manipulate materials to develop a grounding of experience with the phenomena. They identify and develop concepts, processes, and skills through these explorations.

Step 3. Explain. Students analyze their explorations and put the abstract experiences into a communicable form. They clarify their understanding through reflective activities and have opportunities to verbalize their conceptual understanding or to demonstrate new skills or behaviors.

Step 4. Elaborate. Students expand on the concepts they have learned, make connections to other related concepts, and apply their understandings to the world around them. These connections often lead to further inquiry and new understandings.

Step 5. Evaluate. The teacher determines whether learners have attained understanding of concepts and knowledge. Evaluation and assessment can occur at all points along the continuum of the instructional process.

The five-E inquiry model is based on the constructivist approach to learning. It can also be used with students of all ages.

Inquiry gives students the opportunity to learn and practice skills associated with critical thinking (see Chapter 10). Developing the ability to think is becoming increasingly important in this information age. Unfortunately, traditional instruction emphasizes rote memorization instead of application, analysis, synthesis, and evaluation. Inquiry activities equip students with the necessary knowledge, skills, and confidence to identify and solve real-life problems. Figures 8.5 and 8.6 offer examples of an inquiry lesson for young children and the five-E inquiry model.

Suchman Inquiry Learning

J. Richard Suchman's inquiry learning approach, the Inquiry Development Program, was designed entirely around the concept of inquiry. This junior high school oriented program emphasized physical science and developed the basic processes associated with inquiry (data generating, data organizing, and idea building).

The main feature of the **Suchman inquiry** was the concept of a "discrepant event," or filmed physics demonstration whose outcome was contradictory to what was expected. A common example showed a teacher filling a bottle to the brim with water and placing a 3-by-5-inch piece of cardboard over the mouth of the bottle. The bottle was then inverted, with the cardboard held firmly over the mouth. When the teacher removed the hand supporting the cardboard, the water remained in the bottle—with the cardboard firmly attached—even though the cardboard was not supported in any way. The title of each of these filmed demonstrations asked why the outcome of the demonstration occurred. The teacher's role was to develop an environment where inquiry could take place.

The original Suchman inquiry approach has changed in two ways. First, today's teachers usually demonstrate the discrepant events live. Second, students receive more guidance from the teacher than did the students in the original program. But the basic purposes of the inquiry program, which were the development of skills in searching and data processing and the development of concepts through analysis of concrete problems, have not changed.

The Suchman inquiry approach focuses on the process by which information is acquired, rather than on the final information. The problem-solving process associated with this approach occurs in three steps: (1) analyzing the episode, (2) gathering information, and (3) reaching conclusions.

FIGURE 8.5	Inquiry Lesson for Young Children

Grade level: K–1

Description: Young children should explore an awareness of themselves in a social setting. This lesson lays the foundation for the study of school and family life.

Prior to this lesson, the children learned about families so they have an understanding about different types of families. In this lesson, children will speculate about where families live, examine pictures of different types of houses and locations, and draw conclusions.

Materials: Dollhouse, flipchart, pictures of different types of homes

Instructional Objectives:

Students will

- Speculate about where families might live.
- Describe different types of homes based on a set of pictures.
- Describe simple differences and similarities among ways people live in different locations.
- Develop a general statement indicating that families live in a variety of homes that provide for family needs.

Procedures:

1. Introduction and motivation
   a. Place the dollhouse in the center of the classroom. Ask the following: If this were a real house, how would a family use it?
   b. Allow children to describe how the rooms might be used. Ask the following: Why is it important for families to have a place to live? Important reasons may include sleep, eat, keep warm, and play.

2. Have students develop some guesses
   a. Ask the following: Where do people live?
   b. Students may respond that people live in houses. If so,
      i. Write the word *houses* on the flipchart.
      ii. Stimulate guessing. Ask: Does everyone live in the same type of house?

3. Looking at pictures
   a. Say the following: Those are really good ideas. Let's look at some pictures of houses and see if we can get some more ideas.
   b. Show pictures: (a) suburban house, (b) complex in city, (c) trailer house, (d) apartment house, (e) farmhouse. After each picture, ask: Tell me about this house. Point out differences in style and location.
   c. Possible problem: Children unfamiliar with apartments may be confused about how families live in these buildings. Use the school as a comparison with the classrooms as apartments. Houses have rooms; apartments have rooms.

4. Adding to our list
   a. Ask the following: Did we learn about some new houses?
   b. Say the following: Let's add those homes to our list.

5. Conclusion
   a. Let's go back to our BIG question. Where do people live?
   b. Ask the following: What can we say about where people live?
   c. Outcome: People live in a variety of homes that provide for family needs.

6. Assessment
   a. Did the class develop the conclusion?
   b. Who participated in the discussion?

7. Possible follow-up activities
   a. Have children find and cut out pictures from magazines, brochures, catalogs, and old books that show different homes.
   b. Have children draw a picture of their home and have them talk about it with the class.

FIGURE 8.6	Five-E Inquiry Model Lesson

Topic: Earthquakes

Materials: Internet, resources science books

Objectives:

Students will:

1. Explain what earthquakes are and what causes them.

2. Identify events caused by the movement of the earth plates.

Procedures:

Engage: Has anyone in class ever experienced an earthquake or seen one in the news? Have you ever felt the ground move under your feet? Have you ever been involved in an accident?

Explore: In small groups, explore the Internet and/or read the class book and other available books on earthquakes and what causes them.

Explain: Each group presents a summary of what they have found.

Elaborate: What other events are caused by earth plate movement?

Evaluate: Each group will make a formal presentation on plate movement and the ramifications of such movement.

Analyzing the Episode. A Suchman session is initiated by having students view a discrepant event presented by the teacher or by one of Suchman's films. Next, the teacher asks the class for ideas, guesses, or hypotheses about what happened. Students are allowed to ask as many questions as they wish as long as they follow these rules:

1. They can only ask questions that can be answered with a yes or no.

2. One student at a time can ask as many questions as he or she wants without being interrupted by the class.

3. The teacher will not respond to a question that asks for support of a student-originated theory or hypothesis.

These rules give students the freedom of establishing a sequence and pattern of questions that, in turn, will help lead them to possible hypotheses.

Gathering Information. Next, students formulate their own hypotheses and gather data to support or refute the hypotheses. During this stage, teachers phrase questions that encourage students to conduct experiments to identify essential conditions and to verify answers—for example, "Would the object sink in a different kind of liquid?" and "Would a heavier object sink in the liquid?"

The Suchman inquiry approach requires a supportive atmosphere. Students conduct any reasonable tests or experiments to check on the validity of their proposed hypotheses. Although the teacher does provide some information, students seek data without help from the teacher. Thus, in the typical Suchman inquiry session, students work independently, conducting experiments, reexamining the discrepant event, engaging in questioning sessions with the teacher, and evaluating the data.

Reaching Conclusions. Based on the resultant data, students draw their own conclusions and attempt to explain the cause of the observed phenomenon. In addition, they try to determine why the conditions were necessary for the final outcome.

The Suchman inquiry technique can be a valuable tool in a teacher's repertoire. By seeing how problems are solved in the classroom, students learn how to solve problems in other areas of their lives.

Benefits of Inquiry Learning

The inquiry method of teaching has several unique benefits. First, there are no rigid guidelines, so students are encouraged to develop creative solutions to problems. In fact, students sometimes address tangential problems that have little to do with the original problem. Thus, investigations can be as original and limitless as students' imaginations.

Second, inquiry stimulates student interest and challenges them to solve problems to the very limits of their abilities. They are not penalized for lack of content knowledge. Students are free to use the skills they do possess to reach their own solutions.

Last, because the problem-solving process celebrates individuality and creativity, it is impossible to fail in inquiry learning. Students carry out the approach to the best of their abilities and then stop without being penalized for not reaching a predetermined solution. Thus, students' self-confidence is enhanced.

FORRESTER: A REFLECTIVE CASE STUDY

Forrester looked out his window to watch a robin feed her young in a nest precariously perched under the eave near his classroom. His mind took flight as he puzzled over how to best deliver his unit on conserving the earth's resources. Should he recycle his lecture notes from last year? Forrester knew he could talk until he was blue in the face, but would that inspire his students to internalize the importance of being stewards of the environment? There had to be a better way!

Using what you have learned in this chapter, describe two other instructional strategies Forrester could use to provide an authentic learning experience for his students. Be ready to share.

Limitations of Inquiry Learning

Inquiry tends to appear, and sometimes tends to be, chaotic. It is possible that a class of 25 students might simultaneously pursue 25 different activities addressing a single problem. Although actively engaged students generally cause few problems, inquiry can appear to

"Mrs. Broderick isn't as user-friendly as our teaching machines."

SOURCE: Created by Martha Campbell.

be an undisciplined process in which little learning is taking place. Anticipating and locating materials can be difficult because it is impossible to anticipate all the resources that students will require in one inquiry lesson. Indeed, some students may want to conduct experiments, whereas others may want to conduct research in special reference books. Whatever the need, you must try to anticipate students' needs and make the materials available. This isn't an easy task.

As with discovery learning, giving students the freedom to engage in problem solving is very time consuming. Moreover, depending upon the strategy they employ, some students will finish quickly while others will not want to stop their investigations.

One difficulty unique to inquiry is evaluation. Because you must provide grades, you need some criteria on which to base your evaluation. This problem can be overcome, to some extent, by using a rubric with generic criteria and by having students create progress portfolios documenting their activities.

This completes the discussion of the various heuristic teaching methods. Table 8.2 summarizes these methods. Review the summary, and complete Reflect and Apply Exercise 8.2.

TABLE 8.2	Heuristic Methods
Method	**Description**
Discovery	Intentional learning through supervised problem solving following the scientific method
Inquiry	Flexible yet systematic process of problem solving
Suchman inquiry	Inquiry approach whereby students are presented with and asked to explain discrepant events

REFLECT AND APPLY EXERCISE 8.2: Discovery and Inquiry

Reflect

- Contrast discovery and inquiry learning.
- What are the strengths and limitations of discovery and inquiry learning?
- What are the teacher's roles in discovery and inquiry learning?

Apply

- Can all elementary and middle school students be given the freedom needed to make discovery and inquiry learning successful? Is not, why not? If yes, what are some areas of concern that must be overcome?
- What level of problem solving would work best at the elementary level? Middle school level?
- What difficulties could you encounter in implementing the discovery learning method? Inquiry learning method?

Because the teacher and environment are so important to the success of the indirect approaches to instruction, let's take a brief look at these two factors before we go on to integrated teaching methods.

REFLECTIONS ON TEACHER PRACTICE 8.2: Problem Solving

1. How can issues in the life of students be connected to lessons? Which curriculum areas would be most difficult to make life connections?

2. Would researching issues be appropriate at all grade levels? Why? At what grade level is it most appropriate?

Try to work in some of your students' personal interests into your teaching. I have been pleasantly surprised by the connections my students could make and the inquiry projects they have done when learning about things that MATTER to them (if they can see WHY and HOW they matter, unlike some school info, which you might need to connect to them more closely).

One interesting research project I did required students to select an event in history (recent, ancient, local, global . . . whatever) and research. The goal was to figure out as much as possible about the event, including how the student's life was affected by the event, positively or negatively, directly or indirectly. They needed to consider the possibilities of how their lives would be different, had the chosen events not taken place.

Another project that involved all students integrated history and science (in many cases), language arts, and technology (they presented their projects on hyper studio). I had students research the building of the local mall, the Holocaust, Columbine, and dozens of other great topics. The only criteria I required for topic selection were: The topic MUST BE appropriate for school; and You MUST show some logical connection to your life (This helped me to give reasons why Charles Manson was NOT a great choice; I didn't accept "If he hadn't done what he did, I wouldn't be researching him—that's how he affects me.").

—Amy, middle-level teacher

Please visit the Student Study site at **www.sagepub.com/mooreteachingk8** *for additional discussion questions and assignments.*

ADDITIONAL CONSIDERATIONS

When using authentic approaches to instruction, you need to facilitate students' academic and emotional efforts by establishing a classroom environment conducive to individualized problem solving. Participatory methods require that students are given a certain amount of freedom to explore problems and arrive at possible solutions. Such freedom takes time—days or even weeks. State curricular mandates require you to cover a certain amount of content, however. Therefore, you may opt to intersperse problem-solving sessions with regular, teacher-directed lessons.

Planning and Monitoring Authentic Instruction

The problem-solving process requires careful planning and continuous monitoring. You must work diligently to help students precisely define the problem, clarify related issues, access available resources, and form conclusions. Facilitate their systematic investigation of problems by teaching them how to apply appropriate problem-solving strategies. Monitor students' efforts by requiring them to submit periodic progress reports related to their investigative progress.

Authentic methods require an open classroom environment that supports alternative perspectives and risk-taking. Provide plentiful encouragement; turn mistakes into learning opportunities; and encourage diverse, creative approaches. Maintain an orderly environment and high expectations. Promote cooperation, trust, self-control, and conviction. Develop a close working relationship with your students. Be constantly alert for social issues and research roadblocks.

These interactive, constructivist approaches motivate students to make good behavioral choices because of their active involvement, intellectual stimulation, and social interaction. Indeed, these strategies can even encourage and empower the most disheartened students. However, some students do not respond well to the open, unstructured activities. Every school has some students who, because of factors outside your control, will choose to misbehave. You must take every opportunity to interact with your students one-on-one and to really get to know them as individuals. Try to connect their personal experiences and interests to class events whenever possible. This will be a challenge, but even the most recalcitrant students have special interests and talents that you can tap.

Technology in the Authentic Classroom

Computers can be valuable instructional tools in the authentic classroom. During authentic lessons, teachers and students can use software such as Power Point, Timeliner, Kidspiration, and Inspiration. Students can create WebQuests (http://webquest.org/index.php) and TrackStars (http://trackstar.4teachers.org/trackstar/index.jsp) to guide self-directed studies of safe websites related to topics of interest. Individuals and small groups can create PowerPoint presentations to share the results of their self-directed studies. Video clips are also available on Encyclomedia, YouTube, TeacherTube, and United Streaming. Specialized assistive technology (AT) is also available to accommodate students' special needs during the instructional process.

This completes our discussion of the various authentic teaching strategies. Complete Application Activity 8.2 to further explore the use of authentic instructional strategies at the grade level you expect to teach.

APPLICATION ACTIVITY 8.2 Authentic Instruction

List the authentic instructional strategies presented in Chapter 8, and indicate how valuable each approach would be for the grade level you expect to teach. Use this scale: (1) appropriate and useful, (2) limited usefulness, and (3) not appropriate and not useful. Provide rationales for your ratings. Be ready to share.

SUMMARY

This chapter covered authentic teaching methods. The main points were as follows:

The Discussion Method

- Discussions stimulate students' thinking, develop their ability to articulate their own ideas, and teach them to consider others' perspectives.

- Teachers facilitate discussions by setting them into motion and monitoring their progress.

- Discussions can be whole class or small group. One of the major problems of whole-class discussions is that a few students tend to dominate. Small-group discussions result in more student-to-student interactions.

Heuristic Methods

- Heuristic methods actively involve students in their own learning and result in higher degrees of intrinsic motivation.

- The heuristic modes of discovery and inquiry essentially represent different types of problem solving.

Additional Considerations

- Teachers act as facilitators of the problem-solving process.

- Active participatory methods require close teacher–student relationships and an open, risk-taking classroom environment.

- Technology can be a valuable instructional tool in the authentic classroom.

DISCUSSION QUESTIONS AND ACTIVITIES

1. **Authentic Methods.** When is it appropriate to use authentic methods? Consider the objectives and purpose of the instruction as well as the students themselves.

2. **Discussion Topics.** Generate a list of topics that would be appropriate for discussions. Which would work best for whole-class discussions? Small-group discussions? Explain your rationales.

3. **Textbook Examination.** Examine a textbook or curriculum guide and identify several possible topics for a discussion lesson. What kinds of questions would you use to (a) begin the lesson, (b) keep the discussion rolling, and (c) wrap up the lesson?

TECH CONNECTION

Authentic teaching typically focuses on real-world issues and problems. Students often prefer learning by *doing* instead of learning by *listening* to a teacher. Teachers can use technology to make authentic learning activities even more motivating. Complete the following application activities to help identify technology ideas that will strengthen authentic teaching:

- Find a lesson plan related to a topic you plan to teach one day. Convert that lesson by using one of the authentic instruction models found in this chapter. Identify ways technology could be used to further strengthen the lesson. You might want to access the following Internet URL websites for ideas www.teachnology.com, www.edzone.net/~mwestern, http://wtvi.com/teks, and www.eduref.org/Virtual/Lessons/index.shtml. Form groups of four or five to share ideas. Create a wiki or PowerPoint slide show to share your group's findings with the class.

- Using one or more available search engines, search the web and locate a discussion lesson plan appropriate for the grade level you expect to teach. Dissect the lesson's component parts. What are the lesson's strengths? How could it be improved?

CONNECTION WITH THE FIELD

1. **Classroom Observation.** Visit several public school classrooms. Keep a record of the different methods used. What authentic methods did you observe? Was there a pattern?

2. **Inquiry Lesson.** Design an inquiry-based lesson plan. Describe how you will help students in each of these stages:
   a. Identifying the problem
   b. Working toward solutions
   c. Establishing a solution
   d. Teaching the lesson

3. **Teaching.** Prepare and teach a mini lesson using an authentic method. Access **www.sagepub.com/mooreteachingk8** and use the microteaching guidelines and forms to plan and analyze your mini lesson.

4. **Teaching Analysis.** Make a videotape of your mini teaching lesson; then critically analyze it with your peers. Access **www.sagepub.com/mooreteachingk8**, and use the mini lesson analysis forms to evaluate the lesson.

STUDENT STUDY SITE

Visit the Student Study Site at **www.sagepub.com/mooreteachingk8** for these additional learning tools:

- Video clips
- Web resources
- Self quizzes
- E-Flashcards
- Full-text SAGE journal articles
- Portfolio Connection
- Licensing Preparation/Praxis Connection

CHAPTER 9

Using Integrated Teaching Methods

Today people remember 10% of what they hear, 20% of what they read and about 80% of what they see and do.

—Jerome Bruner

Before We Begin

What is something you learned by actually doing it? What skills in your future classroom might students learn best through doing? Be ready to compare your view with classmates.

OVERVIEW

Americans are fixated by food. We salivate while watching Emeril Lagasse whip up incredible edibles on the Food Network. We read recipe books full of eye-tempting, perfectly presented pastries. The true joy of food, however, comes from cooking and eating it in person. We have studied how teachers can whet students' intellectual appetites through formal teacher presentations and self-directed learning activities. To create true educational epicureans, students need to experience a balanced diet of assorted teaching strategies. Therefore, in this chapter we'll examine these **integrated directed teaching** strategies: demonstrations, the **Socratic method**, **concept attainment**, **cooperative learning**, **simulations** and games, **individualized instruction**, **independent study**, and mastery learning.

OBJECTIVES

After completing your study of Chapter 9, you should be able to

- describe the purpose, structure, function, and implementation of the **demonstration** method, Socratic method, concept attainment strategy, and cooperative learning method;

- identify and explain the three-step procedure for role-playing and suggest ways to use role-playing in the classroom;

- describe and differentiate between simulations and games and the benefits and limitations associated with their use;

- describe individualized instruction, independent study, and mastery learning;

- identify the benefits and limitations associated with individualization of instruction; and

- describe the purpose of integrating **drill** and **practice** activities and technology into instructional delivery.

Because teachers teach and students learn in multiple ways, it is imperative that teachers develop an extensive repertoire of effective teaching strategies beyond traditional teacher presentation and student recitation. When teachers combine direct instruction with self-directed learning, it is called integrated directed teaching. Together, the teacher and students blend telling, showing, and self-exploration into a meaningful, intrinsically motivational approach. The teacher provides the information, and students engage in activities that require them to assume responsibility for their own learning, construct their own meaning, and think critically.

Teachers empower students to become self-directed learners by providing them with opportunities before, during, and after instruction. They emphasize self-direction by teaching and engaging students in decision-making and problem-solving opportunities, encouraging students to reflect about their thinking and learning processes, and engendering a self-confident, "I can do this" attitude. Furthermore, they nurture students' independence and confidence by providing activities addressing various learning styles (see Chapter 2). Students' and teachers' efforts are enhanced by their ubiquitous access to all forms of information sources, demonstrations, library and research materials, technology, the Internet, and tutorials over high-speed networks.

When teachers who are entrenched in using direct teaching methods gradually blend teacher-directed and self-directed learning activities in their classrooms, students learn that they can be in charge of their own learning some or most of the time. Self-direction depends on who makes the learning decision—what is to be learned, who should learn it, what methods and resources should be used, and how the success should be measured. As such, varying degrees of self-directness are possible. Complete Application Activity 9.1 to further explore the levels of self-directness.

An excellent starting point for developing self-directed learning is through demonstrations, the Socratic method, concept attainment, and cooperative learning. These initial experiences can be followed with simulations and games and individualized instruction, which give students even more control over their own learning.

THE DEMONSTRATION METHOD

Teachers use the demonstration method when they stand before the class, use objects or displays to share information, and discuss what is happening or has happened. This method is especially advisable when there is danger involved in students' use of equipment or materials. Teachers often use demonstrations to save time, show proper use of equipment, detail procedural steps, or visually represent a complicated concept. Even though the only person usually directly involved with the materials is the demonstrator, students like this approach because it actively engages more senses and piques their interest. When possible, students should assist the presenter or, even better yet, conduct the demonstrations themselves to ignite more interest and increase student involvement. For example, first graders would enjoy helping the presenter grind wheat into flour, knead dough, and bake bread. Seventh grade teams could develop demonstrations exploring scientific principles such as magnetism.

Teachers and students can conduct demonstrations in most content areas. For example, a teacher could demonstrate the stages of the water cycle, how to use hundreds blocks to build large numbers, or how to "throw" a clay pot. Essentially, the technique deals mostly, but not totally, with showing how something works or with skill development. Demonstrations may be made by teachers, students, video clips, or a sequence of pictures. Whatever technique is chosen, a demonstration should be accompanied by a verbal explanation or follow-up discussion. One type of demonstration, however, asks students to observe without interactions. This method is referred to as the **inquiry demonstration.**

The inquiry demonstration is similar to the Suchman inquiry approach (see Chapter 8) or the Socratic method (see the next section of this chapter) because students observe the demonstration in silence. These observations are then followed up with teacher questioning, a whole-class discussion, or students conducting experiments. Students are asked to think logically, make inferences, and reach conclusions.

REFLECTIONS ON TEACHER PRACTICE 9.1: Seeking Quality

1. How can you help students take responsibility for their own learning and behavior?

2. How can students be taught to objectively evaluate each other and themselves?

How do we get kids to work toward quality rather than just completion? I struggled with this for a long time, and this year I finally really and truly got it: AUDIENCE and REFLECTION.

The journey started with a series of PowerPoint presentations to the class. After each group presented, I asked the audience to share each presentation's strengths and areas that needed improvement. It was slow going at first; I had to remind them time and again that their critiques had to be specific so the presenters would know what to repeat and what to avoid in another situation.

I went through this process several more times with various pieces of work. My kids developed better on task behavior, became more likely to use the rubric while they were working, and my students' comments were more specific. Better yet, more students were completing projects, and the projects themselves were of higher quality. The only thing I was not happy with was presentation skills; though the kids would point out lack of eye contact, volume, and so on in their critiques, I didn't see the same sort of improvement as in the projects themselves.

As a result, with the last presentation I had kids work with their partners to score each presentation with the rubric. While content was included, the bulk of the points were focused on volume, enthusiasm, eye contact, speaking clearly, and so forth. The kids filled out the rubrics, made comments at the bottom, and then we shared our thoughts in discussions. As a result, I saw more kids actively working on volume, eye contact, and enthusiasm, among other things.

They have become very good evaluators, and no one wants to be evaluated poorly by their peers. We've developed a common language and understanding of what makes quality work, and the kids are judging solely on the work and not who the presenter is. As they work, I push them to answer the question, "Is this good enough?" themselves, using the scoring guide and their own experiences. I can honestly say it has helped AND, if we don't present something we've done in class, they always want to know why. We put those items on the wall, and the discussion continues after class.

It is a process. I did A LOT of modeling, demonstrating the appropriate way to give praise and make suggestions. If a student made a particularly insightful/ interesting/appropriate comment, I'd point to their comment as the type we were looking for. I ALWAYS start with the positive, no matter how dreadful the presentation is; we found good things to say about students with one slide out of the required eight, incomplete work, and so on. There is always a strength, a place to start, and while I had to connect the dots for them at first, they've gotten really good at doing it themselves. Of course, they still really enjoy pointing out the flaws, BUT they do it in a completely objective, supportive manner. I wonder if they zero in on the negatives so easily because that's what they've seen modeled for them by their teachers through the years?

It is just not okay to treat others poorly in my classroom or in my presence. I've tried to model what I want from them at all times. We sometimes believe kids know how to act, and while they might be able to describe it, putting it into practice is an entirely separate matter. We must teach, model, and practice how to talk with each other thoughtfully.

As I've thought all of this over, I've realized how important it is to teach kids to become their own evaluators. They came in so dependent on me to tell them what was good and what needed improvement. If I am *really* going to teach them, I need to teach them to evaluate themselves and hold themselves to high standards. In the end, it's not about me, it's about them learning how to recognize and work for quality—for themselves.

—*Ellen, middle-level English/language arts teacher*

Please visit the Student Study site at **www.sagepub.com/mooreteachingk8** *for additional discussion questions and assignments.*

SOURCE: www.middleweb.com. Reprinted with permission.

Students need the opportunity to work together and to learn from each other.

How can you use demonstrations in your future classroom? Begin with a strong set induction that generates interest, shares academic expectations, and perhaps defines important terms. You might want to tell students what they should look for during the demonstration, but don't give too many details about what is going to happen—you don't want to ruin their anticipation!

Following the introduction, complete the demonstration as simply and directly as possible. If you are demonstrating the proper use of equipment or explaining a procedure, you should follow the desired action step-by-step, with pauses and explanations (and possibly a handout) to clarify the actions. Occasionally, when you want students to totally focus on the actions taking place, you might want to conduct an inquiry demonstration instead. In fact, it might work best to perform the demonstration silently the first time and then repeat it with explanations. Finally, when conducting classroom demonstrations, keep these guidelines in mind:

1. Go slowly so students can follow.

2. Break complex procedures into small steps. Demonstrate each step separately.

3. Once students understand the components, repeat the entire demonstration.

4. Remember, left and right are reversed, so set up the demonstration from the students' perspective.

Carefully plan and practice your demonstration for success. Be sure your demonstration is doable, your explanation is comprehensible, and your time is manageable. Use semicircular seating arrangements to ensure that every student can see the demonstration. Present high-interest demonstrations to maintain student interest; use questions as needed to clarify concepts and regain wandering attention. After the demonstration, have students walk and talk through the steps to demonstrate their competency and comprehension. Evaluate the effectiveness of your demonstration using the Socratic method.

THE SOCRATIC METHOD

Socrates, an ancient Greek philosopher, is so renowned for his effective teaching strategies that teachers still use the Socratic method today to develop content information. In general, teachers use a questioning-and-interaction sequence to draw information from students until they discover a logical contradiction. Essentially, the Socratic method follows this pattern:

1. Begin with a broad, open-ended question that most students can answer.

2. Ask a series of questions to narrow the range of responses and focus the students' thinking on the target topic.

3. Intersperse periodic summaries of the discussion among the questions to keep the salient points in the forefront.

4. Ask a concluding question to bring students to the desired endpoint.

Socrates used several questioning strategies to prompt pupil ponderings and continue the conversation. Students are asked to clarify their responses by adding more supportive details, question the accuracy of their assumptions, and examine how they arrived at their opinions. During the conversation, they need to honor others' perspectives and explore all the possibilities. Near the end of the conversation, they pause to consider the implications or consequences of their decisions and elaborate upon what the decision or solution means to them.

Socrates' original techniques required individualized teacher–student interactions and relationships. In today's classroom, the teacher usually questions one student first, then another, and another—moving slowly throughout the class (see a sample science script at http://educate.intel.com/en/ProjectDesign/InstructionalStrategies/Questioning/). This dialogue becomes a collective attempt to find the answer to a fundamental question or issue.

The Socratic method can be quite effective in small-group and tutorial sessions.

Consider this dialogue relative to *choice*. Please note that since this is a values clarification dialogue it would be best to conduct it privately to protect the student's dignity.

Teacher:	Suppose your school is having a science fair and you can get class credit for presenting a project. Someone offers to do the science project for you for a price. What do you do?
Mike:	I would pay them and let them do it for me.
Teacher:	What would you do if a science judge asked if it was your work?

Mike:	I paid for it. I would say it was mine.
Teacher:	But wouldn't that be a lie?
Mike:	I did pay for it. So it is mine.
Teacher:	All right, but you know it wasn't really your work. Suppose the judge asks you to verify that you did the actual work.
Mike:	I'd have no choice but to say I didn't.
Teacher:	Suppose it wasn't the science judge, but rather your science teacher who asked, "Mike, did you do all this good work?"
Mike:	I might say, "Yes, I did it."
Teacher:	Okay, why would you say that?
Mike:	Fear of getting no credit.
Teacher:	Does that mean it is all right to have someone else do your work and lie? Then, doctors should be able to do it, your classmates, the president, and your parents?
Mike:	[*Long pause*] Well, no.
Teacher:	Then it is okay for you but not others? Are there different rules for you?
Mike:	[*Longer pause*] No.
Teacher:	What would you think of yourself now that you've said that you would lie to your teacher out of fear? Are you that kind of person? You would pay someone else to do your work. What vision would you have of yourself?
Mike:	Well, what with the thought I have given it today, I would feel bad. Before today, I wouldn't have cared.
Teacher:	Do you have a different image of yourself now?
Mike:	Yes. I think more of myself today than I would have yesterday because I know there's a better me and I should do the right thing.

Essentially, the Socratic method is a process in which ideas are debated until some recognizable clarity (the light) is reached. Teachers must have a clear vision of what they want students to learn; they have an endpoint in mind so they can steer the discussion in that direction.

CONCEPT ATTAINMENT

Concept attainment is an instructional strategy that uses a structured inquiry process. The strategy is based on the research of Jerome Bruner and his associates, who investigated how different variables affected the concept-learning process. To help students develop a concept, teachers provide a set of items (symbols, words, passages, pictures, objects) for student perusal. Students discuss and identify the attributes of each item until they develop a tentative hypothesis (definition) about the concept. Next, students separate the items into two groups, those that have the attribute and those that don't. They test their hypothesis by applying it to other examples of the concept. Finally, students demonstrate that they have attained the concept by generating their own examples and nonexamples. Concept attainment, then, is the search for and identification of attributes that can be used to distinguish examples of a given group or category from nonexamples. With carefully chosen examples, it is possible to use concept attainment to teach almost any concept in all content areas.

To illustrate the concept attainment process, consider the concept of *proper noun*.

- First, the teacher chooses the targeted concept (e.g., proper noun).

- Begin by making a list of both positive "yes" and negative "no" examples: The examples can be written on chart paper, flash cards, or a whiteboard.

- *Positive examples:* Present positive examples containing distinctive attributes of the concept (e.g., Jane, Houston, John, Seattle, United States, George Washington, Honda, Titanic). The examples should emphasize the idea that a proper noun means a *specific* person, place, or thing.

- *Negative examples:* Next present negative or nonexamples of the concept (e.g., table, chair, cat, dog, farm, boy, town, chair). Note the negative examples differentiate *proper nouns* from *common nouns*.

- Designate one area of the whiteboard for examples and one area for nonexamples or post a chart with two columns—one marked YES and the other marked NO.

- Present the first card or example by saying, "This is a YES." Place it under the appropriate column (e.g., Seattle is a YES).

- Present the next card or nonexample and say, "This is a NO." Place it under the NO column (e.g., town is a NO).

- Repeat this process until there are three examples under each column.

- Ask the class to look at the three examples under the YES column and discuss how they are alike. Ask, "What do they have in common?"

- For the next three examples under each column, ask the students to decide if the examples go under YES or NO.

- At this point, there are six examples under each column. Students should begin to hypothesize a name for the concept. These hypotheses are tested with further examples and nonexamples provided by the teacher. Students determine which hypotheses are acceptable and which ones have to be rejected based on the examples. They also can suggest additional hypotheses at this point. The process of presenting examples, analyzing hypotheses, presenting additional examples, and continuing to analyze hypotheses continues until all the hypotheses but one are eliminated.

- Discuss the process with the class. Students should be asked to explicitly define the hypothesis and identify the characteristics. Students are then asked to define a proper noun.

- Next, students apply the concept by classifying examples or generating examples of their own.

- Students analyze their own thinking (metacognition). Ask questions such as, "Did anyone have to change his or her thinking?" or "What made you change your mind?" or "When did you begin to see this concept?"

The concept attainment strategy is based on the assumption that one of the best ways to learn a concept is by seeing examples of it. Because examples are central to the concept attainment activity, special attention must be paid to their selection and sequencing.

COOPERATIVE LEARNING

The evolving constructivist perspectives on learning have fueled interest in collaboration and cooperative learning. As a result, cooperative learning has emerged as a promising instructional approach. Cooperative learning requires that students work together in heterogeneous groups of four to seven members to accomplish a task. Heterogeneous groupings of mixed performance level, gender, and ethnicity that represent a cross section of the entire class work best.

Group members are expected to be interdependent, or reliant upon one another to complete the group's task. Teachers can promote interdependence by designing complex tasks that require multiple minds, providing scarce resources that must be shared, and assigning group roles. Although cooperative learning groups are given considerable autonomy in deciding how to accomplish the task, to ensure that each person contributes to the group effort, grading reflects both whole-group efforts and individual performance. Thus, overachievers do not feel the need to do all of the work and noncontributors aren't rewarded with high grades. Teachers often assign roles and responsibilities to students to encourage cooperation and full participation. Primary students' roles might include leader, reporter, and helper. Intermediate and middle students' roles might include team facilitator, recorder, encourager, materials monitor, taskmaster, quiet captain, and coach. Make sure the assigned roles support the desired learning outcome and that students understand their roles.

Cooperative Learning Formats

Cooperative learning takes many forms. The most common approaches include peer tutoring, group investigation, and the jigsaw strategy.

Peer Tutoring. One of the simplest forms of cooperative learning uses students as supplementary instructors in basic skills areas. After direct instruction, student pairs complete structured assignments to reinforce the new material. Students take turns tutoring and supporting one another's efforts. Although student pairs are usually mixed ability, gifted students also need to have an opportunity to work with their intellectual peers. Another form of two-person interactions is share pairs. The teacher poses a question or short task. After an independent "think time," students share their ideas with a shoulder partner. Volunteers share with the class. This strategy works especially well for opening and closing activities.

Group Investigation. Group investigation involves a combination of independent learning and group work. Heterogeneous student teams work on a common task such as a science experiment, creative dramatic presentation, community project, or artwork. Student groups develop goals, assign individual responsibilities, and complete the projects. When designing group investigations, teachers need to consider topic selection, authentic performance tasks, heterogeneous group formation, implementation, time and materials management, student presentations, and evaluation. Once the investigations have commenced, the teacher's role is to facilitate students' cooperative and academic efforts. Grades are assigned for individual contributions as well as the quality of the final group product.

Jigsaw Strategy. The jigsaw strategy is a cooperative learning activity that helps all students learn a great deal of information in a short amount of time. The teacher selects a topic that has multiple subtopics—for example, the solar system. Each student is assigned a subtopic (e.g., Mars) to study in more depth using the textbook, reference materials, and the Internet. Once their independent research is complete, students form expert teams representing each subtopic. All of the students who studied Mars, for example, convene to share their information. Expert teams cooperatively decide the most important information they wish to share with everyone else. Then students form learning teams comprised of one member from each of the expert teams. Student "experts" share information about their subtopics. The teacher may evaluate students' efforts at multiple junctures—review of individual research results, expert team quizzes, and learning team tests, or cooperative competitions (e.g., Jeopardy game).

MURIEL: A REFLECTIVE CASE STUDY

Muriel was excited and a wee bit anxious about using a cooperative learning activity for the very first time. Her fifth grade students had developed a comfortable learning community and seemed to prefer interpersonal learning activities, so they were poised and ready for a new learning venture. She puzzled over which strategy to use for her lesson on animal kingdoms.

1. Which cooperative learning activity would you suggest for this topic?

2. How could Muriel structure the activity to ensure student success?

3. How can Muriel evaluate students' efforts?

Group work gives students the opportunity to learn important social and cognitive skills from each other.

Cooperative learning can be used to promote higher level learning development inquiry skills, complete major projects or lab work, practice skills, review for tests, and create products or presentations demonstrating what was learned. Members are held accountable for contributing to the group effort and for taking responsibility for their own learning. When structured properly, cooperative learning increases students' achievement and critical thinking skills across all grade levels and content areas. In addition to boosting achievement, cooperative learning builds a learning community by enhancing students' self-esteem, developing their social interaction skills, increasing their tolerance for peer differences, and improving their attitude toward school. All students feel special because they have an opportunity to contribute to their team's efforts using their preferred multiple intelligences and learning styles.

Graphic Organizers

To facilitate team discussions and presentations, cooperative groups can use **graphic organizers**, or tables and charts, to visually represent complex information in a simple, structured display. Graphic organizers can be grouped into three main categories from simple to more complex: (1) sequential (timeline, flowchart, cyclical, hierarchy), (2) single main concept (continuum, argumentation structure, spider maps), and (3) multiple concepts (Venn diagram, matrix). Examples of the three types of graphic organizers can be examined on the web-based student study site (**www.sagepub.com/mooreteachingk8**) or by typing "graphic organizers" into an Internet search engine.

Video Link 9.1: Watch a video about graphic organizers.

Teachers should introduce and model how to use graphic organizers by recording students' responses during whole-class discussions or direct instruction. Once students are familiar with the strategy, cooperative groups can use graphic organizers to facilitate their discussions and to demonstrate what they have learned. The processes of carefully analyzing the information and determining how to construct the organizer increase student comprehension and retention of new information. After multiple encounters with graphic organizers, students can use them independently to organize their learning logs, prewriting outlines, etc.

Table 9.1 summarizes the teaching approaches presented in this section. Review the summary and check your knowledge of this section by completing Reflect and Apply Exercise 9.1.

Through the Eyes of an Expert

Guiding Times to Talk

You know the scene. A classroom packed with students. There's one of you and at least twenty of them, all chattering at once. They're active and engaged while they're doing what *they* want, but what about when you start your lesson? How can you maintain their naturally high levels of enthusiasm while providing structured and meaningful learning opportunities?

"Controlling the chaos" of cooperative learning requires well-developed and practiced procedures, but the benefits far outweigh the preparation time involved! Try these simple, motivating strategies that encourage "time to talk" for specific purposes, while developing habits of respectful discourse in your students.

Perhaps you've incorporated a version of "Think, Pair, Share" in your class. Well, each of these is a slight variation that can be easily integrated into any classroom routine on a daily basis. Instead of calling on one student at a time during class discussions, pose a question or statement for consideration and direct all students to respond as they:

- *Turn & Talk* about the designated topic

- *Say Something* or give an *I Remember* statement about something they feel is especially important

- or, ask students to make a connection to the content by offering a *That Reminds Me* statement

After presenting the question or prompt to the class and directing students to "pair and share" with one another, allow a mere 30–60 seconds for discussion. This enables both partners to briefly respond, yet doesn't typically allow enough time for much distraction from the assigned task. Once you've signaled the class to return to whole-group instruction, you may ask a few individual students to share their responses aloud (as would occur in a traditional class discussion).

For topics in which a lengthier discussion is required, try this "Timed Pair Share" activity called "Talk a Mile a Minute!" For each pair, ask students to designate who will speak first and who will be the listener. (Both partners will have the opportunity to assume both roles.) During the first minute, the speaker may provide a stream of commentary on the topic while the other partner actively listens; he/she may nod and gesture accordingly, but is not permitted to respond verbally. The partners reverse roles for the second minute. During the third minute, each partner is allowed 30 seconds for a closing response. You will be utterly amazed at the demonstration of cognitive engagement that will occur in just over 3 minutes!

By regularly utilizing these few cooperative learning strategies, your students' engagement and motivation will increase effortlessly! So when they get chatty: don't fight it, guide it!

SOURCE: Carol A. Withrow, Elementary Literacy Coach/Writing Instructor—McNabb Elementary School, McNabb Kentucky, Adjunct Instructor—Murray State University (MSU), Assistant Director, Purchase Area Writing Project (PAWP), MSU. Used with permission.

TABLE 9.1   Integrated Methods

Method	Description
Ordinary demonstration	Individual shows and explains something to class
Inquiry demonstration	Individual shows class something without explanation; students observe, make inferences, and reach conclusions
Socratic method	Questioning and interaction to draw information out of students
Concept attainment	Teaching strategy designed to help students learn concepts and practice analytical thinking skills
Cooperative learning	Students work together as a team on assigned tasks

REFLECT AND APPLY EXERCISE 9.1: Integrated Directed Instructional Strategies

Reflect

- What challenges do demonstrations pose for teachers?

- Describe the Socratic method. What are the strengths and weaknesses of this method?

- Describe a time when one of your teachers used the concept attainment or cooperative learning method of teaching. How successful were their efforts?

Apply

- What are some good elementary and middle school demonstration strategies? How can teachers give students a sense of ownership?

- Is the Socratic method a viable teaching method for the grade level you plan to teach? Why or why not?

- Choose a concept you might teach one day. How could you use the concept attainment strategy to teach it? Provide specific details.

- Give a specific example of how you could use each of the cooperative learning strategies presented in this chapter in your future classroom.

SOURCE: Reprinted with permission from ProTeacher, a professional community for elementary school teachers (www.proteacher.net).

REFLECTIONS ON TEACHER PRACTICE 9.2: Cooperative Learning

1. How can students benefit from group work? How can it result in more effective teaching and learning?

2. What potential do you see for group work at the grade level you expect to teach? Is group work more effective at lower or upper grade levels? If so, why? If not, why not?

The key to successful cooperative grouping is keeping the kids on task while they are working. If you make the group sizes reasonably small—no more than three, then you will have more constructive work time. I have found that when you have groups of more than three, somebody in the group is coasting, while others are carrying the weight of the work. I also make sure that the kids work quietly. The more noise there is in the room, the more it seems as if less gets done. Kids get off task so easily, especially when they get noisy and get into the chatting mode. I think that if you give the students a grade for their cooperative work, they will work more seriously. Elect a team leader, and make sure that each person in the group has an assigned job.

I have successfully had kids do maps together. They can also work together in small groups to read the textbook. Each group can pic a section of the text, then report it to the class. Sometimes I have them get together as a small group to play reporter. They report the event as if it happened yesterday. "And in today's news, the colonists dumped tea into Boston harbor. . . ."

—*Wanda, elementary teacher*

Please visit the Student Study site at **www.sagepub.com/mooreteachingk8** *for additional discussion questions and assignments.*

SIMULATIONS AND GAMES

Most modern-day students have grown up playing high-tech games and participating in electronic simulations using arcades, home gaming stations, or Internet gaming sites. Teachers can capitalize upon students' "gaming" interests by including simulations and games as part of their teaching repertoire to create interest, relieve tension, develop skills, evaluate knowledge, and create a classroom learning community. These do not necessarily have to be high-tech venues, having students talk face-to-face to work through simulations and to play games is equally beneficial. Although there is no clear-cut difference between *simulation* and *games*, usually games are played to win, whereas simulations need not have a winner.

Simulations

Simulations present artificial situations that represent reality but remove individual risk. These can be viewed as models of what exists or might exist under manageable and controlled conditions. Teachers can use human simulations (role-playing or sociodramas) or person-to-computer simulations (**educational games**).

Role-playing is an extemporaneous reenactment of a historic, current, or future event or imaginary situation. Teachers begin by giving students a thorough briefing of the

"I like educational toys. I like educational TV. I like educational
reading material. It's education I don't like."

context of the scene—what has led up to this moment? For example, students can re-create the signing of the Declaration of Independence, reenact the first Thanksgiving, or "become" Winnie the Pooh and his friends as they track Woozles. Indeed, students can bring to life historic moments, scenes from short stories or plays, events from the lives of different people, courtroom dramatizations, ethical dilemmas, mock town meetings, or UN sessions. Whatever the episode, teachers need to describe the situation in detail to students and set clear guidelines.

Next, individual or small groups of students assume character roles and spontaneously act out the scene. These simulations develop students' problem-solving skills, enable students to gain insight into others' perspectives, prepare students to deal with difficult situations, and teach students how to make decisions. Because students can "hide" themselves in their roles, teachers can address difficult or sensitive issues without making it too personal.

Afterward, the class analyzes the characters' behaviors and the consequences of their actions. For example, young students could recreate a home fire drill; teens could reenact a peer argument to learn conflict resolution skills.

The *sociodrama* is a form of role-playing that focuses on the various ways a group could solve a problem. For example, students can assume multiple roles to reenact while exploring a volatile issue at a faux town meeting, family situation, or UN session.

Educational Games

One of the best-known educational games is Monopoly, a simulation board game of the real estate business. Educational games involve students in decision-making roles in which they compete for certain objectives according to specified rules. Thus, educational games should reflect real-life situations because they offer students the opportunity to experience

Video Link 9.2:
Watch a video
about motivation.

authentic roles. For example, teachers can form student "families" with assigned roles, lifestyle, and specified income. Family teams compete to see how well they can budget their resources while meeting their family members' needs. The competitive nature of games, however, should be kept in perspective.

Teachers should also consider using appropriate computer simulations and games in the classroom. Simulations and games are beneficial because they actively involve students in their own learning, provide immediate feedback, enable students to practice communication skills, create a high degree of interest and enthusiasm, and promote and reward analytical and critical thinking. They also allow teachers to address a wide range of student capabilities at the same time and allow safe experimentation with a model of the real environment.

Simulations and games are high-interest activities that motivate students to develop new skills and gain new knowledge while they're having fun. In addition to using commercial products, teachers and students can design unique simulations and games. Teachers should play games and think through simulations in advance to ensure their educational validity and to proactively address any possible conflicts or issues that might arise. Well-written guides will facilitate students' educational gaming experiences.

INDIVIDUALIZED STRATEGIES

Because students have varied backgrounds and abilities, they do not learn or master skills uniformly. Therefore, teachers need to customize students' academic experiences through individualized instruction, independent study, and mastery learning.

Individualized Instruction

Ideally, individualized instruction engages students in instructional activities tailored to meet their interests, needs, and abilities. Accordingly, teachers vary the learning pace, instructional objectives, delivery method, or materials to meet the students' needs. One of the simplest ways to individualize instruction is to permit students to work on the same series of short, related activities or lessons at their own pace. High achievers rapidly move through the lessons before participating in enrichment activities. Struggling students move through the lessons more slowly, reworking troublesome areas and receiving assistance as needed.

Teachers also individualize instruction by varying the learning objectives. They administer a pretest to see which students have already mastered the intended outcomes and use these results to tailor activities to meet all students' needs. High achievers progress through a series of lessons on a related topic or a topic of their choice while low-ability students work through the traditional lesson. All students are given dignified, high-interest, authentic tasks.

Sometimes teachers vary the delivery method to individualize instruction while still reaching the desired outcome. One student may rely on a textbook, whereas another may work with tutors. Still other students with learning difficulties may need to work with special teachers. Self-instructional packages, learning centers, and computer-assisted instruction (CAI) are other possible methods that could provide individualized instruction.

Finally, teachers can vary the materials used in accomplishing the objectives. Elementary teachers might use leveled readers whereby all students are studying the same topic (e.g., volcanoes) but reading developmentally appropriate books. Middle school teachers might record the chapter so struggling readers can still learn the textbook information. Using assistive devices such as closed-circuit monitors and "speaking" computer software plus audiovisual resources such as films, CDs, DVDs, and video clips will enhance all students' academic efforts.

Essays and research projects are also an excellent way to individualize instruction because they allow students or small groups of students to pursue areas of interest. Essays can be assigned on broad topics such as patriotism, family heroes, the space program, or the national debt, whereas research projects can be given in such areas as designing a new way to get to school, creating a model of an animal in its natural habitat, or writing and/or performing a play.

Not all individualized instructional efforts need to be teacher-directed. Sociolinguistic theorists propose that many students learn best through peer interactions. Therefore, teachers can individualize instruction through heterogeneous group work, cooperative learning, and mastery learning activities. Also, student assistants can facilitate group work, demonstrate equipment, or direct discussions.

Independent Study

One of the goals of education is to help students become self-directed, lifelong learners. There is no reason for teachers to do what students can do for themselves. Students of all ages benefit from some independent study, or educational activities completed with little or no guidance.

Students need to learn to work independently while teachers are teaching small groups or conferencing with individuals. The length of independent study time varies depending upon the age and maturity of the students. Independent study activities can take many forms. Students may complete independent practice pages related to the content area (e.g., spelling, math computation), respond to assigned readings, visit learning centers, or work on unfinished long-term projects. Students might be especially motivated to pursue inquiry projects on self-selected topics of personal interest.

Teachers should provide special enrichment activities for students who finish their seat-work quickly (and up to standard). Activities could include computer drills, sustained silent reading, jigsaw or Sudoku puzzles, or open-ended learning centers.

Mastery Learning

Before focusing on the mastery learning model, let's review the traditional model of instruction (Figure 9.1). Students who use the traditional model provide the same activity for all students at the same time. They follow a traditional sequence of events: set induction, primary instruction (presentation, discussion, reading, media, and/or seatwork), then closing. At the end of the lesson, teachers evaluate student achievement relative to their intended outcomes.

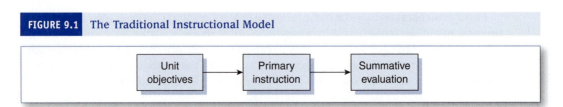

FIGURE 9.1 The Traditional Instructional Model

The mastery learning model also takes a group approach to teaching. However, this model's diagnostic-corrective-enrichment activities provide a high degree of individualization because students learn at different paces and use different materials. As depicted in Figure 9.2, the mastery learning model includes six steps.

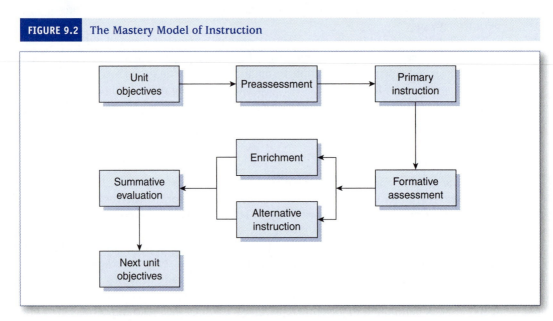

FIGURE 9.2 The Mastery Model of Instruction

Teachers begin by identifying their instructional objectives. Before they deliver the primary instruction, however, they administer a preassessment to ascertain students' prior knowledge of the intended outcomes. After analyzing the preassessment results, teachers provide additional instruction for students who lack prerequisite skills and knowledge (Step 2) before delivering their primary instruction to all students using integrated methods (Step 3). At this point (Step 4), the mastery model parts from the traditional model: Teachers give a formative assessment (progress check or diagnostic test) to identify which students have achieved the desired mastery level and which students are in need of further instruction. Those at the mastery level are directed to enrichment activities, whereas those below the mastery level move on to the fifth step, individual or group remediation activities. Further formative evaluations are an integral part of the alternative instructional sequence. Once the initial alternative activities have been completed, teachers repeatedly check student progress until all students achieve mastery. During this sixth and final phase, all students are given a final evaluation.

The basic structure of the mastery learning model can take two forms. In the first, the enrichments and alternatives parallel each other, with the summative assessment providing closure for the unit. As students achieve mastery, they are routed to the enrichment component until the class is ready for the formal evaluation. The summative evaluation also may be administered to students when the formative evaluation indicates mastery has been achieved. Students who test out early can be involved in other types of individualized activities, or they can work on the next set of unit objectives on an individualized basis.

Effectiveness of Individualization

Under the right conditions, the mastery learning approach leads to higher student achievement at any grade level. When used as the only method of instruction, however, this method has not proven superior to traditional methods.

Teachers' decisions on whether to use individualization should be guided by their students' unique needs and by the nature of the learning task. Students need to be self-motivated, independent, critical thinkers who would benefit from long periods of individualized instructional activities. Therefore, teachers need to use a combination of traditional and individualized instructional strategies to keep all students on task and to meet all students' developmental and academic needs. If carefully designed and monitored, individualization can be effective at providing needed remediation or enrichment. Students can work at their own pace on assignments geared to their ability, for example, but receive direct instruction from the teacher with the rest of the class. The greater active involvement in their own learning generally results in a higher level of interest, better motivation, and a feeling of independence and self-discipline.

DRILL AND PRACTICE

Drill and practice activities strive to increase performance accuracy and speed through systematic, repeated "workouts" in targeted skill areas. Drill focuses upon helping students internalize basic knowledge for future instant recall; practice is concerned with improvement of skills. Thus, one drills multiplication facts but practices playing scales on the violin.

To internalize newly learned concepts and skills, students need to have multiple drill, practice, and application opportunities at the outset, followed up by periodic reviews. Therefore, teachers need to systematically provide drill and practice sessions as an integral part of curricular activities, not as time fillers. Teachers should provide activities that match the students' ability levels, hold them accountable, and make it clear that students are expected to work independently with minimal teacher intervention.

TECHNOLOGY INTEGRATION

Effective teachers integrate technology throughout the curriculum to motivate students while accommodating their special needs and to teach and practice new skills. **Computer-based instruction (CBI)** has been expanding rapidly as an innovative "tech"-nique for accomplishing these goals. CBI uses a structured curriculum; it allows students to work at their own pace, provides frequent feedback and positive reinforcement, and measures performance quickly.

"We're going to need a new computer in our class today.
I hope I'm the one it replaces."

SOURCE: Created by Martha Campbell.

To develop students' technological and academic proficiency, teachers should provide daily CBI activities that remediate, practice, and extend information presented in class. CBI can and should be applied in all content areas in the elementary and middle school. For example, after reading *The Mitten*, students can extend and enrich their reading skills by visiting Jan Brett's website. SpongeBob Squarepants Typing and Mavis Beacon Teaches Typing programs can teach elementary and middle school students how to type. Students can vicariously experience pioneers' perspectives while traveling westward via the Oregon Trail. They can dissect frogs using V-Frog, refine visual/spatial and directional skills with One Key Logo, and practice their math skills using Speedway Math or Gnarly Math.

Table 9.2 summarizes the self-directed techniques covered in this section. Review Table 9.2, and check your knowledge of this section by completing Reflect and Apply Exercise 9.2.

REFLECT AND APPLY EXERCISE 9.2: Individualized Instruction

Reflect

- What is individualized instruction? What are some pros and cons of individualized instruction?

- Did any of your past teachers involve you in individualized instruction? If so, how successful was it? Did you like this instructional approach?

Apply

- What challenges does individualized instruction pose for elementary teachers? Middle school teachers?

- How would you prepare students to participate in individualized instructional activities?

Computer labs as a supplement to classroom teaching offer students opportunities for practical application of instruction.

TABLE 9.2	Self-Directed Approaches
Method	**Description**
Computer integration	Using computers to enhance curriculum learning
Simulations and games	Models of artificial situations and events designed to provide no-risk experiences for students
Individualized instruction	Instruction tailored to interests, needs, and abilities of students
Independent study	Activities carried out with little or no guidance
Mastery learning	Diagnostic-corrective-enrichment model where students work on objectives until mastery is achieved
Drill and practice	Development of automatic and/or improved performance

This completes the discussion of the various integrated teaching strategies. Complete Application Activity 9.2 to further explore the use of integrated instructional strategies at the grade level you expect to teach.

APPLICATION ACTIVITY 9.2 Integrated Instruction

List the integrated instructional strategies we addressed in this chapter. Rate the usefulness of each strategy for the grade level you expect to teach. Use this rating scale: (1) appropriate and useful, (2) limited usefulness, and (3) not appropriate and not useful. Explain your ratings.

SUMMARY

This chapter focused upon integrated teaching methods. The main points were as follows:

- Integrated directed strategies give students some control over their own learning.

The Demonstration Method

- Demonstrations can be effective when used appropriately. Prepare the materials in advance. Practice the demonstration before class. During the presentation, go slowly, repeat components, and keep it simple and focused.

The Socratic Method

- The Socratic method of teaching is designed to draw information from students through the use of questions. Teachers can use the Socratic teaching when interacting with individuals, small groups, or the entire class.

Concept Attainment

- The concept attainment strategy uses a structured inquiry process. Students learn concepts by comparing and contrasting the attributes of examples and nonexamples.

Cooperative Learning

- Cooperative learning has emerged as a promising instructional approach. Forms of cooperative learning include peer tutoring, group investigation, and the jigsaw strategy.

- Graphic organizers can be valuable teaching aids when students are working in groups.

Simulations and Games

- Simulations are problem situations that represent reality.

- Role-playing helps student consider the motives behind actions and behaviors.

- Educational games involve students in decision-making roles.

Individualized Strategies

- Individualized strategies include individualized instruction, independent study, and mastery learning, and effectiveness of individualization. These techniques are tailored to fit students' needs and abilities.

- Teachers can individualize instruction by allowing students to work at their own pace on different objectives, using different materials, and assigning essays or research projects.

- Mastery learning represents a model of instruction where students continue their work on unit objectives until mastery is achieved.

Drill and Practice

- Drill and practice provide students with needed accuracy and/or speed. Drill is usually concerned with instant recall, whereas practice is more often concerned with skill improvement.

Technology Integration

- Technology should be integrated throughout the curriculum.

- CBI is used to teach a wide range of skills across the content areas.

DISCUSSION QUESTIONS AND ACTIVITIES

1. **Demonstration Topics.** Generate a list of demonstrations that would be appropriate at the grade level you expect to teach. For each item, specify who should perform the demonstration: (T)eacher, (S)tudent, (B)oth.

2. **Integrated Directed Methods.** When is it appropriate to use integrated directed teaching methods? Consider your instructional intent, as well as the students themselves. Would mastery learning be appropriate for the students you expect to teach? Why or why not?

3. **Role-Playing.** Identify some core values that could be taught using role-playing (e.g., honesty, fairness, citizenship).

4. **Educational Games.** Suppose a parent criticized your use of games in the classroom; prepare a response entitled "Why Our School Uses Games."

5. **Individualized Strategies.** If individualized strategies are so important and beneficial, why are they not implemented by all teachers? Provide rationales for your reasons.

TECH CONNECTION

Teaching can be viewed as making connections between the real world and various aspects of the curriculum. Complete these application activities to discover ways to use technology to help students make real-world connections.

- Find an online lesson plan that uses direct instruction. How could it be changed to reflect one of the integrated instruction models found in this chapter? How could technology further enhance the lesson? You might want to access the following Internet URL websites for ideas www.teachnology.com, www.edzone.net/ ~ mwestern, http://wtvi.com/teks, and www.eduref .org/Virtual/Lessons/index.shtml. Form groups of four or five to share ideas. Use PowerPoint and SMART Board technology to share your group's findings with the class.

- Access www.enchantedlearning.com/graphicorganizers. Review and analyze the graphic organizers presented on this site. Which organizers would be useful for you at the grade level you expect to teach? Cooperatively complete a graphic organizer related to the concept featured in the lesson plan you just revised in the application activity. Be ready to share.

CONNECTION WITH THE FIELD

1. **Teacher Interviews.** Visit with several classroom teachers, and discuss with them how they use integrated directed instruction. Do they use individualized strategies extensively? Why or why not?

2. **Classroom Observation.** Visit several public school classrooms. Keep a record of the different methods used. What integrated directed methods did you observe? Was there a pattern? Were drill and practice used?

3. **Teaching.** Prepare and teach a mini lesson using the demonstration method. Use the **microteaching** guidelines and forms in Appendix A to plan and analyze your mini lesson.

4. **Teaching Analysis.** Make a videotape of your mini teaching lesson; then critically analyze it with your peers.

STUDENT STUDY SITE

Visit the Student Study Site at **www.sagepub.com/mooreteachingk8** for these additional learning tools:

- Video clips
- Web resources
- Self quizzes
- E-Flashcards
- Full-text SAGE journal articles
- Portfolio Connection
- Licensing Preparation/Praxis Connection

CHAPTER 10

Teaching Effective Thinking Strategies

In the twentieth century, the ability to engage in careful, reflective thought has been viewed in various ways: as a fundamental characteristic of an educated person, as a requirement for responsible citizenship in a democratic society, and, more recently, as an employability skill for an increasingly wide range of jobs.

—Kathleen Cotton

Before We Begin

Today's students will become tomorrow's leaders. What are some local, national, and global issues that they will be expected to solve? How can teachers equip students with the thinking skills they will need to overcome these challenges? Be ready to compare your view with classmates.

OVERVIEW

When our founding fathers signed the Declaration of Independence, they not only declared freedom from taxation and tyranny but they also declared freedom from ignorance. In direct contrast to the European social caste system of education, they envisioned a free public school system that would create an educated citizenry who could make informed decisions supporting the democratic system and American way of life. To make the American dream a reality for all citizens, it was necessary and even desirable to provide students with a sound education in basic knowledge and skills.

In today's information age and global society, knowing basic facts and skills isn't enough to meet new challenges and to solve increasingly complex problems. Tomorrow's future citizens must learn *how* to think so they can function responsibly and solve problems in ways that respect others, society, and the world. Undoubtedly, this goal requires teachers to explicitly teach the thinking skills deemed necessary for a lifetime of continuous learning and leadership.

How can teachers equip students with these thinking skills? In *The Prophet*, Kahlil Gibran (1989) told us, "If the teacher is indeed wise, he does not bid you enter the house of his wisdom, but rather leads you to the threshold of your mind." These words suggest that thinking skills must be placed high on the educational agenda as one of the most essential skills needed today. This chapter will focus on teaching students how to think. A wide variety of thinking skills will be examined; however, we will emphasize the ideas, methods, and issues related to **critical thinking** and **creative thinking**.

OBJECTIVES

After completing your study of Chapter 10, you should be able to

- define *thinking* and differentiate among the various categories of thinking skills,
- explain the four stages of the creative thinking process and various difficulties that can hinder the process,
- define and describe *metacognition*,
- describe different approaches and activities that can be used in teaching thinking skills,
- explain the eight behaviors that exemplify "nonthinking," and
- describe the role of the teacher in modeling and teaching thinking skills.

When teachers prepare lessons, they need to consider not only the content knowledge they want students to master but also the basic learning *skills* they want students to acquire. Thinking skills provide a foundation for remembering information, incorporating knowledge, acquiring motor skills, and developing values and attitudes. Many of these skills can be taught as general learning strategies, independent of specific content knowledge.

Students' achievement increases when they are taught how to use thinking skills across multiple disciplines. Therefore, teachers need to provide plentiful opportunities for students to develop their proficiency in using thinking skills in a variety of contexts. Students are more likely to internalize these skills if they are actively involved in the learning process, can apply what they have learned in a meaningful way, and assume responsibility for their own learning.

THINKING SKILLS

What are thinking skills? How can teachers teach students *how* to think? These are difficult questions to answer. Indeed, there are as many definitions of *thinking* as there are thinkers. In fact, education authorities have expressed strong feelings about what it means to "think" beyond mere replication of information. David Perkins (1986) of Harvard University says that thinking is a combination of problem solving, decision

Students must learn to be responsible for their own learning.

making, reflecting, and making predictions. Matthew Lipman (1988) suggests that thinking is a way to edit, rearrange, examine or think about experiences. Ernest Boyer (1983), president of the Carnegie Foundation, states that thinking cannot be separated from good language.

Although it is true that all cognitive acts require thinking, thinking skills involve much more than rote memorization; they require the generation of new information as well. Indeed, many believe that it is possible to teach students the creative thinking skills they will need to become effective problem solvers and leaders. In this chapter's discussion, we will consider thinking as the act of withholding judgment to use knowledge and experience to find new information, concepts, or conclusions. With this definition in mind, let us explore the different types of thinking.

Categories of Thinking

When deciding which thinking skills to address, teachers need to consider what thinking skills students will

---

REFLECTIONS ON TEACHER PRACTICE 10.1: Thinking Games

1. What is "thinking" ability?

2. How do we use our thinking ability every day? Why might we need to address thinking in school?

To engage my students in thinking, I have my class work in pairs to construct a game about our state. I give them a rubric when I explain the lesson that outlines what they are expected to include (for example: game pieces, strategy, at least 15 cities mentioned, at least 15 facts about the state, etc.). An old clothes box makes a great box for storage of the game! The game construction worked out great and the kids had fun working on the project.

I was really impressed with some of the game ideas students came up with. On the day they were due, each pair had to present their game to the class. Then we had a "game day" and I let them play their games for part of the afternoon. We also kept them in the room for extra things to do during indoor recess. I plan to use the same idea again and students will get to pick different states.

—*Tracy, elementary school teacher*

Please visit the Student Study site at **www.sagepub.com/mooreteachingk8** *for additional discussion questions and assignments.*

SOURCE: Reprinted with permission from ProTeacher, a professional community for elementary school teachers (www.proteacher.net).

need to apply to their current and future real-life experiences. Instead of trying to "cover" all the skills superficially, teachers should concentrate on teaching a few skills thoroughly. To ensure that the full spectrum of thinking levels is represented in all content areas, effective teachers refer to Bloom's (1956) *Taxonomy of Educational Objectives* (see Chapter 4). This facilitates their efforts to address and assess multiple levels of thinking through well-designed instructional activities.

Critical Thinking

Many formal classroom activities focus upon developing students' critical thinking skills. Students reference their personal value systems while evaluating messages and judging the integrity of conflicting information from different perspectives. Well-cultivated critical thinkers formulate vital, precise questions of inquiry, interpret information against relevant criteria, think open-mindedly within alternative systems of thought, and communicate solutions to complex problems.

Critical thinking is more complex than ordinary thinking because it is based on standards of objectivity and consistency. Students must be taught to change their thinking (a) from guessing to estimating, (b) from preferring to evaluating, (c) from grouping to classifying, (d) from believing to assuming, (e) from inferring to inferring logically, (f) from associating concepts to grasping principles, (g) from noting relationships to noting relationships among relationships, (h) from supposing to hypothesizing, (i) from offering opinions without reasons to offering opinions with reasons, and (j) from making judgments without criteria to making judgments with criteria. For additional information about characteristics of critical thinkers, visit this site: www.ncrel.org/sdrs/areas/issues/envrnmnt/drugfree/sa3crit.htm.

In our consumer-based society, one motivational way to develop students' critical thinking skills is by teaching them to analyze samples from newspapers, magazines, television, and the Internet for evidence of propaganda, misleading statements, faulty reasoning, doublespeak, euphemisms, biased or one-sided reports, false assumptions, avoidance of issues, exaggerated statements, and emotional appeals. They could demonstrate their understanding by developing and advertising faux products using propaganda or persuasive tactics. These activities require both lower and higher levels of thinking because students must have basic information upon which to base their judgments.

Creative Thinking

Creative thinking can lead to "fasten-ating" results! As George de Mestral removed sand burrs from his dog's coat after a nature walk, he realized the tiny hooks could lead to a new form of fastener—Velcro. Spencer Silver invented a new adhesive, and Arthur Fry realized it could be used for removable page markers, resulting in the invention of Post-it Notes. All people have the potential for "Aha!" or "Wow, guess what I just figured out?" experiences. Such creativity occurs when people discover seemingly incomprehensible connections between natural events, existing ideas, or different disciplines. This occurs when the "creative" right brain generates ideas and images while the

"Cafeteria duty."

"logical" left brain critiques and evaluates. It is during the creative processes that the two halves of the brain seem to communicate best. Before we can decide how to develop students' creative thinking skills, however, we must discuss what, exactly, creativity is.

Creative thinking can be both a process and a product. Creativity is a process whenever a person connects existing bits of existing information to arrive at a new understanding, relationship, understanding, or idea. Creative thinking is a *product* when a person realizes an original concept resulting in the production of a new invention or theory. For the student, this could be the creation of a poem, a game, or an unusual use for a household object. Ideally, all creative thinking expands people's intellectual horizons.

Curiosity, imagination, discovery, and invention are all synonymous with creative thinking. Although it may not be possible to teach a person how to be creative, it is possible to provide activities that enhance opportunities for creative thinking.

During the creative process, people progress through four stages of creative thought: (1) preparation, (2) incubation, (3) illumination, and (4) verification. Numerous thinking skills are used during each of these stages of the creative process. In fact, the greater the flexibility in thinking provided, the greater the possibility for developing students' creative thinking ability.

During the first stage, preparation, the creative thinker investigates seemingly disparate information until a major relationship begins to appear among events, objects, or ideas. This hypothesis causes the individual to ponder and meditate as the thinker moves into the second stage: incubation. The individual spends time allowing images from the unconscious to surface. Sometimes this stage is short-lived, moving the creative thinker into the "Aha!" or illumination stage. Suddenly, the "I've got it" or "Now I know" arises. At this stage, the individual may feel confident and regain equilibrium, eager to pursue new questions and additional related ideas. During the final stage, the creative thinker seeks out ways to verify and test the idea. Figure 10.1 summarizes the four stages of creative thinking.

FIGURE 10.1 Stages of Creative Thinking

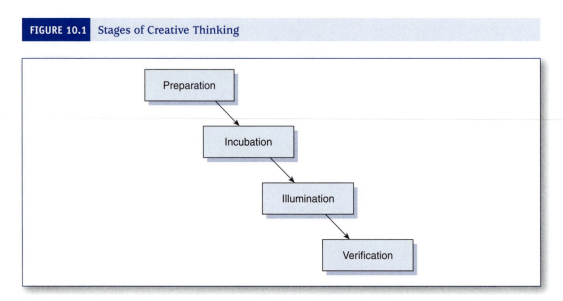

Eminent creative persons, and others less prominent but no less creative, have expressed frustration and disconcerting feelings while struggling with a puzzling concept that later led them to a discovery or "Eureka!" feeling. Here are some other difficulties creative thinkers have reported experiencing:

1. Creative thinkers frequently report they have difficulty finding words to describe the original, complex images. Certainly, not all creative insights must be expressed in words; they can also be expressed visually or kinesthetically.

2. Many people cannot permit themselves to let their imagination "go" in childlike play, even momentarily. The ability to relax, laugh, and play with new ideas with an unrestricted attitude is an important characteristic of creative thought.

3. Some thinkers tend to overanalyze instead of synthesize, which hinders creative thinking. Whereas analysis is helpful during the early stages of creativity, synthesis is necessary in pressing forward through the development of new, original ideas.

4. Creative thinkers sometimes "jump the gun" to synthesize before analysis of the facts is complete. This can create "thinking blocks," which hinder the consideration of other valuable possibilities.

5. Many creative thinkers fear others won't appreciate their inventions and ideas. It takes courage to be an independent thinker. This does not mean, however, that independent thinkers never experience doubt or misgivings. Even the most eminent creative thinkers of our time have experienced these feelings.

6. A frequent complaint of creative thinkers has been that they get too many ideas at one time. This avalanche of information stresses the individual. The thinker needs to shelve some thoughts to focus upon successfully completing one or two ideas.

To confront and overcome these difficulties, teachers must set the stage for student success by creating a nonjudgmental risk-taking environment, providing students with opportunities for creative thinking in all content areas, and encouraging their creative attempts. Although some students might develop critical thinking and creative skills on their own, most students will need assistance.

Metacognition

Metacognition can be simply defined as "thinking about thinking." Metacognitive skills include invisible thinking skills and study skills such as self-interrogation, self-checking, self-monitoring, and analyzing, as well as memory aids (called mnemonics) for classifying and recalling content.

Video Link 10.1:
Watch a video about thinking about thinking.

When students use metacognitive skills, they monitor their progress in learning new material, correct misconceptions, analyze the effectiveness of their learning strategies, and change learning behaviors when necessary. They use self-reflection, self-responsibility, and initiative to determine whether a cognitive goal has been met. Metacognitive strategies come into play when cognitions fail, such as the recognition that one did not understand what one just read. Such an impasse should activate metacognitive processes as the learner attempts to rectify the situation.

Using metacognitive strategies enhances students' ability to learn. When students do not have metacognitive skills, they don't evaluate their comprehension of material, examine problems in depth, revise work, or make personal connections with the material. Take reading, for example. Students often read a page (or a whole chapter!) in a textbook without comprehending a single thing. They simply go on to the next page or chapter, thinking that merely reading the words on a page is enough. They need to learn to reread difficult pages until the main concept is understood or flag a difficult passage to ask for clarification from the teacher.

Students can be taught strategies for self-assessment and problem solving. For example, students might be stumped by a math application problem. What do they do? Perhaps they could look for clues in the problem's wording, try using drawings or manipulatives, or revisit earlier sections of the chapter to determine what math strategy to use. These are all examples of metacognitive skills; students need to learn how to know when they are not understanding and how to correct themselves. Other metacognitive strategies that students can be taught to use include the following:

- Predicting what is likely to happen
- Deciding if something makes sense

- Consciously identifying what they already know

- Determining how performance will be evaluated

- Estimating the time required to complete a task

- Planning study time into their schedule and setting priorities

- Making a checklist of what needs to happen when

- Organizing materials

- Using outlining, mnemonics, and diagramming

- Reflecting on the learning process, noting what works best

- Monitoring learning by questioning and self-testing

- Providing their own feedback

- Maintaining high concentration and motivation

- Using online tools and resources to gather information

Although many students will develop adequate metacognitive skills, some will not. All students need an opportunity to learn to think about their own thinking processes and to apply learning strategies to address misperceptions. They can develop self-questioning strategies so they can talk themselves through instructional activities, asking themselves or each other the questions teachers might ask. Teachers can teach students metacognitive strategies by modeling "think-alouds" as they present new material (e.g., when composing a collaborative summary of a shared experience or as they discuss a literary character's actions). As students become more skilled at using metacognitive strategies, they become confident, independent learners, and their achievement increases. Students realize they can pursue their own intellectual needs and discover that a world of information is at their fingertips. The teacher's task is to acknowledge, cultivate, and enhance the metacognitive capabilities of all students. Complete Application Activity 10.1 to explore the emphasis put on thinking skills in your state.

APPLICATION ACTIVITY 10.1 Thinking Skills Standards

Access the state content standards (competencies, benchmarks) for the grade level and area(s) you expect to teach. What types of thinking skills are stated? What changes would you make in the amount of emphasis put on developing thinking skills in your state? Do your classmates agree?

The concepts regarding thinking skills are summarized in Table 10.1. Review the summary and complete Reflect and Apply Exercise 10.1.

TABLE 10.1	Thinking Skills
Concept	**Description**
Thinking	The act of withholding judgment to use knowledge and experience in finding new information, concepts, or conclusions
Critical thinking	The ability to analyze complex situations critically, using standards of objectivity and consistency
Creativity	The capacity for producing imaginative, original products or ways of solving problems
Metacognition	The skill of thinking about thinking

REFLECT AND APPLY EXERCISE 10.1 Thinking

Reflect

- What is thinking?

- Some experts contend that few schools teach students to think critically and creatively. Does your own experience support this view? If you agree with the experts, why isn't critical and creative thinking more widely or effectively taught?

Apply

- How can you show your future students that they can be successful thinkers? Share your ideas with your class.

- Generate some ideas for materials and support that would help your future students to develop their thinking skills. Share your ideas.

- How do you use metacognitive strategies in your life? How can you model it for your students?

THINKING SKILLS INSTRUCTION

When you teach thinking skills in your future classroom, you will need to be open to all possibilities and all avenues of learning. You must be willing to explore, question, take risks, and experiment. Otherwise, how can you lead students through the same processes?

Begin by creating individual lessons focusing upon a few particular thinking skills. Enhance your lessons by using instructional technology, such as multimedia presentations, to promote higher order thinking skills. Then, as your experience and confidence grow, consider emphasizing thinking skills throughout your curriculum.

Students should be given the opportunity to ponder issues related to classroom instruction and to present alternative ideas.

Should you teach thinking skills separately or infuse them into specific content areas? There are pros and cons to both approaches. People who favor the separate approach believe that thinking skills deserve to be taught separately like reading and writing. Advocates of the infusion approach state that some thinking skills lend themselves to certain disciplines, so they should be taught in conjunction with the discipline's content. Perhaps the answer to this issue is to use both the separate and infusion approaches.

The Separate Approach

Reuven Feuerstein (1980), an internationally known cognitive psychologist, stated that students who are unable to see relationships or comparisons between ideas need focused instruction targeting specific thinking skills. As such, many educators prefer the separate approach when introducing the new thinking skill because it may be difficult for students who are unfamiliar with a skill to focus on the learning of a new skill and on learning of content at the same time.

When using the separate approach, you should model the new thinking skill. For example, when teaching students about classification demonstrate the skill by doing a whole-class classification activity. Provide a list of classification steps to facilitate students' efforts. For example, if students are classifying miscellaneous buttons, the steps might read like this:

- Find two buttons that have something in common.

- Label them as a group.

- Could any other buttons fit into that group?

- Find two other buttons that have a different thing in common. Label them as another group.

- Continue the process until all buttons have been classified.

During the classification process, ask for whole-class responses to each of the steps to demonstrate that multiple answers can all be correct. Class input is one of the most important aspects of teaching the classification skill as a thinking skill. As students make suggestions and form their own classifications, gradually release responsibility to students by allowing them to arrive at answers and provide rationales for their decisions. Once the initial introductory activity has been completed, provide students with an opportunity to practice the skill independently, so you can evaluate their individual classification skills.

The Infusion Approach

Teachers use the infusion approach when they teach the desired skill in conjunction with the regular curriculum. In effect, this approach requires that students transfer the newly acquired skill to the regular content being studied. For example, students could apply their newfound classification skills to what they are currently learning. Facilitate students' efforts by talking through the classification process in this new context as a whole class. Then assign an independent assignment for students to complete in your content area in which they can apply the skill. For example, students could use *Kidspiration*, *Inspiration*, *Excel*, or online graphic organizers to categorize rocks, organize animals by kingdoms, or classify foods into different good groups.

Assistive Technology

Many teachers use assistive technology (AT) and computers as essential instructional tools to develop students' critical thinking strategies. AT devices may include adaptive keyboards, assistive-writing programs, eye-gaze technology, interactive SMART boards, screen readers, touch screens, tablet PCs, talking calculators, Braille translation software and printers, closed-circuit televisions, text-to-voice and voice-to-text software, TDD/TTY for phone service, voice amplification devices, wireless headsets and amplifiers, and switches. The classroom use of listening centers, **technology learning centers**, and **virtual field trips** can also help develop critical thinking skills.

Technology-centered instruction can be regarded both as "minds-on" (complex thinking) and as "hands-on" (practical) activities. Indeed, computer tools can be viewed as mind tools as they facilitate complex thinking as students develop procedural, communication, and research skills. When students use technology as a tool or support for communicating with each other, they are in an active role of recipient of information. Thus, technology use often allows students to actively think about information and make choices.

Critical Thinking Instruction

During the critical thinking process, students challenge assumptions and explore alternative possibilities. Assumptions are the cultural truths that students have assimilated into their value systems without examination. These assumptions influence how they interpret situations and perceive solutions to problems. Consequently, to become critical thinkers, students need to be willing to think beyond their cultural norms, examine old ideas in new ways, and challenge old ways of thinking. This task may be difficult because it is often inherently disruptive to personal values and beliefs. Perhaps that is why sometimes critical thinking activities are strongly resisted.

You can use direct, specific instruction to help students develop open-minded attitudes toward alternative perspectives. Without such instruction, there is little hope for dismantling the concepts our society has outgrown—for example, previously held conceptions about racism, family structure, and women's roles in society. Although many misconceptions about areas such as these still exist, an important aspect of teaching thinking is the modeling of the open-minded attitude you hope to foster. Remember, you are not trying to impose your own beliefs upon your students. Rather, you are providing opportunities for students to think about their views and the views of others; students must arrive at their own final decisions. Without this atmosphere of respect, it is impossible to model the concepts you desire to teach.

Students can examine assumptions during small-group work. Give each group a list of "loaded" questions. After gathering responses from each member, groups report areas of

Through the Eyes of an Expert

Modeling Critical Thinking in the Classroom

Critical thinking needs to begin early. Beginning in primary grades, create a *community of inquiry* by implementing the following best practices. Model and use critical thinking vocabulary and terms.

Use critical thinking terms like *observe, research, estimate, evaluate.*

The first few times the new thinking words are used, the teacher should explain what they mean. Other critical thinking words include *devise, formulate, invent, validate, assess, interpret, conclude, prioritize,* and *critique.*

- For example, your first grade class has just measured and recorded the height of an average student (A) who just turned five and an average student (B) who is almost six. You say, "Based on the data we observed and recorded, how tall can we predict "A" will be when she is almost 6?"

Use questioning skills that elicit critical thinking.

Use open-ended, productive questions in the classroom. Reproductive questions elicit just one right answer and often require lower level thinking. Open-ended questions allow students to construct and produce knowledge, which they can then assess and validate.

- In what ways might we observe that the season is changing?
- What would happen if spring followed fall?
- What are different ways we can gather data for this research?
- How will you know if you are correct with your conclusion?

SOURCE: Dr. Joy Navan, professor of Education; director, Center of Gifted Studies, Murray State University, Murray, Kentucky. Used with permission.

Use the tools and the skills of professionals in the discipline.

Mathematicians, scientists, social scientists and other professionals are critical thinkers. Students need to sense and practice the critical thinking skills of the disciplines that they study. Educators can facilitate the development of effective thinking and provide early career exploration by implementing problem-based learning that calls on students to use the research protocol of different fields of inquiry.

- The following scenario is an example of a problem-based learning project for Social Studies students. "You are the town historian for your city. You have been asked to work with a committee to choose a person from your town's history and to design a memorial for that person." Students would then (1) define the problem, (2) collect data through researching historical documents, (3) analyze the data to decide on the historical figure, (4) design a memorial that represents the figure's achievements, and (5) present the results.

agreement and disagreement during a whole-class discussion. The following statements are examples of loaded questions:

What assumptions might you make about. . .

- a person who wears shabby clothes?

- a person with multiple piercings, tattoos, and green hair?

- a person who rides a Harley?

- a classmate who receives a D on a report card?

- somebody who keeps falling asleep in class?

By challenging personal assumptions, students develop the societal consciousness and rational thinking skills they will need to become thoughtful, future citizens. Challenging these personal assumptions and questioning internalized truths can be both liberating and threatening. It may seem demeaning to students' capacity for valuing, believing, and developing moral codes, however, when they discover that the absolutes they hold to be true are not necessarily absolutely true. The development of completely new thought patterns that differ from past thinking structures can even create momentary imbalance. Therefore, you might find it necessary to help students broaden their thought structures beyond the confines of their own culture, without weakening their desire to believe in, and form, values. The goal is not to destroy but to refine. Above all, remember that, sometimes you, too, will pass through these disruptive processes as a teacher–learner.

Regardless of the approach you choose for teaching critical thinking skills, you need to be prepared to circumvent these eight roadblocks, or nonthinking behaviors, that might impact the development of your students' critical thinking skills:

1. *Impulsiveness.* Students may blurt out the answer without having enough information, or they impulsively base their decision on the first thing that enters their minds without considering alternatives. In other words, they "leap before they look" without adequate thought. These students think, but they fail to consider consequences of their inferences, hypotheses, or decisions on information presented.

2. *Overdependence on the Teacher.* Students sometimes raise their hands as soon as the teacher finishes explaining the assignment. These students won't try the concept first but, rather, say, "I don't understand this" before even attempting to read the instructions. These students often fail to pay attention during group instruction and insist that the teacher provide individual instruction at their desks.

3. *Inattentive Behavior.* These students start working but don't stay on task. They need constant prompting, their attention span is short, and their attention constantly wanders, seemingly into "space." They rarely finish assignments and demonstrate a lack of self-motivation.

4. *Restless Rusher.* Restless rushers get very little meaning out of assigned tasks; rather, they rush through their work, sacrificing accuracy for the sake of finishing first. When asked questions pertaining to the assignment just finished, they pause and reply, "I don't know." When they are prompted to redo the work, they rush through the second time just as quickly as the first time. These students differ from impulsive students in that they usually don't base their responses on past or similar experiences and jump the gun as impulsive students do; instead, they concentrate only on turning in the work.

5. *Dogmatic, Assertive Behavior.* These students fail to consider another's point of view. Basic assumptions are never questioned, and they always think their perceptions are the only correct ones. Because they think their views are already perfect, they see no reason for considering or listening for other possibilities.

6. *Rigidity, Inflexibility of Behavior.* These students are reluctant to give up old strategies that have worked for them in the past, even when they prove inadequate in the new situation. For example, students might be requested to perform a certain task, and they may reply that it's not the way they learned to do it last year.

7. *Fearful, Lack of Confidence.* These students rarely respond to questions that require anything other than one right answer. When asked to answer a question that calls for higher-order thinking skills or to voice their thoughts during a brainstorming activity, these students are afraid to express themselves because they are fearful of expressing their own views. Despite their seeming lack of confidence, they usually won't seek extra help.

8. *Responsibility Forfeiture.* Because these students are afraid to take risks or assume responsibility, they want the teacher to provide one right way of accomplishing all learning tasks. These grade-conscious individuals are not afraid to approach their teacher for specific guidelines; by obligating the teacher in this way, the students shift responsibility to the teacher and relieve themselves from thinking for themselves.

Often, you will need to prescribe thinking activities to alter these behaviors and promote self-confidence and mental growth. Let's now look at some of the activities that could be used in correcting faulty thinking habits.

YOUR TURN: A REFLECTIVE CASE STUDY

We have explored behaviors that can impede the development of students' development of creative and critical thinking skills. Do the following for this chapter's case study:

1. Create an imaginary student who is exhibiting two or more of the difficulties associated with creative thinking or the nonthinking behaviors that affect critical thinking.

2. Write a case study scenario where this student is experiencing academic or personal distress because of these mental roadblocks. Write the scene as if you were watching it as a teacher.

3. Trade scenes with a classmate. Discuss ways an effective teacher could help the creative, critical thinkers in crisis.

Thinking Skills Activities

Teaching thinking skills requires open-ended activities in which no single, correct answers are sought. Although there are many areas, categories, and thinking operations that could be approached, let's examine some of the concepts that could address the eight nonthinking behaviors.

Video Link 10.2: Watch a video about brainstorming.

Brainstorming

Brainstorming is an excellent way of promoting fluent and flexible thinking at any grade level (see Chapter 8). Give students a real or imaginary problem to solve. Some topics might include the following:

1. How can you create a zoo environment where animals are living in as natural a setting as possible without eating one another?

2. It's your mother's birthday, and you only have $5.23 in your pocket. What can you give her for a birthday present?

3. In what ways are addition and multiplication alike?

4. How could you change a car to make it more energy efficient?

5. Name as many words as you can that have the long *e* sound.

The goal of brainstorming is to produce as many responses as possible. Give students an opportunity to brainstorm independently first before asking for whole-class responses. Create a supportive atmosphere by accepting and appreciating all responses and withholding praise or judgment. Encourage your students to "piggyback," or add onto each other's ideas. Emphasize that not all responses will be of high quality because the aim is for quantity. Piggybacking upon others' ideas encourages flexible thinking.

Flexible Thinking

Flexible thinking activities stretch the mind into considering possibilities beyond the usual responses. Begin by defining an area for examination. Ask students to put their five senses to work in thinking about how many different ways they could use an item. For example, how could they use a garden hose on a desert island? Inspire them to ask themselves questions that take forms such as these:

What if _____?

Suppose that _____?

How is _____ like _____?

If you were _____?

Another outstanding thinking skill that improves students with impulsive behaviors is cause-and-effect considerations, or forecasting activities.

Forecasting

Instruct students to brainstorm all possible causes and effects of a certain action. For example, students could ponder the connections between what they eat and their general health. This requires that students make inferences about cause and effect by considering what could be or might be. Afterward, students examine the quality of each prediction, choose the best cause and effect, and provide reasons for their choice. Giving rationales promotes students' **inductive thinking**.

Inductive Thinking

Inductive thinking activities can be helpful for students who frequently fail to check their responses to determine whether their generalizations can hold up against data. During inductive thinking, students collect, organize, and examine data. Then they identify common elements before making generalizations based on inferences found in the data. For example, students could "read between the lines" of a selected newspaper article and then to state a generalization based on information known about the article. If possible, provide students with newspaper articles from different areas and by different authors to further check the generalization against data. Making inferences is closely related to finding generalizations.

Inference Making

When people make inferences, they must provide possible consequences, conclusions, or implications from a set of facts or premises. Inference-making requires thinkers to provide a rationale for their thoughts about a situation based on similar associations with past experiences. People's basic assumptions play a key role in the inferences they make. Questions that call for inference-making ask students to provide their personal opinion. "Why do you suppose?" and "What do you think someone should do?" and "What do you suppose was meant by . . . ? Why?" are all questions frequently used in promoting inference-making. As with forming generalizations, however, it is important that you ask students to supply evidence or provide reasons for the inference they make. Even when basic assumptions are examined, it may be necessary to determine whether inferences are

"Of course I believe that a teacher should offer a positive role model; however. . ."

based on clear, meditative thinking or whether they are the product of assertive, dogmatic rigidity. Therefore, students also need practice in logical thinking.

Logical Thinking

During logical thinking activities, students begin with assumptions or concepts and generate step-by-step ideas to arrive at an endpoint or a solution. Students use their prior knowledge or acquired patterns of thinking to examine the presented information and analyze supportive details to arrive at a conclusion. Students can develop logical thinking skills by reflecting upon well-written mysteries, working Sudoku puzzles, solving online logic problems (search for "logic puzzles"), or completing an activity such as the one shown in Figure 10.2. Students might even enjoy creating their own logic puzzles to challenge classmates.

Deductive Thinking

Whereas inductive thinking requires students to make generalizations based on data, **deductive thinking** asks students to consider the generalizations given and provide supporting data. Most thinking activities will be incomplete until students provide a rationale for their responses.

Deductive thinking is crucial in a democratic society that demands a responsible citizenry capable of making informed decisions because it requires students to evaluate the merit of an activity, object, or idea. Teaching students to identify possible outcomes, define standards of appraisal, and make judgments based on careful consideration are all-important elements of instruction. When students are called on to decide among objects or alternatives, decision-making and problem-solving steps will help them reach conclusions.

| FIGURE 10.2 | Sample Logical-Thinking Activity |

LADYBUG COUNTING SQUAD

1. The ladybug counting squad is showing their counting skills to the school. The more spots a ladybug has the greater the counting ability.
2. Carefully read the clues below. Then identify each squad member's name in logical sequence of counting ability.

Assumptions: (clues)

1. Connie Counter is their best counter.
2. Susie Small Stuff is the least skilled counter.
3. Legs is second only to Connie Counter in counting skill.
4. Antenna Mary is between Carrie the Nose and Legs in counting skill.

Problem Solving

Problem solving involves six steps: (1) defining the problem, (2) collecting data, (3) identifying obstacles to the goal, (4) identifying alternatives, (5) rating alternatives, and (6) choosing the best alternative. Problem-solving models can be developed that guide students through these important steps. For example, divergent questions might be developed that discourage students from supplying one "right" answer. Also, brainstorming should be an important aspect of each step. Students should consider the following questions as they carry out the problem-solving steps:

1. What is fact, and what is opinion?

2. Is there only one right way?

3. Do the examples prove the rule?

4. Just because two things happened together, does this prove one is the cause of the other?

5. Is it possible that personal feelings are causing you to rule out possibilities?

Sometimes guides with similar questions help new problem solvers organize problem-solving activities. Students record alternatives then critically consider their choices. Teachers can teach this skill at all grade levels and in all content areas. Examples might include the following:

1. Find a way to take care of the classroom pet during weekends and school vacations.

2. Design a new playground.

3. Find a solution to uneven air-conditioning in the school.

4. Discover why plants die in the school cafeteria and correct the situation.

Decision Making

Decision making involves the thinking skills needed in choosing the best response from several options. It involves examining advantages and disadvantages, considering all of the steps of problem solving, and evaluating the final decision in relationship to available alternatives and consequences. Basic to decision making are the abilities to observe, interpret, compare, classify, and analyze information. Topics could include choosing a suitable career, selecting the best way to power your school, determining how to catch a mouse, or deciding how to spend the $150 given to your class by the school.

Observing

Observation demands that students watch for a purpose and note objective changes, details, or procedures. Students use their five senses to record data as accurately as possible. The proposition that "you can't believe anything you hear and only half of what you think you see" becomes a reality, as students not only examine their own perceptions and others' perspectives. Students can practice their observational techniques by watching other people interact in a public setting such as a playground or cafeteria. They record every movement, action, and environmental condition. Students can also carefully observe commercials for underlying messages. Close observations of this type lead students to recognize the power of effective persuasion and help them develop open perceptions when attempting to interpret information.

Interpreting

Interpreting requires that students consider how their perceptions might impact their judgments or conclusions. Perceptions are developed through associations with personal experiences and are, therefore, unique to each individual. Interpreting is an important skill to teach directly, because oftentimes people generalize based upon insufficient evidence in their repertoire of basic assumptions. Explain to students that the skill of interpreting depends on drawing inferences from *valid* data. Warn them about the tendency to generalize on the basis of insufficient evidence. Guide them in critically examining information and in differentiating between what is true and what they may believe to be true. Students' first interpretation activities might begin with your presentation of an interesting piece of art. Begin by asking students to list at least four statements that can be made through observing the artwork. Afterward, ask them to share with the class their interpretation of what the artist was trying to convey. After the first student gives personal responses of interpretation, search for other responses that might represent different interpretations. This particular activity prompts examination of the many ways individuals perceive and interpret information. It can further develop students' ability to withhold judgments of absolutes and to consider other alternatives. Thinking skills instruction must include training that fosters open-mindedness, so that students understand that what seems to be unconditionally true in one situation may not be completely true in another.

Comparing

Comparison requires that students examine two or more situations, objects, ideas, or events and seek out relationships, similarities, or differences. For example, they might compare butterflies and moths or the Japanese and Chinese cultures. Venn diagrams (two overlapping circles) provide a framework for such comparisons. After students have learned this skill, provide independent, authentic practice opportunities. Encourage students exhibiting nonthinking behaviors to keep an open mind and compare their answers and beliefs with the opinions expressed by others.

Analyzing

Video Link 10.3: Watch a video about improving thinking.

During analysis, students examine the designated problem, identify its basic elements, and find relationships among its elements before reaching a conclusion. Some teachers ask students to consider how each of these elements relates to the designated problem. Others present a problem along with four steps: (1) identify the whole, (2) identify each part of the whole, (3) organize data related to each part, and (4) state a conclusion based on your analysis. Keep in mind the difference between asking an analysis question and asking a knowledge-level recall question.

While analysis is an important aspect of problem solving and decision making, it is not intended to confine the individual to categorizing only presented information. Students should be encouraged to analyze information for relationships that might otherwise go unnoticed.

Again, the teacher's role in developing students' skills in decision making is to create an atmosphere of acceptance and to support students' struggles as they reexamine internalized values and beliefs. Let's look at one scenario in which a teacher successfully shared classroom decision-making responsibilities with students. This teacher felt so overwhelmed by the demands of classroom record keeping that she created a shared-responsibility system with her students. Each class was divided into three groups, and each group elected an officer to handle the group's record keeping.

Students quickly learned to value honesty and accountability. As a result, each group requested additional officers so they could ensure more of a "check and balance" system. Each of the groups elected three officers—governor, assistant, and secretary—with specific responsibilities. For example, the secretary of each group recorded and collected all makeup work for absentees in the group. When students returned after being absent, they were directed to see their secretary for makeup work. Thus, the group held the secretary accountable for all makeup work. Subsequently, peer responsibility began to increase and be expected among students. Often, secretaries talked with a group member when absenteeism was frequent or was affecting the member's performance in class. Moreover, group norms evolved. For instance, should a student be "impeached" from office when found in error? To what extent should peers be tolerant of shortcomings? The classroom teacher in this situation continued to insist on a shared-responsibility role and required students to use problem-solving and decision-making skills in resolving these problems. Thus, the system provided students with opportunities to practice and refine responsible learning.

When you convey to your students that you view them as responsible persons, you give them an "I can!" sense that helps them view themselves as successful thinkers that nurtures different ways of thinking, believing, and acting. Help them develop the vital sense of responsibility for their own accomplishments and for finding solutions to complex problems.

You need to reassure students constantly that, even though it is important to withhold judgments temporarily, it is important to never "bail out" until they feel comfortable with their personal interpretations and perceptions. You, too, may feel some disequilibrium and may be tempted to shut down or bail out because the challenges your students present have become intense.

REFLECTIONS ON TEACHER PRACTICE 10.2: Critical Thinking

1. How can critical thinking be taught?

2. What is the connection between critical thinking and learning? Between critical thinking and memory?

Critical thinking skills are essential to education and here's a great opportunity for students to develop and use them. How about getting the kids to read the stories and rewrite portions (if not the whole story) to make them "politically correct" by today's standards, such as changing the word "lady" to "woman," or even "womyn," changing job stereotypes, etc. It can lead to interesting dialogues about the changes in societal values and norms. Even if the stories don't need to be run through the "political correctness mill," create an assignment to have them identify specific aspects that make or break a story and why the story (or stories) they have read may or may not be interesting to students of today, as compared to students in 1979.

—Middle school teacher

 Please visit the Student Study site at **www.sagepub.com/mooreteachingk8** *for additional discussion questions and assignments.*

SOURCE: Reprinted with permission from ProTeacher, a professional community for elementary school teachers (www.proteacher.net).

Developing thinking skills requires that you become a more reflective teacher and a model for reflective thinking. Creative and critical thinkers in your future classroom will

- approach subject content and unique situations with a thinking orientation;

- reflect on the meanings, implications, and consequences of what they are learning and doing;

- participate in reflective activities; and

- accept responsibility for their own learning and thought processes.

Learning how to learn and thinking skills development are essential for dealing with life situations. Complete Application Activity 10.2 to explore the use of thinking skills activities at the grade level you expect to teach.

APPLICATION ACTIVITY 10.2 Thinking Skills Strategies

Create a two-column chart of the indirect instructional strategies covered in Chapter 10. Rate the value of each strategy at the grade level you expect to teach using this scale: (1) appropriate and useful, (2) limited usefulness, and (3) not appropriate and not useful. Provide rationales for your ratings.

This completes the examination of various activities for developing students' thinking skills. Complete Reflect and Apply Exercise 10.2.

REFLECT AND APPLY EXERCISE 10.2 Teaching Thinking

Reflect

- Why should thinking skills be part of the elementary school curriculum? Middle school curriculum?
- Contrast the separate and infusion approaches to teaching thinking skills. Is one approach more effective at elementary level? Why or why not? Middle school level? Why or why not?

Apply

- Develop a plan for integrating direct instruction of critical and creative skills, techniques, and processes into your teaching. Share your plan.
- Plan a sequence of learning activities that will lead to successful thinking skills at the grade level you expect to teach. Share your activities.

Creativity should be encouraged in the classroom.

SUMMARY

This chapter focused on teaching thinking skills. The main points were as follows:

- Thinking can be viewed as the act of withholding judgment to use knowledge and experience to find new information, concepts, and conclusions.

Thinking Skills

- Thinking can take place at any one of Bloom's (1956) *Taxonomy* levels: knowledge, comprehension, application, analysis, synthesis, and evaluation.

- The thinking level most appropriate to a specific class depends on the maturity of the students and the needs of the content area. The most commonly taught thinking skills are critical and creative thinking.

- Metacognition can be simply defined as thinking about thinking. Metacognitive skills enable students to better benefit from instruction.

Thinking Skills Instruction

- Thinking skills can be taught separately (separate approach) or by infusing them into the content (infusion approach).

- Direct, specific instruction often proves useful in fostering critical and creative thinking skills.

- Eight behaviors have been identified that negatively affect the development of thinking skills: (1) impulsiveness; (2) overdependence on the teacher; (3) inattentive behavior; (4) restless rusher; (5) dogmatic, assertive behavior; (6) rigidity, inflexibility of behavior; (7) fearful, lack of confidence; and (8) responsibility forfeiture.

- Categories of thinking skills activities include brainstorming, flexible thinking, forecasting, inductive thinking, inference making, logical thinking, deductive thinking, problem solving, decision making, observing, interpreting, making comparisons, and analyzing.

DISCUSSION QUESTIONS AND ACTIVITIES

1. **Thinking.** What type of thinking is emphasized in most schools? Is critical thinking rewarded? Creative thinking? Is school success based on students' ability to think critically? Creatively?

2. **The Environment.** What type of classroom environment would be conducive to developing critical thinking? Creative thinking? What problems can you foresee in establishing this environment?

TECH CONNECTION

Students' thinking skills can often be improved with careful planning and plentiful practice. Complete the following application activities to help you develop strategies for using technology to improve students' thinking skills.

- Use available search engines to research ideas for developing and improving thinking skills at the grade level you expect to teach. Form groups of four or five to share ideas. Use PowerPoint and SMART Board technology to share your group's ideas with the class.

- Select an online lesson plan (www.lessonplanspage.com), and "remodel" it as a critical thinking activity. Describe elements of the remodeled lesson that will develop and reinforce students' critical thinking skills.

CONNECTION WITH THE FIELD

1. **Classroom Observation.** Visit several public school classrooms at the grade level you expect to teach. Keep a record of the techniques used to develop student critical thinking and creative thinking. Share your record with your class.

2. **Interviews.** Interview several teachers at different grade levels. How do they incorporate critical thinking and creativity into their everyday teaching activities? Make a list of ideas you can use when you become a teacher.

STUDENT STUDY SITE

Visit the Student Study Site at **www.sagepub.com/mooreteachingk8** for these additional learning tools:

- Video clips
- Web resources
- Self quizzes
- E-Flashcards
- Full-text SAGE journal articles
- Portfolio Connection
- Licensing Preparation/Praxis Connection
- Part III View from the Classroom
- Part III Public View of Education

Appendix A

Laboratory Experiences

Microteaching and Reflective Teaching

The primary purpose of teacher education is to prepare aspiring teachers for the classroom. Because teaching is such a highly complex profession, however, becoming a skillful teacher takes plentiful practice. Future teachers cannot learn to teach just through classroom lectures and assignments. They need an opportunity to apply teaching principles and processes through application-type activities. In general, there are two ways such practice can be provided: (1) laboratory and (2) field-based experiences.

Laboratory experiences usually take place on campuses whereas field-based experiences generally take place in public or private school classrooms. Of course, field-based experiences provide the most realistic experiences and thus are more desirable. But because public or private school classrooms are not readily available to most methods classes for practice purposes, application-type experiences are most commonly achieved through laboratory practice. Laboratory experiences come in two forms: (1) microteaching and (2) reflective teaching.

Essentially, microteaching and reflective teaching differ only in the complexity of the experience. Whereas microteaching is concerned with the practice of a limited number of skills or behaviors, reflective teaching deals with the total teaching act.

MICROTEACHING

Microteaching is an abbreviated laboratory experience that closely simulates what occurs in public or private classrooms. The teacher trainee teaches four to six students (peers) for 5 to 10 minutes. The main focus of microteaching is to provide a venue for practicing targeted teaching skills and behaviors.

Microteaching is often an integral component of methods classes in teacher preparatory programs whereby the various skills and behaviors addressed are practiced and demonstrated. This technique allows preservice teachers to home in on a particular aspect of teaching by placing it "under a microscope" for close examination. Each session focuses on a specific skill or behavior until a satisfactory level of mastery is demonstrated. Demonstration lessons usually are recorded and critiqued by the teacher trainee and the instructor.

Microteaching simplifies the task of teaching by subdividing multifaceted teaching acts into simpler, less complex components. Because the teacher trainee is teaching a shorter, less complex lesson, he or she can better manage the lesson and focus it on a few major skills in the planning process. In addition, microteaching provides an opportunity for self-analysis and allows for constructive feedback from both the students being taught and an instructor. Recording the microteaching lesson offers a further advantage because the recording can be replayed as many times as necessary, and the viewer can focus on different aspects of a lesson with each viewing.

Microteaching does not just involve getting up in front of a small group and teaching. The experience must be carefully planned. First, the teacher trainee carefully selects teaching skills or behaviors that can be practiced in the short time span. Targeted skills and strategies might include effective questioning techniques, the appropriate application of reinforcement, the effective use of stimulus variation, the implementation of a specific teaching method (discussion, teacher presentation, inquiry, discovery, exposition with interaction, etc.), or some combination of these skills or behaviors.

Second, the teacher trainee chooses an appropriate topic that matches the targeted skill as well as the available instructional time. Not every topic is automatically appropriate for being taught by any method. For example, time constraints dictate that the topic be somewhat narrow—a single concept or subconcept that can be taught in a 5- to 10-minute time span. Therefore, the topic concept must be analyzed carefully in relation to the proposed method, procedure, and allotted time.

Third, the teacher trainee narrows the topic to a single concept or subconcept. Once the concept or subconcept has been determined, the trainee specifies one or more objectives.

The Microteaching Preparation Form in this appendix can be used by the teacher trainee in developing a 10-minute-long lesson.

Finally, the teacher trainee and instructor evaluate the microteaching experience using a form such as the Microteaching Evaluation Form and Microteaching Self-Analysis Form. Some colleges of education might design their own evaluation instruments. The teacher trainee and instructor watch the recording of the microteaching lesson while rating the trainee's performance with respect to established performance criteria. They reflect upon and analyze the session to identify specific teaching skills that need additional practice.

REFLECTIVE TEACHING

In response to a desire to provide quality on-campus laboratory and clinical teaching practice, Cruickshank (1987) developed the concept of reflective teaching. Essentially, reflective teaching is an expanded form of microteaching. Prospective teachers plan, teach, execute, and evaluate a full-length lesson. They focus upon how much their students (peers) learned as well as how satisfied the students were with the instruction. In effect, the potential teacher is called on to analyze and reflect on the teaching act itself.

Specifically, as conceived by Cruickshank (1987), reflective teaching has the following components and characteristics:

1. The total class is divided into groups of four to six students.

2. One student from each group is selected (designated) to teach the group.

3. Designated teachers teach toward *identical* instructional objectives, using their own choice of teaching methods.

4. Designated teachers teach at the same time, either in nearby classrooms or in different parts of the same classroom, and are required to finish within the same period of time (usually 15 to 20 minutes).

5. Designated teachers focus on two things: (1) learner achievement and (2) learner satisfaction.

6. Learners (peers) are asked to be themselves and not to play the role of school-age students.

7. There must be a measurable product (evaluation) resulting from the teaching experience, so that teaching and learning can be determined.

8. A learner satisfaction form is completed by the learners following the administration of the evaluation.

9. After the reflective teaching sessions, the entire class reflects upon and discusses the different teaching acts that took place.

10. The next teacher is selected (designated), and the cycle repeats.

The goal of this process is to improve teaching skills through reflection on what was taught and how well it was taught. Each learner's achievement evaluation and lesson satisfaction is analyzed to elicit information relative to the effectiveness of the designated teacher. Reflection on this information is very instructive to the total class because the students can compare the different methodological approaches and become aware that the effectiveness of the approach depends on the objective(s) and the teacher.

Because practice of the total teaching act is the ultimate goal of reflective teaching, students should be responsible for the development and presentation of a complete lesson. Thus, when planning for a reflective teaching session, the instructor should provide the instructional objective and, in most cases, a common evaluative instrument. The designated teachers, however, should plan a total lesson using a form similar to the Reflective Teaching Lesson Plan Format in this appendix.

Immediate, objective feedback to the designated teachers is a major component in reflective teaching. To maintain objectivity, the evaluation instrument and peer comments focuses upon specific teaching skills, not personal characteristics. The instructor and peers complete an evaluation instrument such as the Reflective Teaching Evaluation Form. Moreover the designated teachers can watch a recording of their teaching efforts while completing a self-assessment using the same Reflective Teaching Evaluation Form. Instructor's and peers' feedback can be used in addressing the areas that the learners found inappropriate in a lesson presentation.

Finally, grades are an important ingredient in any teacher preparatory program. Thus, the Reflective Teaching Evaluation Form should be based on the program criteria for effective teaching. As such, the instructor's, learner's, and designated teacher's self-evaluation of a teaching session can provide input for grades.

MICROTEACHING PREPARATION FORM

Microteacher: _____ Date: _____

Course Title: _____

Use this form for preparation of your lesson. Prepare a copy for your instructor.

1. Concept to teach: _____

_____

_____

2. Targeted teaching skill(s) or behavior(s): _____

_____

_____

3. Specific instructional objective(s): _____

_____

_____

4. Set induction: _____

_____

_____

5. Instructional procedures: _____

_____

_____

6. Closure: _____

_____

_____

7. Audiovisual materials and equipment needed: _____

_____

_____

8. Notes and comments: _____

_____

_____

MICROTEACHING EVALUATION FORM

Microteacher: _____ Date: _____

Subject: _____

Lesson Preparation	5 4 3 2 1
Set Induction	5 4 3 2 1
Targeted Skill/Behavior A: _____	5 4 3 2 1
Targeted Skill/Behavior B: _____	5 4 3 2 1
Closure	5 4 3 2 1
Subject Matter Knowledge	5 4 3 2 1

Rate the teacher trainee on each skill area using this rating scale: (5) skill mastery; (1) much skill refinement needed.

COMMENTS:

MICROTEACHING SELF-ANALYSIS FORM

Microteacher: _____ Date: _____

Concept taught: _____

Rate your teaching efforts on each skill area using this rating scale: (5) skill mastery to (1) much skill refinement needed.

Lesson Preparation	5 4 3 2 1
Set Induction	5 4 3 2 1
Targeted Skill/Behavior A: _____	5 4 3 2 1
Targeted Skill/Behavior B: _____	5 4 3 2 1
Closure	5 4 3 2 1
Subject Matter Knowledge	5 4 3 2 1

Watch the recording of your microteaching session as often as needed to collect data for the following items. Analyze the collected data and draw conclusions with respect to the behavior addressed in each item. Tally the number of times you…

asked convergent questions	
asked divergent questions	
used students' names	
used wait time	
provided verbal reinforcement	
provided nonverbal reinforcement	
switched students' sensory channels	

TEACHER TALK VERSUS STUDENT TALK. As you view your recording, place a tally on the chart to represent who was talking approximately every 3 seconds. If no one was talking or if many people were talking simultaneously, then place a tally in the silence or confusion category. When you have finished, count the number of tallies in each category as well as the total number of tallies in the categories teacher talk and student talk combined. Use the following formulas to determine the percentage of teacher talk and student talk:

- Percentage of teacher talk = (Tallies in teacher talk category/Total tallies in teacher talk + student talk categories) × 100

- Percentage of student talk = (Tallies in student talk category/Total tallies in teacher talk + student talk categories) + 100

Type of Talk	Tally Marks	% of Time
Teacher talk		
Student talk		
Confusion		

Which filler words or sounds did you use ("okay," "you know," or "uh")? How many times did you use each word or sound?

Filler Word or Sound	Tally Marks

REFLECTIVE TEACHING LESSON PLAN FORMAT

Teacher: _____ Date: _____

Course title: _____

Topic: _____

Instructional objective(s): _____

_____

_____

Set induction: _____

_____

_____

Instructional procedures

1.

2.

3.

4.

Closure: _____

_____

_____

Evaluation procedure: _____

_____

_____

Instructional materials: _____

_____

_____

Notes and comments: _____

_____

_____

REFLECTIVE TEACHING EVALUATION FORM

Teacher: _____ Date: _____

Subject: _____

Rate the trainee teaching efforts on each skill area using this rating scale: (5) skill mastery to (1) much skill refinement needed. **Please write additional comments and suggestions on the back.**

Lesson preparation	5 4 3 2 1
Set induction	5 4 3 2 1
Closure	5 4 3 2 1
Subject matter knowledge	5 4 3 2 1
Eye contact	5 4 3 2 1
Enthusiasm	5 4 3 2 1
Speech quality and delivery	5 4 3 2 1
Audience involvement	5 4 3 2 1
Verbal behaviors	5 4 3 2 1
Nonverbal behaviors	5 4 3 2 1
Use of questioning and questioning techniques	5 4 3 2 1
Directions and pacing	5 4 3 2 1
Use of reinforcement	5 4 3 2 1
Use of aids and materials	5 4 3 2 1

During the lesson, how satisfied were you as a learner?

      Very satisfied   Satisfied   Very unsatisfied

    < -- >

What would have increased your satisfaction?

Appendix B

State Licensure/Certification and Reciprocity

Students and teachers often need information related to licensure/certification as they prepare for a teaching career or as they relocate after obtaining certification in a state. Licensure/certification regulations vary a great deal among states. Some states offer relatively few licenses; others offer many. Most states require applicants to pass examinations such as the Praxis II or a state-developed exam before applicants can be granted a regular license. Although some states will grant a temporary license to an applicant licensed in another state, the applicant often has to fulfill additional requirements, such as a specific test or additional courses, to obtain a regular license.

Many changes can be anticipated in teacher licensure practices in the next few years. Indeed, most states are experimenting with and implementing alternative means of authorizing people to teach. Many mid-career professionals are showing interest in pursuing second careers in education. These older applicants have a college education and life experiences that make them attractive as teachers. Requirements for alternative routes to teacher licensure vary greatly. Some alternative certification programs prepare excellent teachers, whereas graduates from other programs leave the profession after a short stay. Here are resources to help you find state teacher certification addresses, telephone numbers, and websites, as well as general information on state reciprocity.

STATE TEACHER CERTIFICATION ADDRESSES

Many states continually revise and pass new legislation relative to teacher licensure and certification. State departments also continuously update and revise their websites. Therefore, instead of providing often outdated state department information in this appendix, we are providing websites with the latest addresses, telephone numbers, state

282

teacher certification requirements, and links to state departments of education. This information is provided at the following sites:

www.education-world.com/jobs/state_certifiction.shtml

www.uky.edu/Education/TEP/usacert.html

These sites should provide the information students and teachers need as they consider relocating or as they move from state to state and seek licensure/certification information.

RECIPROCITY

Due to the growing teacher shortage, some state policy makers are mandating that their state accept out-of-state licenses without additional subsequent requirements. In these reciprocity agreements, one state recognizes the validity of another state's teacher certification program and grants equivalent certification to teachers who have moved from a cooperating state. The nature of the reciprocity agreements vary according to the state partnerships. Not all states have reciprocity. Some states mandate that their state accept certificates issued by the National Board for Professional Teaching Standards (NBPTS) instead.

Many states have signed reciprocity agreements, which allow individuals certified in one state to be certified in others. However, certain requirements such as state or national examinations or state history are not waived. Candidates are usually given provisional certification, which is good for 1 year. They must meet all state requirements during the provisional year before a standard certificate is issued. Reciprocity does not always guarantee that a license will transfer directly from state to state but generally guarantees individuals will be awarded the closest comparable areas.

Glossary

Absolute grading system: Student grades given relative to performance against an established criterion—for example, 90% to 100%, A; 80% to 89%, B; 70% to 79%, C; and 60% to 69%, D.

Active learning: Learning by doing with students engaged in reading, writing, discussing, and problem solving.

Advance organizer: An introductory statement at the outset of instruction that provides a cognitive framework for new information that is to be presented.

Affective domain: Learning domain in *Taxonomy of Educational Objectives* (Bloom, 1956) concerned with values, attitudes, feelings, and emotions.

Analysis: An examination of students' work for possible errors during or following instruction.

Assertive discipline: A classroom management approach developed by Lee and Marlene Canter that states teachers have a right to teach and students have a right to learn.

Assessment: Process of collecting a full range of information about students for the purpose of making educational decisions.

Assistive technology (AT): Special tools designed to assist individuals who have special needs.

Attitudes: Mind-sets toward a person, place, or thing.

Authentic: Learning that is related to students' experiences and to the real world.

Authentic assessment: An assessment procedure that has students demonstrate their ability to perform a particular task in a real-life situation.

Authentic methods: Student-centered instruction with a wide range of participatory activities.

Behavior modification: Shaping behavior by altering the consequences, outcomes, or rewards that follow the behavior.

Beyond discipline: Classroom management approach that replaces the traditional, teacher-centered approach to classroom discipline with a democratic classroom community that recognizes the needs and interest of both teachers and students.

Block scheduling: An instructional delivery pattern that divides schooltime into instructional blocks ranging from 20 to 110 minutes.

Brainstorming: Instructional technique in which small groups of students generate ideas, solutions, or comments related to a specified topic. All initial answers are accepted, no matter how wrong they may seem to the teacher or other students.

Broad questions: Questions that require students to defend or explain their response.

Buzz group: Instructional technique in which a small work group shares opinions or reactions for a short period of time.

Checklists: Assessment instruments used to judge whether or not specified criteria or characteristics are evidenced by a performance or product.

Classroom management: Process of organizing and conducting classroom business to keep it relatively free of behavior problems.

Closure: Activity that summarizes and reviews the lesson's main concepts and brings it to a logical conclusion.

Cognitive domain: Learning domain, in *Taxonomy of Educational Objectives* (Bloom, 1956), that focuses on information, thinking, and reasoning ability.

Cognitive set: Mental framework that promotes positive transfer of new learning.

Cognitive style: The means by which individuals process and think about what they learn.

Competitive evaluation: Evaluation that compares each student's score with peer's scores.

Computer-based instruction (CBI): Individualized approach that uses computers to present instructional information, ask questions, and interact with students.

Concept attainment: Strategy designed to teach concepts through the presentation of examples and nonexamples.

Constructivism: See *constructivist approach*.

Constructivist approach: Approach to learning that actively involves students in constructing their own knowledge and understanding.

Convergent questions: Questions that allow for only a few correct responses.

Cooperative learning: Instructional technique in which students of mixed abilities work together as a team on an assigned task. Interdependence and support for all members of the group is stressed.

Creative thinking: Process of assembling information to develop a whole new understanding of a concept or idea. Four stages generally associated with creative thought are (1) preparation, (2) incubation, (3) illumination, and (4) verification.

Creativity: Capacity for producing imaginative, original products, or ways of solving problems.

Critical thinking: Analyzing complex situations critically, using standards of objectivity and consistency, and arriving at tentative conclusions.

Cumulative records: Paper or electronic files containing information about students' academic history, test scores, vital statistics, and extracurricular activities.

Curriculum: Systematic plan of instruction for a school system. The learning, intended and unintended, that takes place under the sponsorship of the school.

Curriculum mapping: Long-term planning that identifies overarching instructional goals, state-mandated outcomes, methods of assessment, and instructional resources the teacher plans to use to attain the desired results.

Daily lesson plans: Detailed outlines used to structure and sequence instructional activities for a single day.

Decision making: Thinking that asks students to choose the best response from several options.

Deductive thinking: Thinking that asks students to consider given generalizations and provide supporting data.

Demonstration: Instructional method in which the teacher or some other designated individual stands before a class, shows something, and tells or leads a discussion about what is happening or has happened.

Desist approach: Method of classroom management that gives the teacher full responsibility for regulating the classroom.

Differentiated instruction: A teaching theory based on the premise that instructional content, process, and product should be adapted to meet the needs of all learners.

Direct teaching: A structured, teacher-centered approach that is characterized by teacher direction and control, high academic expectations, effective use of class time, and minimal behavioral disruptions.

Discipline: Systematically teaching students to assume responsibility for their behavioral choices.

Discovery learning: Instructional method that focuses on intentional learning through supervised problem solving according to the scientific method. Students are encouraged to learn concepts and principles through their own exploration.

Discussion: Small-group or whole-group activity during which students exchange and share ideas about an assigned topic.

Dispositions: The values, commitments, and professional ethics that influence a teacher's behaviors toward students, families, colleagues, and communities and affect student learning, motivation, and development, as well as the educator's own professional growth.

Divergent questions: Questions that allow for many right responses.

Drill: Fixation of specific associations for automatic recall.

Educational games: See *simulations*.

Empirical questions: Questions that require students to integrate or analyze remembered or given information and supply a single, correct predictable answer.

English as a second language (ESL): English language training for students whose first language is not English. Training is designed to help participants learn English reading, writing, listening, and speaking skills.

English language learners (ELL): Learners who are beginning to learn English as a new language or have already gained some proficiency in English.

Evaluate: Process of obtaining available information about students and using it to ascertain the degree of change in students' performance.

Evaluative questions: Questions that require students to make a judgment or to place a value on something.

Exposition teaching: Teaching method in which some authority—teacher, textbook, film, or microcomputer—presents information without overt interaction taking place between the authority and the students.

Exposition with interaction teaching: Authority-presented instruction followed by questioning that determines whether information has been comprehended.

Factual questions: Questions that require the recall of information through the mental processes of recognition and rote memory.

Focusing questions: Questions used to direct students' attention to a lesson or to the content of a lesson.

Formal curriculum: Intentional learning experiences at school.

Formative assessment: Use of evaluation information to assess and provide feedback on students' progress during the learning process.

Gallery walk: Students walk around the room, reviewing and reflecting upon one another's posted work.

Gifted and talented (G/T) students: Learners with exceptional general intellect, specific academic ability, creative productive thinking, leadership ability, or visual and performing arts talents.

Goals: Broad statements of instructional intent that describe the general purpose of instruction.

Graphic organizers: Pictorial or graphical ways to organize written or oral information.

Halting time: Teachers pause their talking to give students time to think about presented information or directions.

Heuristic approach: Active, reflective teaching methods that involve students in problem solving and comprise modes of discovery, inquiry, simulations, and games.

Inclusion: Practice of including students, regardless of their disabilities, in regular classroom instructional activities.

Independent study: Instructional method in which students are involved in activities carried out with little or no guidance.

Individualized instruction: Instructional method in which instruction is tailored to the interests, needs, and abilities of individual students.

Inductive thinking: Thinking that asks students to make generalizations based on knowledge of specific examples and details.

Informational objectives: Abbreviated instructional objectives that only specify the performance and product.

Infusion approach: Method of teaching thinking skills in which the desired skill is used in conjunction with and incorporated into the regular curriculum.

Inner discipline: Student's ability to exhibit self-control and to make responsible decisions.

Inquiry: Instructional method that focuses on the flexible yet systematic process of problem solving.

Inquiry demonstration: Instructional method in which students are asked to observe in silence.

Inspection method: Grading system in which the teacher creates a frequency distribution of raw scores and assigns grades according to a natural break in the distribution.

Instructional approach: Method of classroom management based on the premise that well-planned and well-implemented instruction will prevent most classroom problems.

Instructional objectives: Narrow statements of learning intent. Includes four components: (1) performance, (2) product, (3) conditions, and (4) criterion.

Instructional strategy: The global plan for teaching a particular lesson. It includes the selected methodology as well as the sequence of instructional activities.

Instructional units: A series of interrelated lessons focused upon common goals.

Integrated directed teaching: Direct instruction combined with self-directed learning.

Learning styles: The sets of cognitive, affective, and physiological behaviors through which an individual learns most effectively. They are determined by a combination of hereditary and environmental influences.

Lesson procedure: Sequence of steps designed to lead students to the acquisition of the desired learning.

Limited English proficiency (LEP): A designation for students with limited ability to understand, read, speak, or write English and whose first or primary language isn't English.

Mainstreaming: Placing students with special needs in general education classrooms full-time or part-time.

Mastery learning: Diagnostic-corrective-enrichment instructional model in which students work on objectives until mastery is achieved. Based on the assumption that every student is capable of achieving most of the course objectives if given sufficient time and appropriate experiences.

Mastery learning system: See *mastery learning*.

Measurement: Assignment of numerical values to objects, events, performances, or products to indicate the degree to which they possess the characteristics being measured.

Mental Operation system: Four-category question model composed of factual, empirical, productive, and evaluative questions.

Metacognition: Cognition about cognition, or "knowing about knowing."

Metacognitive: See *metacognition.*

Methodology: Carefully planned behaviors teachers use to influence learning.

Microteaching: Technique of practicing teaching skills and processes in scaled-down and simulated situations.

Minimum competency tests: Exit tests designed to ascertain whether students have achieved basic levels of performance in basic skill areas—such as reading, writing, and computation—before they can graduate or continue to the next level.

Montessori method: A method of teaching, developed by Maria Montessori, based on a prescribed set of materials and physical exercises to develop students' knowledge and skills.

Multiple intelligences: Howard Gardner's theory that individuals possess many forms of intelligence: linguistic, logical–mathematical, spatial, bodily–kinesthetic, musical, interpersonal, intrapersonal, and naturalistic.

Narrow questions: Questions that solicit factual recall or one right answer.

No Child Left Behind (NCLB) Act: Legislation designed to ensure all public schools provide all students with highly qualified teachers and quality educational experiences and also increased academic accountability and federal support for education.

Noncompetitive evaluation: Evaluation that compares students' progress toward meeting established criteria. Students' scores are not compared with other students' scores.

Norm group: A representative cross section of the intended testing population for a standardized test.

Normal curve: Bell-shaped distribution that reflects the natural distribution of all sorts of things in nature.

Objectives: Anticipated results or products of instruction. Unambiguous statements of instructional intent.

Percentage grading system: Teacher records the percentage of correct responses for each assignment then averages the scores to determine a final grade.

Performance assessment: Assessment in which students perform a task to demonstrate what they have learned.

Point grading system: Teacher allocates points for student assignments and assigns grades according to an established grade range.

Portfolios: Systematic, organized collections of evidence (e.g., projects, written work, and video demonstrations of skills) that document growth and development and that represent progress made toward reaching specified goals and objectives.

Practice: Repeating of specified tasks or skills for the purpose of improvement.

Preassessment: Activities used to ascertain students' prior knowledge about a topic before instruction takes place.

Probing questions: Questions that follow a student response and require the student to think and respond more thoroughly than in the initial response.

Problem solving: Instructional technique that focuses on the intentional elimination of uncertainty or doubt through direct, supervised experiences.

Procedure(s): Sequence of steps designed to lead students to the acquisition of the desired learning.

Productive questions: Broad, open-ended questions with many correct responses that require students to use their imaginations, think creatively, and produce something unique.

Prompting questions: Questions that include the use of hints to aid students in answering or in correcting an initial response.

Psychomotor domain: Learning domain concerned with muscular abilities and skills on a continuum ranging from the simple to the complex.

Public Law 94-142 (PL 94-142): Federal law requiring provision of special education services to eligible students.

Questionnaires: Lists of written statements regarding attitudes, feelings, and opinions to which the student responds.

Rating scales: Assessment instruments listing specific criteria. Evaluators use a scale to indicate the degree to which these criteria are met.

Reality therapy: William Glasser's theory of therapy in which individuals are helped to become responsible and able to satisfy their needs in the real world.

Redirecting: Asking different individuals to respond to a question in light of, or to add new insight to, previous responses.

Reflective teaching: Teacher as an informed and thoughtful decision maker, who analyzes past experiences in planning and teaching and in promoting thinking about the nature of teaching and learning.

Reinforcement: Theory that says the consequences of an action strengthen or weaken the likelihood of the behavior or event.

Relative grading system: Students' grades given relative to performance of other students. Grading on the curve.

Rhetorical questions: Questions asked, with no expected response, to emphasize a point or to capture students' attention.

Ripple effect: Spread of behaviors from one individual to others through imitation.

Role-playing: Instructional technique designed to let students assume the role(s) of individuals in a re-creation of an event or situation.

Rubrics: Scoring guides with specific criteria that establish uniform student evaluation.

Scaffold: Teachers assist students' acquisition of new concepts through modeling, discussion, and structured lessons.

Schema theory: A theory that learners have internal, cognitive frameworks into which they fit new knowledge, concepts, and experiences.

Self-discipline approach: Method of classroom management built on the premise that students can be trusted to evaluate and change their actions so their behaviors are beneficial and appropriate to the self and to the class as a whole.

Self-fulfilling prophecy: Phenomenon in which believing that something will happen causes it to occur.

Separate approach: View suggested by Rueven Feuerstein that students need special, focused instruction on thinking skills.

Set induction: Something a teacher does at the outset of a lesson to get students' undivided attention, arouse their interest, and establish a conceptual framework.

Simulations: Instructional techniques in which students are involved in models of artificial situations and/or events designed to provide no-risk experiences for students. Also referred to as *educational games.*

Socratic method: Questioning-and-interaction sequence used to draw information from students.

Standardized tests: Commercially developed tests that samples students' achievement or behavior under uniform conditions with uniform procedures.

Stimulus variation: Actions, behaviors, or behavior patterns designed to gain and maintain student attention during a lesson.

Student work samples: Collection of students' work over a period of time that offers credible evidence of student learning and teacher effectiveness.

Suchman inquiry: Inquiry approach developed by Richard Suchman whereby students are presented and asked to explain discrepant events.

Summative assessment: Evaluation completed after instruction to determine the extent of student learning.

Task group: Instructional technique in which a group of four to eight students is formed to solve a problem or complete a project.

Teacher effectiveness training (TET): Self-discipline approach to classroom management conceived by Thomas Gordon that stresses establishment of positive working relationships between teachers and students. Focuses upon who owns the problem when it arises—teacher or student.

Teacher presentation: Teacher tells and explains with little or no overt interaction with students.

Teacher testing: Requirement, usually legislatively mandated, that teachers pass a test prior to certification.

Teacher-made tests: Evaluative instruments developed and scored by a teacher for classroom assessment.

Teacher–student planning: Participatory process that directly involves students in instructional planning.

Teaching: Actions of someone who is trying to assist others to reach their fullest potential in all aspects of development.

Technology learning centers: Centers or stations designed to develop student technology skills and/or technology concepts.

Test: Task or series of tasks used to obtain systematic observations regarding ability, skill, knowledge, or performance.

Thematic units: Units of instruction that are organized for interdisciplinary/cross-curricular teaching over a block of time.

Thinking: Withholding judgment to use past knowledge and experience in finding new information, concepts, or conclusions.

Transfer: Students' ability to apply what they have learned in one area to novel learning situations inside and outside of the classroom.

Unit planning: Planning that links goals and objectives, content, activities, resources and materials, and evaluation for a particular unit of study for a course.

Virtual field trips: Guided exploration through the web to local or distance locations.

Wait time: Time needed for students to consider their responses to questions. *Wait time 1* is the initial time a teacher waits following a question before calling for the response. *Wait time 2* is the total time a teacher waits for all students to respond to the same question or for students to react to each other's responses to a question.

Weekly plan: Condensed version of a week's daily lesson plans, written on a short form provided by the school.

Weighted grading system: Assignments are given a letter grade, and all grades are weighted in determining the final grade.

Zone of proximal development (ZPD): A concept attributed to Lev Vygotsky that represents the area between a learner's actual developmental level and his or her level of potential development with outside assistance.

References

Airasian, P. W. (2001). *Classroom assessment: Concepts and applications* (4th ed.). New York: McGraw-Hill.

Allard, H. (1977). *Miss Nelson is missing!* New York: Houghton Mifflin.

Anderson, L. W., & Krathwohl, D. R. (Eds.). (2001). *A taxonomy for learning, teaching, and assessing: A revision of Bloom's taxonomy of educational objectives*. New York: Longman.

Armstrong, D. G. (2002). *Curriculum today*. Englewood Cliffs, NJ: Prentice Hall.

Armstrong, T. (1994). *Multiple intelligences in the classroom*. Alexandria, VA: Association for Supervision and Curriculum Development.

Arons, A. B. (1988, April 9). *What current research in teaching and learning says to the practicing teacher*. Robert Karplus Lecture presented at the National Convention of the National Science Teacher Association, St. Louis, MO.

Ausubel, D. P. (1963). *The psychology of meaningful verbal learning: An introduction to school learning*. New York: Grune and Stratton.

Belvel, P. S. (2010). *Rethinking classroom management* (2nd ed.). Thousand Oaks, CA: Corwin.

Beyer, B. K. (1984). Improving thinking skills: Practical approaches. *Phi Delta Kappan, 65*, 556–560.

Bloom, B. S. (Ed.). (1956). *Taxonomy of educational objectives: Handbook I. Cognitive domain*. New York: David McKay.

Boyer, E. L. (1983). *High school*. New York: Harper & Row.

Canter, L., & Canter, M. (1976). *Assertive discipline: A take-charge approach for today's educator*. Los Angeles: Canter and Associates.

Charles, C. M. (2002). *Building classroom discipline* (6th ed.). New York: Longman.

Checkley, K. (1997). The first seven . . . and the eighth: A conversation with Howard Gardner. *Educational Leadership, 55*(1), 8–13.

Coloroso, B. (2002). *Kids are worth it! Giving your child the gift of inner discipline*. New York: HarperCollins.

Cornelius-White, J. H. D., & Harbaugh, A. P. (2010). *Learner-centered instruction*. Thousand Oaks, CA: Sage.

Crane, C. (2001). General classroom space. *School Planning and Management, 40*, 54–55.

Cruickshank, D. R. (1987). *Reflection teaching*. Reston, VA: Association of Teacher Educators.

Danielson, C. (2007). *Enhancing professional practice: A framework for teaching* (2nd ed.). Alexandria, VA: Association for Supervision and Curriculum Development.

Davis, G. A., Rimm, S. B., & Siegle, D. (2010). *Education of the gifted and talented* (2nd ed.). New York: Merrill.

Dunn, R., & Dunn, K. (1993). *Teaching secondary students through their individual learning styles: Practical approach for grades 7–12*. Boston: Allyn & Bacon.

Ebel, R. L., & Frisbie, D. A. (1991). *Essentials of educational measurement* (5th ed.). Englewood Cliffs, NJ: Prentice Hall.

Evertson, C. M., Emmer, E. T., & Worsham, M. E. (2003). *Classroom management for elementary teachers* (6th ed.). Boston: Allyn & Bacon.

Fantini, M. D. (1986). *Regaining excellence in education*. Columbus, OH: Merrill.

Feuerstein, R. (1980). *Instrumental enrichment: An intervention program for cognitive modifiability*. Baltimore: University Park Press.

Gallup, A. M., & Elam, S. M. (1988). The annual Gallup Poll of the public attitude toward the public schools. *Phi Delta Kappan, 70*(1), 33–46.

Gardner, H. (2003, April). *Multiple intelligences after twenty years*. Paper presented at the annual conference of the American Educational Research Association, Chicago.

Gibran, K. (1989). *The prophet*. New York: Knopf.

Glasser, W. (1965). *Reality therapy: A new approach to psychiatry*. New York: Harper & Row.

Glasser, W. (1977). 10 steps to good discipline. *Today's Education, 66*, 61–63.

Glasser, W. (1986). *Control therapy in the classroom*. New York: Harper & Row.

Gordon, T. (1974). *Teacher effectiveness training*. New York: David McKay.

Green, F. L. (1999). Brain and learning research: Implications for meeting the needs of diverse learners. *Education, 119*(4), 682.

Gregory, G. H., & Kuzmich, L. (2010). *Student teams that get result*. Thousand Oaks, CA: Corwin.

Haller, E. P., Child, D. A., & Walberg, H. J. (1988). Can comprehension be taught? A quantitative synthesis of "metacognitve" studies. *Educational Researcher, 17*(9), 5–8.

Hancock, M. R. (2007). *Language arts: Extending the possibilities*. Upper Saddle River, NJ: Pearson/Merrill Prentice Hall.

Hansen, J. (1999). The effect of elementary teachers' nonverbal behaviors on the teacher-student relationship. *Dissertation and Theses*. (UMI No. 072669)

Harrow, A. J. (1972). *Taxonomy of the psychomotor domain: A guide for developing behavior objectives*. New York: David McKay.

Jacobs, H. H. (1997). *Mapping the big picture: Integrating curriculum & assessment K–12*. Alexandria, VA: Association for Supervision and Curriculum Development.

Jewett, A. E., & Mullan, M. R. (1977). Movement process categories in physical education in teaching-learning. In *Curriculum design: Purposes and processes in physical education teaching-learning*. Washington, DC: American Alliance for Health, Physical Education and Recreation.

Jones, F. (1979, June). The gentle art of classroom discipline. *National Elementary Principal, 58*, 26–32.

Joyce, B., & Weil, M. (1996). *Models of teaching* (5th ed.). New York: McGraw-Hill.

Joyce, B., Weil, M., & Calhoun, E. (2003). *Models of teaching* (7th ed.). Boston: Allyn & Bacon.

Kabagarama, D. (1996). *Breaking the ice: A guide to understanding people from other cultures*. Boston: Allyn & Bacon.

Karnes, F. A., & Bean, S. M. (Eds.). (2000). *Methods & materials for teaching the gifted*. Waco, TX: Pruftock.

Karten, T. J. (2010). *Inclusion strategies that work!* (2nd ed.). Thousand Oaks, CA: Corwin.

Kavale, K. A., Holdnack, J. A., & Mostert, M. P. (2005). Responsiveness to intervention and the identification of specific learning disability: A critique and alternative proposal. *Learning Disability Quarterly, 28*, 2.

Kohn, A. (1996). *Beyond discipline: From compliance to community*. Alexandria, VA: Association for Supervision and Curriculum Development.

Kostelnik, M. J., Soderman, A. K., Whiren, A. P., & Contributor, J. Q. (2010). *Developmentally appropriate curriculum: Best practices in early childhood education* (5th ed.). Upper Saddle River, NJ: Prentice Hall.

Kounin, J. S. (1970). *Discipline and group management in classrooms*. New York: Holt, Rinehart & Winston.

Krathwohl, D. R., Bloom, B. S., & Masia, B. B. (1964). *Taxonomy of educational objectives: Handbook II. Affective domain*. New York: David McKay.

Kryza, K., Duncan, A., & Stephens, S. J. (2010). *Differentiation for real classrooms*. Thousand Oaks, CA: Corwin.

Lambert, L. (2003). *Leadership capacity for lasting school improvement*. Alexandria, VA: Association for Supervision and Curriculum Development.

Latham, N. I., & Vogt, W. P. (2007, March/April). Do professional development school reduce teacher attrition? Evidence from a longitudinal study of 1,000 graduates. *Journal of Teacher Education, 58*, 153–167.

Lipman, M. (1988, September). Critical thinking—What can it be? *Educational Leadership*, 38–43.

Mager, R. F. (1997). *Preparing instructional objectives: A critical tool in the development of effective instruction*. Atlanta, GA: Center for Effective Performance.

McCombs, B. L. (2001, April). *What do we know about learners and learning? The learner-centered framework*. Paper presented at the meeting of the American Educational Research Association, Seattle, WA.

Meyer, C. A. (1992). What's the difference between authentic and performance assessment? *Educational Leadership, 49*(8), 39–40.

Moore, K. D. (2007). *Classroom teaching skills* (6th ed.). New York: McGraw-Hill.

Newman, R. S. (2002). What do I need to succeed? . . . When I don't understand what I'm doing!?: Developmental influences on students' adaptive help seeking. In A. Wigfield & J. S. Eccles (Eds.), *Development of achievement motivation* (pp. 33–53). San Diego, CA: Academic Press.

Nickerson, R. (1985). Understanding understanding. *American Journal of Education, 93,* 201–239.

Nolan, C. (1999). *Under the eye of the clock.* Ukiah, CA: Phoenix.

Oliva, P. F. (2000). *Developing the curriculum* (5th ed.). Boston: Allyn & Bacon.

Orlich, D. C., Harder, R. J., Callahan, R. C., Kauchak, D. P., Pendergrass, R. A., Keough, A. J., et al. (1990). *Teaching strategies* (3rd ed.). Lexington, MA: D. C. Heath.

Ornstein, A. C., Behar-Horenstein, L. S., & Ornstein, S. B. (2007). *Contemporary issues in curriculum* (4th ed.). Boston: Pearson Education.

Perkins, D. N. (1986). Thinking frames. *Educational Leadership, 43,* 4–10.

Posner, G. J., & Rudnitsky, A. N. (2000). *Course design.* New York: Addison-Wesley.

Powell, S. D. (2010). *Wayside teaching.* Thousand Oaks, CA: Corwin.

Rea, P. J., McLaughlin, V. L., & Walther-Thomas, C. (2002). Outcomes of students with learning disabilities in inclusive and pullout programs. *Exceptional Children, 68,* 203–222.

Riding, R. J., & Rayner, S. G. (1998). *Cognitive styles and learning strategies: Understanding style differences in learning behaviour.* London: David Fulton Publishers.

Roberts, P., & Kellough, D. (2003). *A guide for developing interdisciplinary thematic units* (3rd ed.). Englewood Cliffs, NJ: Prentice Hall.

Rothstein, L., Rothstein, L., & Johnson, S. F. (2010). *Special education law* (4th ed.). Thousand Oaks, CA: Sage.

Savage, T. V., & Savage, M. K. (2010). *Successful classroom management and discipline.* Thousand Oaks, CA: Corwin.

Shaughnessy, M. F. (1998). An interview with Rita Dunn about learning styles. *The Clearing House, 71*(3), 141–146.

Skinner, B. F. (1968). *The technology of teaching.* New York: Appleton-Century-Crofts.

Skinner, B. F. (1971). *Beyond freedom and dignity.* New York: Knopf.

TenBrink, T. D. (2003). Assessment. In J. M. Cooper (Ed.), *Classroom teaching skills* (7th ed., pp. 311–353). Lexington, MA: D. C. Heath.

Tomlinson, C. A. (1995). *How to differentiate instruction in mixed-ability classrooms.* Alexandria, VA: Association for Supervision and Curriculum Development.

Tompkins, G. E. (2005). *Language arts: Patterns of practice* (6th ed.). Upper Saddle River, NJ: Pearson Education.

U.S. Department of Education. (2004). *No Child Left Behind: A toolkit for teachers.* Retrieved from http://www2.ed.gov/teachers/nclbguide/nclb-teachers-toolkit.pdf

Vaughn, S., & Fuchs, L. S. (2003) Redefining learning disabilities as inadequate response to instruction: The promise and potential problems. *Learning Disabilities: Research & Practice, 18,* 137–146.

Wiggins, G., & McTighe, J. (2005). *Understanding by design* (2nd ed.). Alexandria, VA: Association for Supervision and Curriculum Development.

Wiles, J. W., & Bondi, J. C. (2010). *Curriculum development: A guide to practice* (8th ed.). Boston: Allyn & Bacon.

Wittrock, M. (Ed.). (1986). *Handbook of research on teaching* (3rd ed.). New York: Macmillan.

Wong, H. K., & Wong, R. T. (1998). *The first days of school.* Mountain View, CA: Harry K. Wong.

Wright, R. J. (2010). *Multifaceted assessment for early childhood education.* Thousand Oaks, CA: Sage.

Index

About the Authors

Kenneth D. Moore grew up in Wichita, Kansas, where he attended Wichita North High School and later taught in the Texas public schools. He received his EdD degree in curriculum and instruction from the University of Houston. Dr. Moore has been involved in teacher education for more than 35 years at both the public school and higher education levels. During his tenure in higher education, he served as dean of teacher education for 12 years and worked closely with school administrators, classroom teachers, student teachers, and teacher education candidates. He has traveled extensively, serving as accreditation consultant and conducting workshops. Dr. Moore has authored three books, numerous journal publications, and an ERIC monograph, and he has presented many papers at regional and national conventions. He has also served as director of the Southwest Regional Association of Teachers of Science, president of the Oklahoma Association of Teacher Educators, president of the Oklahoma Association of Colleges for Teacher Education, and president of the Arkansas Association of Colleges for Teacher Education. He is a past member of the National Council for Accreditation of Teacher Education (NCATE) Board of Examiners (BOE). The texts he has authored include *Classroom Teaching Skills* (6th ed.), *Effective Instructional Strategies: From Theory to Practice* (2nd ed.), *Clinical Supervision: A Practical Guide to Student Teacher Supervision* (coauthored), and *Middle and Secondary Instructional Methods*. Currently, Dr. Moore is semiretired and lives with his wife, Susan, in Vian, Oklahoma, where he pursues his favorite projects, serves as an educational consultant, and continues to write.

Jacqueline Hansen was born in the Rocky Mountains and raised in the suburbs of Denver, Colorado, where she graduated from Arvada West High School. She earned a BA in Elementary Education from Doane College in Crete, Nebraska, before moving to Grand Island, Nebraska, where she taught elementary school for 23 years. While she was teaching full time, she earned two masters degrees in education and education administration from the University of Nebraska at Kearney. She went on to earn an EdD degree in education administration, curriculum and instruction from the University of Nebraska–Lincoln. Now, as a teacher educator at Murray State University, Dr. Hansen strives to teach current and future teachers to love teaching as much as she does. Dr. Hansen has presented at the national and international levels and has authored numerous journal articles and a book chapter. She is past president of the Kentucky Association of Teacher Educators and is a member of Phi Delta Kappa and the International Reading Association. Dr. Hansen is the elementary program coordinator for the College of Education and serves on multiple committees, including vice chair of the Academic Council. As the education writer for the Stamp Services Group of the U.S. Postal Service, she helps to develop education kits correlating with special stamp issuances. Dr. Hansen lives with her beloved husband, Allen, and their four-legged fur people, Tipper, Dixie, and Cat Ballou, in Murray, Kentucky. In their free time, they enjoy exploring the Kentucky countryside on their Harley-Davidson motorcycle and in their Corvette.

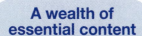